The Small Screen

This book is dedicated to
Harold and Barbara,
in gratitude for their love and support,
as well as my first television set.

The Small Screen

How Television Equips Us to Live
in the Information Age

Brian L. Ott

Blackwell
Publishing

In Chapter 1, "The Times They Are A-Changin'," composed by Bob Dylan. Copyright 1963 by Warner Bros. Inc. Copyright renewed 1991 by Special Rider Music. All rights reserved. International copyright secured. Reprinted by permission.

BLACKWELL PUBLISHING
350 Main Street, Malden, MA 02148-5020, USA
9600 Garsington Road, Oxford OX4 2DQ, UK
550 Swanston Street, Carlton, Victoria 3053, Australia

First published 2007 by Blackwell Publishing Ltd

1   2007

Library of Congress Cataloging-in-Publication Data

Ott, Brian L.
   The small screen : how television equips us to live in the information age / Brian L. Ott.
      p. cm.
   Includes bibliographical references and index.
   ISBN 978-1-4051-6154-1 (hardcover : alk. paper) — ISBN 978-1-4051-6155-8 (pbk. : alk. paper) 1. Television broadcasting—Social aspects. I. Title.

PN1992.6.O88 2007
302.23'45—dc22

                                                      2007005637

A catalogue record for this title is available from the British Library.

Set in 10.5/13.5pt Galliard
by SPi Publisher Services, Pondicherry, India

The publisher's policy is to use permanent paper from mills that operate a sustainable forestry policy, and which has been manufactured from pulp processed using acid-free and elementary chlorine-free practices. Furthermore, the publisher ensures that the text paper and cover board used have met acceptable environmental accreditation standards.

For further information on
Blackwell Publishing, visit our website:
www.blackwellpublishing.com

Contents

Preface

As a communication technology, television is still in its infancy. Unlike mechanical print technology, for instance, which dates back hundreds of years, television did not seriously begin to impact US culture until about the mid-1950s (see Spigel 1992). Although the technical components of television had been developed and patented two decades earlier, only 9 percent of US homes were equipped with television sets in 1950. But that number grew quickly, and by the decade's end the percentage of US households with television sets exceeded the percentage of households with telephone service. In just 20 years (from 1950 to 1970), television adoption had swelled from less than 10 percent to over 95 percent. So, despite its relative youth, television's spread and influence has been swift. In fact, television's invasion of our lives happened so rapidly that there was little opportunity for careful reflection about the character and social function of this new technology as it was developing and being adopted. Thus, when Newton N. Minow, President Kennedy's chairman of the Federal Communications Commission, declared television to be a "vast wasteland" (Minow 1995: 188) in an address to the National Association of Broadcasters on May 9, 1961, his sentiment quickly hardened into the prevailing wisdom (see Schement & Curtis 1995: 113).

The dominance of this view has had at least two notable consequences. First, it delayed television's entry into the academy as a serious object of study. The early view of television as little more than trash culture, commercial fluff, and popular entertainment all suggested that it was unworthy of sustained critical scrutiny and attention (Allen 1992: 4). As a result, television came to play a vital role in our lives long before we understood or had begun to systematically investigate what its role was. Few universities had television studies courses prior to the mid-1980s, and few researchers were exclusively or even principally television scholars. Most of the individuals writing about television prior to the 1980s were journalists, literary critics, or social scientists. Though individual academic studies of television date back to the 1950s and include such famous studies as Theodor Adorno's (1954) "How To Look at Television," nothing approaching a discipline or field of "television studies" took shape until the 1990s (Brunsdon 2006). In 1989, on the fiftieth anniversary of its first broadcast of a television signal to the American public, David Marc, one of the nation's first professional television critics, recounts, "I was apparently the only person teaching at a major accredited college in the United States unconcerned enough about my personal status to acknowledge it" (1995: 137). Subsequently, Marc appeared on *60 Minutes, The Today Show,* and *The CBS Evening News with Dan Rather* (via a pretaped interview by Bernard Goldberg), where he challenged the notion that television is just entertainment.

By the time television became a legitimate object of academic study, it faced a second challenge, namely that it had already been judged "as both origin and symptom of social ills" (Brunsdon 2006). According to John Corner, "The overwhelming rationale for most research into television has undoubtedly been anxiety about its influence. This was true of the earliest studies and remains the case today, despite there now being many different kinds of research questions concerning influence" (1999: 4). Corner goes on to suggest that studies of television can loosely be grouped into two categories: those that concern its broad political impact and especially the erosion of democracy, and those that examine its broad social influences, particularly with regard to violence, education, and socialization. Many of the studies that fall into the first category are informed by the Marxist tradition of the Frankfurt School and explore the industry of television and its operation within a capitalist economic system. Books such as Todd Gitlin's (1983) *Inside Prime Time* and Douglas Kellner's (1990) *Television and the Crisis of Democracy* are illustrative of this intellectual current. Studies of the second stripe were shaped by two distinct intellectual traditions: social-scientific research and cultural studies. Despite their methodological differences, however, both camps were concerned largely with the social *effects* and/or *functions* of television.

Social scientists sought to quantify, for instance, the effects of exposure to television on the attitudes, beliefs, and behaviors of children. Based on empirical studies of audiences often conducted over many years, researchers such as William Schramm et al. (1961) and George Gerbner et al. (1982) statistically charted television's various influences, ranging from the promotion of passivity to social acculturation. The television scholarship that grew out of the cultural studies tradition drew its inspiration from the Centre for Contemporary Cultural Studies (CCCS) at the University of Birmingham, the work of Raymond Williams, and the film journal *Screen* (see Fiske 1992: 284). Influenced by the work of Louis Althusser and Antonio Gramsci, CCCS scholars were particularly interested in the relation between culture and ideology. Stuart Hall's (2006) analysis of television's communicative process in his "Encoding/Decoding" monograph was, at the time of its initial publication in 1972, among the first attempts to think about how television programs work to reproduce prevailing ideologies. Hall's theory was later field tested by David Morley (1980) in an ethnographic study of television viewers. These and other key studies of television raised a series of important questions about what constitutes a television "text," the relation between texts and audiences, and the tension between domination and resistance – issues that would inform John Fiske's (1987) groundbreaking *Television Culture* and continue to be debated today.

Much of the scholarship conducted on television in the 1990s – continuing in the cultural studies tradition – involved ideological analysis of individual programs, specifically with regard to depictions of race, gender, sexuality, and class. These studies frequently demonstrated TV's perpetuation of stereotypes, as well as its reproduction of White capitalist patriarchal hegemony (see Heide 1995: 147–8; Jhally & Lewis 1992: 135; McKinley 1997: 235; Press 1991: 173–5). Corner (1999) notes that television criticism tends to be "informed by fears of cultural damage," " 'critical' both in the sense that it works within an intellectual tradition of arts analysis and appraisal and in the sense that it is negative about television in whole or in part" (7). There is not much scholarship on television, then, that *begins* with the premise that television's social influence can be positive and productive, as well as negative and harmful. It is this assumption that television's influence may be both positive and harmful that perhaps best distinguishes *The Small Screen* from previous television criticism. Unlike the vast majority of existing scholarship, I am specifically interested in television's pro-social effects and functions, in the way popular television enhances viewers' lives beyond its obvious capacity to inform, educate, and entertain.

That I come to television from a different starting point and perspective does not mean that I think the previous research on television is mistaken. On the contrary, I find most of the television scholarship I have cited in the preceding paragraphs to be careful and compelling. Many of the critiques that have been leveled against television over the past 50 years are fair, accurate, and deserving of our attention. But I do think that the existing research on television has, at times, obscured and even missed television's broad social benefits. That belief, above all, is what compelled me to write this book. My aim is not to serve as an apologist for or trumpeter of TV. Rather, my aim is to illustrate that we return to this medium again and again not only to be entertained (though that is one reason), but also to find symbolic resources for confronting and managing the difficulties we face in our everyday lives. *The Small Screen* is a case study of that process at a very particular time, the latter stages of the transition from the Industrial Age to the Information Age, and in a very particular place, US American culture.

The central argument advanced in the book is that the primetime television programs of the 1990s afforded viewers an array of symbolic "equipments" for negotiating the psychological challenges brought on by the rise of informationalism. Drawing upon and extending Kenneth Burke's (1941) theory of "Literature as Equipment for Living," I demonstrate that television is a mode of public discourse that repeatedly stages or dramatizes contemporary social concerns and anxieties. In watching their own troubles played out over and over, viewers acquire resources for working through those troubles even if they are unaware of them. Television functions like a therapist, diagnosing our deepest fears and worries, and providing substantive and formal strategies for overcoming them. In my analysis of 1990s programming, I find television to be a quite sophisticated therapist, one capable of offering different strategies to different viewers. My argument, then, is one premised on the idea of symbolic action – the notion that engaging in a behavior symbolic of some other behavior can produce psychological comfort and resolution similar to that created by actually engaging in the other behavior. The same way that *writing* (not mailing) an angry letter to an ex-lover can help one resolve his/her feelings of anger, *watching* television can help one resolve feelings of discomfort about the social world.

My analysis is not limited purely to the realm of symbolic action, however. I am also interested in cognition and how repeated exposure to particular mediums, technologies, or forms may shape and condition the way we process information and thus our social world. In *The Small Screen*, I argue that in addition to providing viewers with symbolic resources for managing their sense of self and confronting the unique psychological challenges of living in the Information Age, television also trains us – trains our consciousness – to cope with the ever-increasing volume of information and speed at which it inundates us. Just as television offers viewers a diversity of therapeutic strategies, it fosters a range of logics, of ways to manage and make sense of our information-laden landscape. Viewers are, I further contend, drawn to the television programs that they are, at least in part, because those programs teach them to process the world in a way that is useful and meaningful to them. This component of my study integrates elements of medium theory with psychology and studies of the mind.

Despite my interest in how viewers use television in their everyday lives, my study falls well outside the boundaries of the "uses and gratifications" (UG) tradition begun in the 1960s and still common today. While I share UG's general interest in how media meets the needs and desires of audiences, my study differs from this tradition both in its assumptions and approach. UG research is rooted in three basic assumptions: people use media for their own purposes; people recognize these purposes and can identify them; and despite some variations, general patterns of use can be identified (Williams 2003: 177; see also McQuail 2000: 387–8). It is the second premise that I find troubling. Unlike UG research, I believe that viewers' social needs and desires lie deep in the unconscious. I contend that viewers are drawn to and derive symbolic resources from television in ways of which they are largely unaware. As such, it makes no sense for me to study audiences, which is the standard method or approach in UG. Although I am interested in what viewers derive from their viewing choices and experiences, I'm uncompelled that viewers can accurately name and articulate it. Thus, this is a text-based, rhetorical study that seeks to illuminate the "psychology of the audience" by attending to recurring patterns within television and culture. The novelty of my approach is that I attempt to understand media use by studying the collective unconscious of a society as expressed in TV, rather than the conscious motivations of individuals. In so doing, I avoid the critique often leveled against UG that by focusing on individuals it loses "sight of the social dimension altogether" (Williams 2003: 178).

To meet these aims, the book is organized in the following way. In chapter 1, I provide a broad overview of the epochal social changes taking place during the 1990s. I then identify my central aims, along with the way I conceptualize and approach television throughout the study. Chapter 2 undertakes a detailed investigation of the Information Age. Based on an analysis of changes in the production, format, and flow of information, I map the contours of the emerging technological and economic landscape. Chapter 2 concludes by examining how the shift from industrialism to informationalism has fueled social anxieties such as information overload, placelessness, technological guilt, acceleration, and cultural fragmentation. The remainder of the book is concerned with identifying the symbolic and cognitive resources with which television furnishes viewers for confronting and resolving the anxieties associated with life in the Information Age. In chapter 3, I examine television shows that are generally welcoming in attitude toward the new social paradigm. Specifically, I chart the shared characteristics of these programs, which I refer to collectively as hyperconscious TV. Drawing on an analysis of generic archetypes and a close reading of *The Simpsons*, chapter 3 concludes by identifying the unique equipments of hyperconscious TV. Chapter 4, by contrast, concerns nostalgia TV or those shows whose general orientation toward the new social paradigm is reluctant. After identifying the chief traits of this genre, I engage in a close reading of *Dr. Quinn, Medicine Woman* as a generic exemplar. Chapter 4 ends with an assessment of the equipments offered by nostalgia television. In the fifth and final chapter, I compare and reflect on the social, ontological, and epistemological consequences of nostalgia and hyperconscious television. I conclude the book by commenting on and speculating about the television of today and tomorrow, and its continuing role in political and social life.

Having described the outline of the book, I would like to reflect briefly on the style of writing. Writing is, of course, both individual and cultural, meaning that it bears the unique marks of its author as well as the imprint of various cultural influences. My own writing tends to be rather informal, almost conversational – an aspect that I hope will encourage students and general readers who love television to pick up *The Small Screen* and consider the complex ways that television enhances our lives. Culturally, the style of the book reflects the norms of various communities to which I belong. As a media critic, I hope that the book speaks to other media scholars and extends, enhances, and contributes to our understanding of the role television plays in society. As a teacher, I have tried to define and explain technical and discipline-specific terms and concepts as they arise in the book. My purpose is not just to advance an academic argument about television, but also to present viewers with another vocabulary, another set of resources, for engaging television. Finally, and perhaps most significantly, the book is heavily sourced, drawing frequently on the research and insights of others. This is not accidental. It is, I believe, where the practice of writing is heading. Like television, this book alludes continuously to what Umberto Eco (1984) calls the "already-said." Academic writing (whether consciously or not) is far more indebted to the intellectual work and resources of the past than most scholars would like to admit. I joke with my students that if you have not yet found your argument in the existing literature, then you have not yet done sufficient research. The halls of academia are every bit as information saturated as society writ large; they are overflowing with concepts, models, theories, and increasingly specialized information. It is an environment in which scholarly insight derives as much from redescription and recombination as from originality.

In addition to the many scholars that I cite, this book has been greatly influenced by a number of individuals, to each of whom I owe a debt of gratitude. I first want to thank the editors at Blackwell, along with the external reviewers, for the care they have shown in handling this manuscript. In particular, I would like to extend a special thanks to Elizabeth Swayze for her encouragement and support, as well as to Haze Humbert, Ken Provencher, and Cameron Laux for their feedback and editorial assistance throughout the publication process. I also wish to thank my home institution, Colorado State University, for granting me a research sabbatical to write the initial draft of this book, and the students and faculty in the Department of Speech Communication for creating an all too rare climate of community and family. To my colleagues, I offer my heartfelt appreciation for your many years of kindness, thoughtfulness, and support. As I turn, finally, to those closest to me, I know that there is no way I can adequately express my appreciation for the many ways you have each enriched my life. But please know that I will be forever grateful to each of you. To Eric Aoki and Lisa Kernanen, thank you for lending a supportive ear on those occasions when I have needed it most. To Shannon Velasquez, thank you for bearing burdens that no friend should ever have to bear. To Susan Sci, thank you for helping me to discover true bliss. And finally, to Greg Dickinson – friend, colleague, and all around kick ass guy – thank you for so thoroughly being you. Each and every day of our friendship, I learn something from you, whether it be as insignificant as *The New York Times*'s review of the latest film or as grand as to how to be a better person and to live a happier, healthier life.

Chapter 1

Television and Social Change

Come gather 'round people
Wherever you roam
And admit that the waters
Around you have grown
And accept it that soon
You'll be drenched to the bone
If your time to you
Is worth savin'
Then you better start swimmin'
Or you'll sink like a stone
For the times they are a-changin' (Dylan 1964)

It is now becoming clear that the United States is moving into a new era –
the information age. (Dizard 1982: 2)

We believe that a new stage in history – the Information Age – is about to
be "unveiled." (Davidson & Rees-Mogg 1999: 14)

The Times They Are a-Changin'

In 1964, at the height of social unrest in the United States, music legend Bob Dylan sang, "the times they are a-changin'." The song was a message to the political establishment that social change was inevitable, and it became a popular anthem at both Civil Rights marches and antiwar demonstrations throughout the latter part of the decade. But even those who were fighting for social change at the time probably did not fully appreciate the scope and depth of the changes that were already taking place around them, or the eerie prophetic quality of Dylan's lyrics. What better metaphor, after all, is there to describe social life in the information society of the twenty-first century than a deluge? Society today is awash in information, and if individuals do not start swimming then they will, as Dylan warns, most certainly "sink like a stone." This book is about the seismic social shift that has been occurring over the past 50 years, about the psychological anxieties that accompany the transition to this new social order, and about the role primetime television played in assisting people to negotiate that transition during the crucial decade of the 1990s.

In *The Great Disruption* (1999), professor of international politics Francis Fukuyama observed that, "Over the past half-century, the United States and other economically advanced countries have gradually made the shift into what has been called an 'information society,' the 'information age,' or the 'postindustrial era' " (3). Although gradual, this shift, notes Fukuyama, has been every bit as significant as the shift from an agricultural society to an industrial society was during the eighteenth century. Media and communication scholars James W. Chesebro and Dale A. Bertelsen (1996), however, date the previous shift of this magnitude even earlier, arguing that not since the development of the printing press in 1455 and the spread of literacy has society undergone such a fundamental change (6; see also Dockery 1995: 13). So, which is it? Is this the greatest social shift since the eighteenth or fifteenth centuries? The answer depends upon one's standard of measurement.

If, on the one hand, social change is measured in terms of the economic mode, then the current shift signals the third period since the Middle Ages. The first economic mode of the modern era was agrarianism and involved subsistence farming in small villages. This mode was followed by industrialism; farms were turned into factories, and manufacturing and production fueled the economy (Davidson & Rees-Mogg 1999: 15; Dizard 1982: 2; Hardt & Negri 2001: 280; Toffler 1980: 20, 26). In the most recent mode, industrialism has given way to informationalism in which the economy is service-oriented and consumer driven (Naisbitt 1982: 1, 11–12, 14–15; Pritchett 1994: 1, 5). If, on the other hand, change is assessed in terms of the prevailing communication technology, then the present shift is only the second major shift in all of human history. The first shift was from a primarily oral culture to a primarily print-based culture

(Ong 1988: 78–108). The current shift is from a print to an electronic or digital culture. So both claims are, in their own ways, correct. In economic terms, the current shift is the most profound in 300 years. In communication terms, the current shift is the most dramatic in 600 years. Unit of measurement notwithstanding, the present shift inflects on all spheres of social life, from education and politics to science and religion.

The seeds of this shift were present as early as the 1960s, not so much in the Civil Rights and Peace movements as in the economic movement from standardized mass production and Fordism to flexible accumulation and the rapid development and adoption of new information technologies. The unprecedented spread of television was, for instance, dramatically changing how US Americans received their news and spent their leisure time, while the invention of the microprocessor would soon forever alter the nature of work. In brief, the shift from an industrial society to an information society is nothing short of *paradigmatic* (Barker 1988). It is a fundamental restructuring of how individuals make sense of themselves and of their world.

As with all paradigm shifts, social commentators find themselves struggling for a language to describe the emerging social order, a practice that often results in a vast and disparate array of new terms and concepts. Among the early and more popular phrases used to describe the new social order were "postmodernity" and the "postmodern condition," era, or age.[1] Social critics and cultural historians such as Jean-François Lyotard (1984) and David Harvey (1990), for instance, employed these phrases to describe the ever-changing conditions of knowledge and economic development in late capitalist societies. The terms "postmodernity" and "postmodern condition" have received substantial criticism since their coinage, less for what they attempt to describe than for their unfortunate implication of an abrupt and clean break with the previous social order, as though all of the elements of modernity magically disappeared overnight. Though the transition from the previous social order to a new one has been dramatic, it has also been gradual, and indeed is still ongoing in many social spheres. The sociologist Daniel Bell's (1973) phrase, "the post-industrial society," suffered a similar fate by defining the new social order not by what it affirms, but by what it negates and supersedes. Attempting to correct for this bias, other prominent contenders have included the Space Age, the Atomic Age, and futurist and social commentator Alvin Toffler's (1980) generic "The Third Wave." So far, however, none of these concepts appear to have demonstrated the same cultural caché as "The Information Age" (Lash 2002: 1–2; Mazarr 2001: 2).

As is likely evident from the subtitle of this book, I too have a predilection for this particular phrase, as it highlights what I take to be the most important feature of the new social order: the radical explosion of information. Chapter 2 explores in depth the material causes and psychological consequences of this information explosion. Although it is not clear and probably not important where the phrase "Information Age" originated, it is now used widely to refer to the present era, having entered the popular lexicon of everyone from journalists to presidents. In September 1995, President Bill Clinton was quoted in the *New York Times* as saying, "In the information age, there can be too much exposure and too much informa-tion. . . . There's a danger that too much stuff cramming in on people's minds is just as bad for them as too little, in terms of the ability to understand" (quoted in Shenk 1997: 17). The President's remarks highlight not only the recognition that we now live in an information era, but also that the shift to this new social order carries with it profound challenges. Change, be it personal or social, is always dis-ruptive and unsettling. "Even in slight things," explains sociologist Eric Hoffer (1963), "the experience of the new is rarely without some stirring of foreboding. . . . In the case of drastic change the uneasiness is of course deeper and more lasting. We can never be really prepared for that which is wholly new. We have to adjust ourselves, and every radical adjustment is a crisis in self-esteem" (1). In 1970, Alvin Toffler intro-duced the notion of "future shock" to, in his words, "describe the shattering stress and disorientation that we induce in individuals by subjecting them to too much change in too short of time," for long before most, he saw us plunging into "a roaring current of change, a current so powerful that it overturns institutions, shifts our values, and shrivels our roots" (4, 3).

Toffler's metaphorical gesture to a rushing river with the phrase "roaring current" extends Dylan's metaphor of a deluge by adding the component of velocity to volume. The disorientating character of the current paradigm shift arises, then, from both the magnitude and the speed of change. That social change has been occurring rapidly does not contradict the claim that it has also been occurring gradually. The term "gradual" does not refer to the velocity, but to the type of change. An automobile, for instance, can race up a gradual incline at 60 miles per hour or putter along at only 15. Gradual change occurs continuously in increments or steps, as opposed to abrupt change, which occurs instantaneously in one fell swoop, such as an automobile driving off a cliff. While nearly 3,000 years passed between the development of the phonetic alphabet and movable-type mechanical printing, a mere 400 years passed between mass printing and the first electronic mode of communication (Chesebro & Bertelsen 1996: 18). So, while the paradigm shift to the Information Age has been gradual, progressing steadily in increments, it has also been dizzyingly quick by historical comparison. Given the extremely disruptive and disorienting character of change – especially rapid, epochal change – culture's inhabitants seek out "tools" to help them cope with the specific anxieties brought about by social change.

Those tools come in the form of language and other symbols. As philosopher and literary critic Kenneth Burke (1941) explains, art forms – which broadly can be taken to mean symbolic forms or discursive patterns – function as *"equipments for living"* (304). Put another way, people confront and resolve the difficulties of their lives, whether individual or collective, by using signs, by *talking* their way through them, by "coming to terms" with them. Talk or discourse, elaborates cultural critic Barry Brummett (1985), serves as equipment for living to the extent that "it articulates, explicitly or formally, the concerns, fears and hopes of people ... [and] insofar as the discourse provides explicit or formal resolutions of situations or experiences similar to those which people confront, thus providing them with motives to address their dilemmas in life" (248). When a social group faces a shared challenge, such as a social paradigm shift, they look for resolution in "popular" or "public" discourse. Public discourse is, of course, rarely uniform, particularly on matters of great social importance. Rather, several major discursive patterns may arise in response to any particular situation. Different discursive patterns provide different sets of symbolic tools or equipment for resolving social concerns.

In this sense, discursive patterns function as screens, what Burke (1968) has specifically referred to as "terministic screens" (45). Screens are essentially filters, allowing some material to pass into view and consciousness and blocking out other material. By framing the world or an event using particular "terms" or vocabularies, terministic screens furnish people with specific attitudes and thus motives for confronting real-life situations. In a public debate regarding foreign policy, for instance, an "us vs. them" discourse is more likely to lead to war than to peace because it creates a terministic screen of conflict rather than cooperation. Since persons can select from among available and competing discursive patterns to address any given problem, individuals often resolve the same public problem quite differently. Although different terministic screens provide different symbolic equipments or mental attitudes for negotiating change, terministic screens are always historical. Symbolic forming is linked to the environment in which it occurs, meaning that "new cultural forms of representation" are always arising to address the perceived problems of an era (Harms & Dickens 1996: 211). "The conventional forms demanded by one age," elaborates Burke (1953), "are as resolutely shunned by another" (139). Building upon the idea that discourse serves as equipment for living, this book examines how television equipped and continues to equip viewers to address the challenges of living in the Information Age.[2]

Television as Public Discourse

> *Several theorists have made a compelling argument that public discourse in the United States is dominated by the influence of television. (Brummett 1991: 4)*

> *In order for a viewer to enjoy and to participate in a televisual fantasy, that fantasy must live out premises that are somehow meaningful to the viewer. In short, fantasies, and their appeal, are not random; they respond to felt needs and desires. (Dow 1996: 193)*

Television was not and is not, of course, the only mode of public discourse that furnishes individuals with a set of symbolic resources for managing the transition to the Information Age. So, why dedicate a whole book to studying that relationship? My answer is twofold. First, by the 1960s, television had become a ubiquitous and central outlet for both news and entertainment. I wish to be careful about drawing too harsh a distinction between news and entertainment, however, as the two have become virtually indistinguishable in the past 15 years with the rise of "McNews" and "Infotainment" (Bennett 2005: 92–8; Day 1996: 11–24). Second, the specific nature of television as a communication technology is uniquely suited to provide symbolic resources for confronting the anxieties associated with the Information Age. Both of these points deserve elaboration.

Although less than 10 percent of US homes had television sets in 1950, that number had risen to nearly 90 percent by the end of the decade. To put this growth into perspective, consider that more television sets were sold, roughly 70 million, than children were born, about 40.5 million, in the United States during the 1950s. In fact, in *Bowling Alone* (2000), sociologist Robert Putnam recounts that it took television a mere seven years to go from 1 percent penetration in American homes to 75 percent, a rate of adoption that exceeds that of the telephone, automobile, vacuum cleaner, air conditioner, radio, refrigerator, and VCR (217). As television became more ubiquitous, it also became more central to daily life, first as the focal point of family leisure and entertainment, and later as the primary outlet for news and information. As television spread, newspaper circulation declined dramatically, leaving TV to dominate the political arena (see Schement & Curtis 1995: 110, 116). Most communication scholars today agree that the televised debates between John Kennedy and Richard Nixon in 1960 forever altered American political campaigns by favoring a "telegenic style" (Croteau & Hoynes 2003: 233–4).[3] Likewise, TV news coverage of Vietnam, in bringing the gruesome images of death into American living rooms, fueled antiwar sentiment and influenced US foreign policy.

The spread and influence of television only intensified in subsequent decades, as the increasing availability of cable and the expansion of networks and content providers affected both *why* and *how much* television people watched.[4] The percentage of Americans who watched television for no particular reason, other than to see "whatever's on," increased from 29 percent in 1979 to 43 percent by the end of the 1980s (Putnam 2000: 222). In 1988, researchers estimated that the typical American watched an average of 6 hours of television a day, a figure that had jumped to 7 hours by the start of the 1990s (Harvey 1990: 61; F. Williams 1988: 25). By mid-decade, 60 percent of US homes had both cable television and more than one television set, Americans were spending more than half their free time watching television or over 40 hours a week, and children were spending more time watching television than they were in a classroom (Bellamy & Walker 1996: 1; Grossman 1995: 93; Swerdlow 1995: 7). Indeed, according to professor of culture, media and sport Ellis Cashmore (1994), children who spend as *few* as 22 hours a week watching television will actually have spent twice as much time with TV as they have spent in a classroom by the time they finish school (1). Given these statistics, it is not hard to understand why professor and media critic Neil Postman (1985) claimed in his national best-selling book, *Amusing Ourselves to Death*, that:

> There is no audience so young that it is barred from television. There is no poverty so abject that it must forgo television. There is no education so exalted that it is not modified by television. And most important of all, there is no subject of public interest . . . that does not find its way to television. Which means that all public understanding of these subjects is shaped by the biases of television. (78)

Postman's observation speaks both to the pervasiveness of television and to the influence of television on our habits or "structures" of thinking, on the very ways we process information. "*Every medium of communication creates and presents a unique view of reality,*" elaborate Chesebro and Bertelsen (1996), and therefore, "*Habitual use of specific media systems privileges certain worldviews, perspectives, orientations, or viewpoints*" (22, 24).[5]

Print culture provides a useful example of this point. Prior to the advent of television and other electronic and digital media, information was distributed predominantly through the written word. Since print is highly sequential, one must read the words in a particular, predetermined order to make meaningful sense of them. Opening a book to a random page and reading backwards would likely result only in confusion. But many television viewers think nothing of tuning into a program already in progress, and then channel surfing (in either direction) as they continue to watch. Traditional print media are also tied to physical modes of transportation, and are therefore more closely bound to geography. In the centuries following the invention of the printing press, information traveled slowly and was often several days or even weeks old by the time it arrived at its final destination. Furthermore, the transit of printed information tended to be unidirectional, moving from a clear message source to an intended and identifiable destination. The sequential character of printed material as well as its mode of distribution, argues Edmund Carpenter, "encouraged an analytical mode of thinking with emphasis upon linearity" (quoted in Chesebro & Bertelsen 1996: 24; see also Ong 1988). As such, the rise of the printed word is often credited with the rise of rationality, causal reasoning, and scientific thinking (Croteau & Hoynes 2003: 308).

Television, which is "structured" differently than print media, therefore privileges a different way of knowing. Unlike the highly sequential character of language, images favor a logic of simultaneity. When viewing an image, one processes multiple signs *at once* as opposed to processing them in a sequential, authorially determined manner. Moreover, the editing of televisual images through cutting and rapid montage prominently features gaps, breaks, and ruptures, rather than the uninterrupted coherence of most traditional print media. Professor of theology and ethics Stanley Grenz (1996) explains it this way:

> A typical evening newscast, for example, will bombard the viewer with a series of unrelated images in quick succession – a war in a remote country, a murder closer to home, a sound bite from a political speech, the latest sex scandal, a new scientific discovery, highlights from a sporting event. This collage is interspersed with advertisements for better batteries, better soap, better cereal, and better vacations.... By offering its collage of images, television unintentionally juxtaposes the irreconcilable. (34–5)

Television programs are themselves endlessly "interrupted" by commercials. As *Time* magazine columnist Pico Iyer (1990) observes, "The average American, by age 40, has seen more than a million television commercials; small wonder that the very rhythm and texture of his [*sic*] mind are radically different from his grandfather's" (85). Unlike print media, television is not bound by geography, its images instantly transmittable over great distances by way of cable, broadcast, satellite, or optical fiber. The near instantaneous transmission of images from around the globe often fosters a sense of "telepresence" – the feeling of being somewhere else. Finally, television's occularcentrism or image consciousness, unlike the verbocentrism and literate consciousness of print media, fosters an emotional, participatory, and sensual logic of the body, rather than a rational, detached logic of the ego (Romanyshyn 1993: 341).

The ubiquity of television and its unique logic as a communication medium has had wide-ranging social consequences. Perhaps nowhere are these consequences more apparent than in the political sphere, where entire political campaigns are reduced to 10-second sound bites and presidential candidates are "packaged" into 30-second campaign spots. Although computers and the internet are rapidly coming to play an ever more pivotal role in American politics, most scholars agree that television is the technology that exerted the greatest influence on our political system during the decade of the 1990s. In 1995, for instance, former president of PBS and NBC Lawrence Grossman (1995) called television "the most influential communications medium in history, its images the most widely received, its impact on our political system the most profound" (93). Communication scholar Frederick Williams (1988) claims that, "Our national and regional politics are carried out largely via the medium of television" (25), while professor of communication and government Roderick Hart (1994) contends that, "television redefines how we feel about politics. Not what we *know* about politics, but how we *feel* about politics. Not *what* we feel about politics but *how* we feel about politics" (151). By blurring the distinction between news and entertainment, television's images, according to Hart, make Americans feel informed about, active in, and clever toward politics. For television scholar John Fiske, the relationship between news, politics, and entertainment is better described as *implosion* than as *blurring*, however. Whereas blurring suggests confusion, implosion suggests collapse. He argues that the "reality" of the Clarence Thomas hearings in 1991 "included their televisuality" – that "there was no 'real' Senate hearings that television then represented; the way that people behaved in them and the conduct of the hearings themselves was televisual. Had there been no television, the hearings would have been different" (Fiske 1994: 2).

As a result of television's influence on politics and other social spheres, Neil Postman (1985) claims that the ascendancy of television is "the most significant American cultural fact of the second half of the twentieth century," adding that "We now live in a culture whose information, ideas and epistemology are given form by television," that, "television is the command center of the new epistemology" (8, 28, 78). I am in full agreement with Postman that television constitutes a new way of thinking, of processing information, and of making sense of our world. I also agree that this new paradigm is coming to supplant the old paradigm. Where I differ with Postman is in my judgment of this shift. Postman (1985) deeply laments it, because, for him, television's way of knowing undermines rational debate and literacy (80; see also Croteau & Hoynes 2003: 308–9). Television, he argues, privileges the novelty of information over the relevance of information, leading to a predicament of powerlessness. The pleasures of television's images, in turn, narcotize us against our condition of indifference and helplessness (Postman 1985: 99–108; see also Romanyshyn 1993: 348). Postman is not alone in his sweeping condemnation of television's paralyzing effects. For Hart (1994), television creates a false sense of empowerment; its dramatic images and fast-moving pictures foster a "sense" of motion and participation in politics without actual involvement (154–7). Many other critics have also denounced television, disparagingly referring to it as an "idiot box" or "boob tube" and to its frequent viewers as "couch potatoes" (Bignell 2004: 20; see also Davis 1993).

Whereas Postman and his supporters perceive the logic of television as disturbing and disabling, I view it as absolutely essential to successfully managing the challenges of life in the Information Age. Postman's critique of television is rooted in the standards of the old paradigm, namely linear rationality, seamless continuity, and focused concentration (Romanyshyn 1993: 344–53). His critique of TV is nostalgic for a rapidly fading paradigm, one that he consistently romanticizes throughout his work. Postman's (1999) romanticized vision of the past is perhaps most evident in his book, *Building a Bridge to the Eighteenth Century: How the Past Can Improve Our Future*, in which he argues for a return to Enlightenment principles.[6] I contend, by contrast, that it is both unfair and unwise to assess television's role in society based on the same set of standards that were valued in the age of industrialism and print consciousness. A more suitable standard for evaluating television is the extent to which it equips persons to healthily live in the era of images and information. "The point," notes psychologist Robert Romanyshyn (1993), "is to appreciate whatever positive transformations in consciousness are being brought about by changes in our technological ways of knowing... Television, like the book, incarnates a collective psychological condition" (344). That is not to say that television's way of knowing is universally positive either. Certainly, we need to be insistently aware of how any mode of communication constrains as well as enables our ability to lead healthy public and personal lives.

In addition to romanticizing the past, both Postman and Hart's critiques of television perpetuate a false binarism between entertainment and information. For Postman (1985), television is incapable of informing the public because "Entertainment is the supra-ideology of all discourse on television. No matter what is depicted or from what point of view, the overarching presumption is that it is there for our amusement and pleasure" (87). But this perspective wrongly assumes that information and entertainment are mutually exclusive. Further, it perpetuates the long-standing philosophical bias that anything pleasurable is also anti-intellectual and pacifies the masses. Frankfurt School scholars Max Horkheimer and Theodor W. Adorno (2001) made one of the earliest and most notable attacks on the pleasures of media in the *Dialectic of Enlightenment*, which first appeared in English in 1972. "Pleasure always means not to think about anything," they argued, "Basically it is helplessness. It is flight; not, as is asserted, flight from a wretched reality, but from the last remaining thought of resistance" (144). While attacks like this one on the media became common in the 1970s, the broader academic assault on pleasure has a much longer philosophical legacy. German philosopher Friedrich Nietzsche (2000), for instance, documents that the entire history of Western philosophy is characterized by the repression of the Dionysian spirit of revelry, ecstasy, and pleasure in favor of the Apollonian spirit of order, rationality, and self-control.

The danger of the entertained/informed and pleasurable/rational dichotomies is that they erect a hierarchy in which only one type of knowledge, thinking, and literacy is valued. While I would certainly concede to Postman that traditional book or print literacy has been declining over the past 50 years, I would note that visual and digital literacy has been increasing over the same period of time (see Elkins 2003). The key question, then, becomes which form of literacy is more useful and valuable in society *today*? To answer that question, the present study adopts Kenneth Burke's notion of terministic screens and examines how television functions as what might be termed "imagistic screens." As has been noted, television is an important mode of public discourse today, and thus functions as an information filter. Our televisions "screen" information, providing us with specific vocabularies or orientations toward the world. These vocabularies, in turn, shape our attitudes toward specific situations and problems. The precise manner that television filters information is unique both to the medium of television and to the particular sociohistorical context. Television, for instance, screens information differently than scientific monographs do, not least of all by privileging story and image over exposition and words. Moreover, the manner in which television filters information today is different than the way it did 40 years ago, just as the manner in which television screens information in the US differs from the way it does in other countries. Consider, for example, the dramatic differences in coverage of the Iraq War on CNN and Al-Jazeera.

This book concerns how primetime television in the US screened information in the 1990s and, more specifically, what vocabularies and thus symbolic resources it provided for assisting US Americans to negotiate the disorienting transition from the Industrial Age to the Information Age. In *Attitudes Toward History* (1984), Kenneth Burke explains that there are two basic attitudes or orientations toward any human situation, yes and no. Burke (1984) refers to these most basic of attitudes as "frames of acceptance" and "frames of rejection," noting that:

> one defines the [current] "human situation: as amply as his [*sic*] imagination permits; then, with this ample definition in mind, he singles out certain functions or relationships as either friendly or unfriendly. If they are deemed friendly, he prepares himself to welcome them; if they are deemed unfriendly, he weights objective resistances against his own resources, to decide how far he can effectively go in combating them. (3–4)[7]

Similarly, there are two basic attitudes toward the rise of the Information Age: "accept the universe" or "protest against it" (quoted in Burke 1984: 3).[8] In his book *Cosmopolis: The Hidden Agenda of Modernity* (1990), philosopher Stephen Toulmin describes the choice this way:

> Approaching the third millennium, we are at the point of transition.... Placed at this transition by changes beyond our control, we have a choice between two attitudes toward the future, each with its own

"horizons of expectation." We may welcome a prospect that offers new possibilities, but demands novel ideas and more adaptive institutions; and we may see this transition as a reason for hope, seeking only to be clearer about the novel possibilities and demands involved in a world of practical philosophy, multidisciplinary sciences, and transnational or subnational institutions. Or we may turn our backs on the promises of the new period, in trepidation, hoping that the modes of life and thought typical of the [Industrial] age of stability and nationhood may survive at least for our own lifetimes. (203)

Primetime television programming in the 1990s reflected these same two attitudes toward the future and toward the Information Age in particular. These attitudes, these ways of screening information, I argue, are represented broadly by the categories of "hyperconscious television" and "nostalgia television."[9]

The underlying attitude of hyperconscious television is a welcoming, playful one – "one of imagination . . . [of] *facing* the future, and so asking about the 'futurables' open to us" (Toulmin 1990: 203). The general attitude of nostalgia television is, by contrast, a sentimental, serious one – a reluctant "*backing into*" the future (Toulmin 1990: 203). The notion of "backing into" the future suggests eyes fixed on the past, an idealized past that one longs for more and more as it recedes into the distance. Despite the difference between these two televisual attitudes, as a mode of communication, television is often considered "the postmodern medium *par excellence*" (Joyrich 1992: 229; O'Day 1999: 112). It is important at this juncture to distinguish between the terms "postmodernity" and "postmodernism." Whereas "*postmodernity* alludes to a specific historical period," according to Marxist literary critic and theorist Terry Eagleton (1996b), "*postmodernism* generally refers to a form of contemporary culture" (vii). Elsewhere Eagleton (1996a) notes, "Postmodernism proper can then best be seen as the form of culture which corresponds to this world view [of postmodernity]" (201–2; see also Sarup 1993: 131–2). So, while I prefer the phrase "Information Age" to "postmodernity" as a descriptor for the historical period that we currently inhabit, I am comfortable using the term "postmodernism" to describe the culture of television specifically. "In fact," as Stanley Grenz (1996) explains, "the spread of postmodernism parallels and has been dependent on the transition to an information society" (17). Unlike the term "postmodernity," for which there exists more popular and accurate alternatives to describe the present era, the term "postmodernism" is, at present, the most widely accepted descriptor of the aesthetics that increasingly characterize cultural forms. Moreover, postmodern cultural forms are relatively distinct from their modern predecessors, and though not all cultural forms today are postmodern (many books, for example), television decidedly is.

One of the key features of postmodern art or cultural forms is "aesthetic exhaustion" – the principle that every artistic style has been tried at some point. Thus, postmodern art, such as television, explain communication scholars Richard Campbell and Rosanne Freed (1993), "comes in two flavors – ironic or nostalgic" (81).[10] Typically, postmodern cultural forms either endlessly recombine previous styles in an ironizing manner or seek to recover and rehabilitate a lost style in a sympathetic new guise. In both cases, postmodern art plunders the past, chiefly modernism, which unlike postmodernism is characterized by a *succession of distinct* artistic styles, including but not limited to romanticism, realism, impressionism, post-impressionism, symbolism, art nouveau, expressionism, fauvism, cubism, orphism, futurism, dadaist, surrealism, etc. A second identifying feature of postmodern art is the implosion of the relation between images (representations) and reality (the material world). Modern art conceives of images as a partial reflection of, a distortion of, or an imperfect substitute for reality. But image and reality remain distinct concepts. Selective and biased, images construct reality in particular ways. Postmodern art, by contrast, is on the order of simulation – "the generation by models of a real without origin or reality," a condition in which the image "bears no relation to any reality whatever" (Baudrillard 1983: 2, 11). The image *is* reality, or rather, the image is hyperreality – the realer than Real.

Both the categories of hyperconscious and nostalgia television reflect these defining features of postmodern art and therefore can be thought of as postmodern forms. As postmodern forms, hyperconscious and nostalgia television "screen" the world, and thus orient us toward the world, through a postmodern lens. Hyperconscious television *savages* the past, shamelessly stealing and mixing preexisting styles and genres. It revels in reference and reflexivity. Its impulse toward the present is one of reverie and it may therefore be thought of as belonging to realm of postmodern imagination. Nostalgia television, by contrast, *salvages* the past, rescuing it from obscurity and obliteration. It deals in sincerity and authenticity. Its impulse toward the present is pessimistic and it may therefore be thought of as belonging to the realm of postmodern nihilism.[11] So, there it is, yes and no. These are the basic televisual attitudes toward the rise of the Information Age during the 1990s. Even though the attitude of nostalgia television reflects a "frame of rejection," it still provides people with a set of symbolic resources for coming to terms with the world. To the extent that conflict and chaos are resolved, Burke (1984) goes on to say that frames of rejection are really just subcategories of frames of acceptance (21). It is also worth noting that nostalgia television is not the most extreme frame of rejection expressed in the 1990s. Other public discourses quite literally said "no" to the changes occurring around them by urging individuals and families to turn their TV sets off (see Mander 2002). One popular bumper sticker during the 1990s put it succinctly: "Kill your TV."

Before turning to a discussion about the precise scope of this study, I want to clarify a few aspects of my approach. One of the central ways that this study differs from many previous studies of television is in its approach to the matter of television genres. "Genre," according to John Fiske (1987), "is a cultural practice that attempts to structure some order into the wide range of texts and meanings that circulate in our culture" (109). Stated another way, genres are classes of messages that share common traits or characteristics. Traditionally, television genres have been taken to be self-evident, as "programs appear to fall 'obviously' into clear generic categories – cop shows, soap operas, sitcoms, hospital dramas, quiz and game shows, and so on" (Fiske 1987: 109). This view of genre is rooted in what media scholar Jane Feuer (1992) calls a "historical" perspective and involves categories that are widely recognized, accepted, and utilized by television's producers and audiences (140). To date, television critics have tended simply to adopt these culturally recognized genres. Such an approach is fine for some purposes. But it often misses the deeper, more unconscious patterns shared by television programs, patterns that influence audiences largely without their awareness and thus in an uninhibited way.

Therefore, this study approaches genre from the less common "theoretical" perspective, in which the critic, rather than television's producers or audiences, identifies and illuminates the generic boundaries of television (Feuer 1992: 140). This study begins with the premise that rhetors or message creators find themselves in unique rhetorical situations, whose exigencies or constraints limit the modes of appropriate response (see Bitzer 1986). From this viewpoint, recurring patterns in messages are a consequence of perceived situational demands. Karlyn Kohrs Campbell and Kathleen Hall Jamieson (1978) capture this sentiment in their definition of genres as "groups of discourses which share substantive, stylistic, and situational characteristics. Or, put differently, in the discourses that form a genre, similar substantive and stylistic strategies are used to encompass situations perceived as similar by the responding rhetors" (20). Thus, genres can be thought of as sets of identifiable responses to specific sociohistorical contexts. This study classifies television series according to their general response to the Information Age. Based on the basic attitudes of yes and no, I have identified the genres of hyperconscious and nostalgia television. Although some television programs reflect the less common attitude of "maybe" and hence do not fit cleanly into either generic category, these programs tend to blend the traits of the two genres I discuss.

Kohrs Campbell and Jamieson (1978) describe the potential social benefits of genre analysis in the introduction to *Form and Genre*:

> The critic who classifies a rhetorical artifact as generically akin to a class of similar artifacts has identified an undercurrent of history rather than comprehended an act isolated in time.... One may argue that recurrence arises out of comparable rhetorical situations, out of the influence of conventions on the response of rhetors, out of universal and cultural archetypes ingrained in human consciousness, out of fundamental human needs, or out of a finite number of rhetorical options or commonplaces. Whatever the explanation, the existence of the recurrent provides insight into the human condition. (26–7)

But precisely what "insight into the human condition" can genre analysis reveal? To answer this question, we must reflect on the social functions that genre performs for viewers. Genre creates a sense of security and a feeling of shared values among viewers through familiarity (conscious or unconscious), rhythm, and the pleasure of recurrence (Batra 1987: 4). To the extent that social change or even the perception of social change generates specific social anxieties, the recurrent patterns of television genres help viewers to process change and to impose order on their world. This order aids individuals in making sense of their lives and their place in the world. In short, it assists them in forming collective and individual identities. As media scholars Stuart Kaminisky and Jeffrey Mahan (1985) explain, "The word genre simply means order. All things are ordered by human beings so they can be dealt with. . . . We are bombarded by experiences. We want to make sense out of things, so we start putting them [often unconsciously] in order. The order may be shared or may be individual" (17, 20). The link between genre and identity has been confirmed in various studies. Ira Glick and Sidney Levy (1962) have found a strong correlation between viewer preference for specific television genres and sex, age, and class, and Henry Jenkins (1988) has found that female fans of the typically male-dominated science-fiction genre often recode its stories through the generic lens of romance. So, studying television genres is about studying how people name, order, and adapt to their environments, whether consciously or unconsciously.

A second feature of my approach and one that further distinguishes it from much of the current research on television is that I combine an analysis of content with a consideration of the formal properties of TV as a communication medium. In the past decade, television criticism has tended to focus almost exclusively on the content, and in particular the story and dialogue, of television shows. Critics, animated by an interest in the hegemonic function of television, have attended carefully to the underlying ideological messages communicated by TV. Often examining individual programs in isolation, critics have identified the values and beliefs communicated about race, gender, sexuality, and class. This has generated a massive and compelling body of scholarship. But, as with all approaches, it exhibits certain limitations and blind spots. It tends, for instance, to ignore the way that individual television programs participate in a larger and endless televisual flow – the seemingly uninterrupted and nondiscrete character of television programming (Williams 1974: 81–90). As such, it is ill equipped to comment on the broader patterns of the flow itself. Content studies of television, be they social-scientific or humanistic, also tend to neglect the increasingly diverse viewing practices of audiences. The multiplication of television networks and the technology of the remote control, for example, have profoundly altered television viewing, initiating the practice of "channel surfing" and, in some cases, even allowing viewers "to watch several shows simultaneously" (Flitterman-Lewis 1992: 217; see also Burgin 1996: 22).

In response to these blind spots, I consider the patterns that cut *across* individual shows, as well as *across* popular historical genres. I inquire into the implications of televisual flow and into the implications of camera framing, editing, and mosaic visuality. I also take seriously the notion that *different viewers view television differently* (Kellner 1995: 237), drawing both on personal observations of viewing habits and on the unique structured invitations to viewing proffered by ancillary TV technologies such as the remote control, VCR, and TiVo. In short, I treat television as a symbolic system in which programming content is made meaningful based on the manner in which it is produced, packaged, and processed in a particular socio-historical context. This perspective has a number of implications. Viewing television as a symbolic system implies that television both structures (orders) and is structured (ordered) by our society. Television does not lie outside of the realms of culture and history and must therefore be viewed contextually. Claims made about television and about its social function in the past cannot simply be taken as unchanging and universal. Television is not the same technology it was 40 years ago and it is not used in the same ways or for the same purposes. It borders on the absurd to assume that today's interactive, digital cable medium with hundreds of channels and 24-hour programming functions the same ways as an analog broadcast medium once dominated by three networks each with limited programming.

A second implication of viewing television as symbolic system is that it provides viewers both with models of identity and with actual resources for crafting identities (Ott 2003a: 58). In *Media Culture* (1995), critical theorist Douglas Kellner asserts that the routines, rituals, traditions, and myths of our daily lives fashion the ways in which we create and maintain our identities. Furthermore, he argues that in the culture of informationalism television assumes many of the functions traditionally ascribed to myth and ritual, and subsequently works to resolve social contradictions and provide us with a meaningful sense of self (237–8). Communication professor Jim Collins (1995) offers a similar assessment in *Architectures of Excess: Cultural Life in the Information Age*. According to Collins, identity depends on a sense of self-location and the rise of information technologies has radically disrupted our traditional sense of space and time. As such, Collins (1995) argues that self-location can only be established through "imageability," which involves "envisioning the self in relation to the array of contemporary cultural production" such that mutable memories and geographies are reconfigured to serve as immutable points of reference (259). In different ways, Kellner and Collins are saying the same thing, namely that persons craft a meaningful sense of self from the cultural resources available to them. The present study identifies the various ways that television equips viewers to manage the threats to coherence and identity reflected by the shift to the Information Age.

Finally, viewing television as symbolic system suggests that television adopts general attitudes *toward* and provides specific strategies *for* working through social concerns. Television is, according to Roger Silverstone (1994), crucial to our ability to manage everyday life, to preserve a sense of continuity and the reliability of things, and to find the necessary distance between us and the various threats to that continuity, either by denying them or absorbing them (1–3). Operating from this perspective, Barry Brummett (1980) has variously demonstrated how specific symbolic forms "invite us to experience part of life in a particular way" (64). Based on an analysis of news coverage of John Delorean's arrest on federal drug charges in 1982, for example, Brummett (1984b) showed how certain symbolic forms provide the public with strategies for resolving feelings of guilt (227). In another study, he illustrated how audiences use haunted house films to overcome feelings of anomie and disorientation (Brummett 1985: 247). Similarly, in looking at the genres of hyperconscious and nostalgia television, this study seeks to give an account of how we, as a society, confronted the challenges of transitioning to the Information Age. Television's role of in this process was, I argue, uniquely important during the decade of the 1990s.

The decision to limit this study to 1990s television is motivated by three factors. First, as I elaborate in chapter 2, the decade of the 1990s was the height of the transition from the Industrial Age to the Information Age. At the start of the decade, *Time* magazine columnist Lance Morrow (1991) wrote, "The 1990s have become a transforming boundary between one age and another, between a scheme of things that has disintegrated and another that is taking shape" (65). From the emergence of the World Wide Web and subsequent dot-com boom (the dot-com bust coming after the 1990s) to the restructuring of global capital and changing habits of consumers, forces of change that had been developing for decades in relatively separate social spheres suddenly converged. By the turn of the millennium, society found itself on the down side of change, living more in the new paradigm than the old. Second, changes in television as a technology and mode of communication were particularly momentous and far-reaching in the 1990s. Basic cable steadily replaced broadcast television, and a fourth major network, FOX, challenged the long-standing dominance of the Big 3. The rise of the FOX network not only rewrote the rules of "acceptable" television content with its irreverent programming – a challenge to the cultural conservatism of the 1980s,[12] but also challenged the conventional belief that a major network had to appeal to the "masses" to be successful. By the close of the decade, television had demonstrated the power of "niche" marketing. Third, no one has written a cultural history of 1990s television yet. Frankly, until very recently, academics lacked sufficient historical distance and perspective to begin accurately identifying the cultural contours of the preceding decade.

Decades are, of course, arbitrary boundaries imposed on the flow of time by historians and cultural critics. That said, there are a number of identifiable cultural trends that broadly cut across the spheres of science, religion, technology, sports, politics, and popular culture during the 1990s. At this point, I want to briefly highlight three of those trends, as they each in their own way contribute to the anxieties and challenges of living in the Information Age. The first trend is a deep skepticism and/or distrust of universals, absolutes, objective truth, and traditional centres of authority (see Eagleton 1996b: vii; Lyotard 1984: xxiv). In mathematics, physics, and biology, this attitude was evident in the growing popularity of chaos theory, which developed special computing techniques to explore erratic, discontinuous, complex systems.[13] In religion, Americans increasingly articulated a preference for an eclectic "personal spirituality" over the "wholesale acceptance of traditional Christianity" represented by organized religion (O'Keeffe & Waller 2003: 93). Meanwhile, on television, FOX's *The X-Files* (1993–2002) regularly expressed a profound mistrust of governmental authority and presented an elaborate web of intersecting story lines that seemed to raise more questions about the "Truth" than it answered – a motif characteristic of David Lynch's highly unconventional series, *Twin Peaks* (1990–1), a few years earlier.

A second cultural trend in the 1990s was the erosion of traditional social and conceptual boundaries.[14] In many ways, it was a decade without boundaries. In science, cloning, the Human Genome Project, and Viagra challenged the boundaries between "copy" and "original," "fake" and "authentic," while the 1992 Presidential Campaign confounded the boundaries between politics and entertainment. Vice-presidential candidate Dan Quayle found himself critiqued by actress Candice Bergen after he had disparaged her television character Murphy Brown in a political speech.[15] Likewise, Bart Simpson skewered George Bush on the night of his acceptance speech at the Republican National Convention in retaliation for Bush's comment on the campaign stump that "We need a nation closer to *The Waltons* than *The Simpsons*" (quoted in Fiske 1994: 121). During this same campaign, democratic challenger Bill Clinton took his "political message" to *The Arsenio Hall Show* (1989–94), where he played his saxophone. From the coverage of celebrity scandals to presidential indiscretions, the news was transformed into "infotainment." Acceptable "moral" boundaries also seemed to be collapsing as television explored anything and everything scatological in shows like *The Ren and Stimpy Show* (1991–5), *Beavis and Butt-head* (1993–7), and *South Park* (1997–).

A third important cultural trend in the 1990s was a fascination with spectacle (see Debord 1995). Culture in the nineties glowed red hot, as image and surface were privileged over substance and depth. Indeed, "the supreme formal feature of [postmodern culture]," according to Jameson (1991), is "the emergence of a new kind of flatness or depthlessness, a new kind of superficiality in the most literal sense" (9). The sporting world witnessed an explosion of novel, adrenaline-producing X-treme sports such as street luge, sky surfing, and snowboarding, in which "style" was elevated to the same level of importance as athletic ability (*The Digital Decade: The 90s* 2000: 80). Similarly, the technology-laden NASDAQ stockmarket index doubled from November 1998 through March 2000, gaining roughly 75 percent annually (Alcaly 2004: 163), as individuals invested in "flashy" dot-com companies, many of which had never shown any gross profits. In the news, the more salacious and often sexual a story, the more journalistic attention it received. In addition to nonstop coverage and analysis of the O. J. Simpson trial, two of the decade's most memorable news personalities were Lorena Bobbitt and Joey Buttafuoco. After years of spousal abuse, Lorena Bobbitt severed her husband's penis and then threw it out a car window. Investigators located the penis and doctors reattached it, enabling John Wayne Bobbitt to find fame in a best-selling porno video titled, *John Wayne Bobbitt, Uncut* (1993). The Joey Buttafuoco story was equally abject, featuring an affair with then 17-year-old Amy Fisher, who shot Buttafuoco's wife, Mary Jo, in the face. This "news" story almost immediately generated made-for-TV movies on NBC, CBS, and ABC. But perhaps the most egregious celebration of spectacle in the 1990s was the nightly replaying of images of laser-guided bombs dropping on Baghdad during Operation Desert Storm.

In addition to being limited to 1990s television, this study is also restricted to primetime television programming, or those shows that aired between the hours of 8:00 p.m. and 11:00 p.m. Eastern Standard Time (EST) on Mondays through Saturdays and between the hours of 7:00 p.m. and 11:00 p.m. EST on Sundays. Historically, this is the period that has garnered the largest and most diverse television audience. The study is further limited by focusing primarily on the programming of ABC, NBC, CBS, and FOX. I say "primarily" because I do discuss a few shows that I think were particularly important in the 1990s that aired on the WB, UPN, USA, and MTV. But I do not give these networks equal attention, as they did not deliver nearly the audience share of the other four networks, and in the case of the WB and UPN – both launched in 1995 – did not carry complete primetime line-ups until near the end of the decade. Finally, this study does not examine the programming on pay cable networks such as HBO and Showtime. Regrettably, this excludes innovative series such as *Sex in the City* (1998–2004) and *The Sopranos* (1999–), which emerged at the decade's end. The exclusion of such programming from this study can be justified, however, by the fact that 1990s pay cable programming did not enjoy nearly the critical acclaim or broad viewership that it does today. Of the roughly 98 million television households in 1990, only 39,902 or about one-fiftieth of 1 percent were pay cable subscribers.

As I hope is evident by this point, television simultaneously contributes and responds to a broader social landscape. Thus, before it is possible to understand the precise manner in which primetime television in the 1990s equipped viewers to adapt to life in the Information Age, we must first understand the unique social landscape of that age. Toward that end, in next chapter, I undertake an examination of the changing technological and economic conditions and how they shaped and molded that landscape.

Notes

1 "The twenty-first century will be characterized as the 'postmodern age'" (Dockery 1995: 13). "In fact, we are apparently experiencing a cultural shift that rivals the innovations that marked the birth of modernity out of the decay of the Middle Ages: we are in the midst of a transition from the modern to the postmodern era" (Grenz 1996: 2).

2 In the 1990s, individuals increasingly found such equipments for living in media and popular culture. "A wide range of texts in a variety of media have undertaken the project of imaging postmodern cultures in order to make the terrain more comprehensible to its inhabitants" (Collins 1995: 34). According to Lawrence Grossberg, " 'the popular' is precisely the site of the most powerful postmodern forms, not only in textual forms, but in relations between the text and insertion into people's everyday lives. It is the way real people experience popular texts that is important. These texts are inserted into real experiences and used to make sense of ordinary lives" (quoted in Cathcart 1993: 302).

3 The notable exception to the belief television viewers and radio listeners responded differently to the debate is David L. Vancil and Sue D. Pendell (1987).

4 Chronicling the spread of cable television, Nancy Signorielli (1991) notes that, "Cable systems first appeared in the early sixties as a way to ensure a good signal for broadcast television. Their major sweep of the country, however, did not come until the eighties when the percentage of homes with cable jumped from 20.5 percent in 1980 to 56.0 percent in 1990.... Cable channel capacity (the number of available channels on the system) has also undergone considerable change, going from 12 channels in the sixties, to 35 channels in the seventies, to 54 channels in the eighties" (125–6). More specifically, Thomas Schatz (1992) reports that, "the number of cable households rose from 19.6 million in 1980 to 55 million in 1990, with pay subscriptions increasing from 9 million to 42 million during the decade" (25).

5 "Great changes in human consciousness have always accompanied changes in the forms of communication human beings use to create their social relations. The last great shift in communications technologies, from oral to script to print culture, came at the dawn of the modern era and changed forever the nature of human consciousness" (Rifkin 2000: 203–4; see also Croteau & Hoynes 2003: 308–9; Sreberny-Mohammadi 1995: 23–38).

6 See especially chapter 5, "Information," in which Postman (1999) claims "Language makes sense only when it is presented as a sequence of

propositions" (88). For an overview of Postman's position, see Brummett 1991: 8–9.

7   Burke (1984) offers the following helpful example; "These names [for situations or persons] shape our relations with our fellows. They prepare us *for* some functions and *against* others, *for* or *against* the persons representing these functions. The names go further: they suggest how you shall be for or against. Call a man a villain, and you have the choice of either attacking or cringing. Call him mistaken, and you invite yourself to attempt setting him right" (4).

8   In *The Third Wave* (1980), Alvin Toffler noted, "Whether we know it or not, most of us are already engaged in either resisting – or creating – the new [Information Age] civilization. . . . Millions are already attuning their lives to the rhythms of tomorrow. Others, terrified of the future, are engaged in a desperate, futile flight into the past and are trying to restore the dying world that gave them birth" (22, 25).

9   I am indebted to Jim Collins (1992) for the term "hyperconscious" as a descriptor for contemporary television. But whereas Collins uses the term to describe a particular feature of television, namely its ironic self-reflexivity (333–4), I use the term to refer to a constellation of generic conventions that include eclecticism, intertextuality, and reflexivity. The idea of "nostalgia television" derives from Fredric Jameson's (1983) discussion of the "nostalgia film" (116–17).

10 Jim Collins (1995) makes a similar observation about contemporary film, noting that recent genres "represent contradictory perspectives on 'media culture,' an ironic eclecticism that attempts to master the [semiotic] array through techno-sophistication, and a new sincerity that seeks to escape it through fantasy technophobia" (155; see also Hutcheon 2002: 177–9).

11 I am not using the concept of "nihilism" in the sense first given it by Nietzsche to refer to "the dissolution of any ultimate foundation" (Vattimo 2004: xxv). Rather, I am using it more generally simply to refer to a global pessimistic worldview (see Jameson 1991: 250).

12 The cultural conservatism of Ronald Reagan's America, as reflected in the popularity of 1980s television shows such as *Family Ties* (1982–9), *The Cosby Show* (1984–92), and *The Golden Girls* (1985–92), witnessed a backlash in the 1990s on FOX with shows like *Married . . . With Children* (1987–97), *The Simpsons* (1989–), and *The Family Guy* (1999–2002), which offered a different view of the American family.

13 Chaos theory began to emerge as a new (and interdisciplinary) science in the 1970s with the notion of the Butterfly Effect, which famously advanced the idea of sensitive dependence on initial conditions. It held that very minute differences in the initial conditions of a system would result in drastically different outcomes. At first, this idea was rejected by

mainstream, classical science. It did not become well accepted until the early 1990s. See Best & Kellner 1997: 216–22; Gleick 1987.

14   Postmodern culture is often associated with "the effacement of the boundary between art and everyday life; the collapse of the hierarchical distinction between high and mass/popular culture" (Featherstone 1991: 7; see also Best & Kellner 2001: 134; Mazarr 2001: 11–13; Strinati 1995: 223–6).

15   *Life* magazine characterized 1992 as "a year dominated by a presidential race, a firestorm in LA and a single mom named Murphy." Although these three events may, at first glance, appear unrelated, they repeatedly converged in 1992. It began on May 19 when incumbent vice-presidential candidate Dan Quayle, speaking to the Commonwealth Club of California, suggested that Murphy Brown's single motherhood was a symptomatic cause of the LA riots. The events converged again when the character of Murphy Brown remarked in primetime, "I couldn't possibly do a worse job raising my kid alone than the Reagans did with theirs," and yet again when Candice Bergen, accepting an Emmy for her portrayal of Murphy Brown, mockingly thanked the Vice-President. The three events converged a third time when *Time* staff writer Richard Zoglin (1992b) reported that "the gang-stomping of Dan Quayle at the Emmy Awards ceremony two weeks ago resembled a Rodney King beating by the Hollywood elite" (44; see also Morrow 1992: 50).

Chapter 2

Life in the Information Age

An information bomb is exploding in our midst, showering us with a shrapnel of images and drastically changing the way each of us perceives and acts upon our private world.... we are transforming our own psyches. (Toffler 1980: 172)

A weekday edition of The New York Times *contains more information than the average person was likely to come across in a lifetime in seventeenth-century England. (Wurman 1989: 32)*

By the year 2000, 97 percent of what is known will have been discovered or invented since today's college sophomore was born. (McCain 1998: 2)

The Information Explosion

For the past 40 years, the United States and other technologically advanced Western nations have been undergoing seismic economic, social, political, and cultural changes. At the heart of those changes lies a common force: the radical and previously unprecedented explosion of information. In fact, according to Peter Large in his book, *The Micro Revolution Revisited*, "More new information has been produced in the last 30 years than in the previous 5,000" (quoted in Wurman 1989: 35). This dramatic proliferation of information has created a condition that social critics alternatively refer to as "data smog," "radical semiurgy," "supersaturation," "semiotic excess," "information glut," and "the infobog" (Best & Kellner 1991: 118–19; Collins 1995: 5; Gitlin 2001: 15–18; Naisbitt 1982: 24; Shenk 1997: 27;

Tetzeli 1994: 60). Despite their diverse terminological preferences, analysts concur that we now live in a society whose very contours are shaped by, indeed defined by, the seemingly endless array of signs and information that constantly bombard us. "Whatever else this new age is," declares Ellen Meiksins Wood (1996), "it is the 'information age.' " The information explosion did not arrive without warning. In 1962, urban sociologist Richard Meier correctly predicted that society would confront a deluge of data within the next half-century (7; see also Edmunds & Morris 2000: 20; Shenk 1997: 24). A year later, he was already talking about communication saturation and the challenges of communication overload (Meier 1963).

To understand how the information explosion has changed and continues to change our society, it is vital that we first define the concept of information. Information refers to the vast array of semiotic material produced and circulated in society. The key word in this definition is *semiotic*, which suggests that information is a "structured" set of signs rather than a "random" collection of symbols or data. Defined in this way, information includes everything from the messages we read on billboards and the conversations we have with our friends to the images we see on television and film and the music we listen to on the radio. Information can be presented or re-presented in a variety of formats from words and images to sounds and binary code. But it is only information to the extent that it has meaningful structure – the capacity to communicate. As physicist Hans Christian von Bayer (2004) explains, "a random collection of zeroes and ones is not information; it is only when those symbols are organized into distinct patterns that the information emerges" (4). When a computer converts an image into binary code, it is simply displaying the same information in a different format (a structured pattern of zeroes and ones). Information, therefore, refers to a collection of signs or symbols that have *form*, that are literally *in-formation*. "Information is," observes von Bayer (2004), "the infusion of form on some previously unformed entity, just as de-, con-, trans-, and re-formation refer to the undoing, copying, changing, and renewing of forms. Information refers to molding or shaping a formless heap – imposing a form onto something" (20).

Information should not be confused with knowledge or facts, however. Knowledge implies learning, understanding, and enlightenment, which are not defining characteristics of information generally. Likewise, facts are a specific type of information that assume a certain degree of contextual "accuracy" or "truth." While accuracy may be a defining characteristic of fact, it is not an essential element of information. Information only requires meaningful form, which is why individuals and institutions can both *intentionally* communicate information that is inaccurate (e.g., dis-information) or *unintentionally* communicate information that is inaccurate (e.g., mis-information). One of the greatest dangers or potential pitfalls of life in the Information Age, then, is that all information will be treated equally. Never before has it been so important that citizens learn to critically assess information – to evaluate its credibility, relevance, and value before acting on it. But because all information, regardless of its accuracy or knowledge value, has form, mathematicians have developed ways to quantify the production of information, which is how we know that the gentle but relentless drizzle of information has recently swelled into a thunderous downpour (von Bayer 2004: 3, 6). In the words of architect, graphic designer, and business analyst Richard Saul Wurman (1989), "[Information] has become the single most important word of our decade, the sustenance of our lives and our work" (38).

Information's heightened salience in our everyday lives is a consequence of changes in its production, format, and flow. *Production* refers to the generation of "new" information, a process that has undergone two significant changes in the past 40 years. First, the development of new information technologies, especially computing technologies, has considerably reduced the *cost* of producing information (Seabrook 1997: 182). Advances in word processing and desktop publishing have, for instance, made it far simpler and cheaper to publish printed material by reducing the time required to enter data, edit it, and typeset it for printing. As a result, we have seen a dramatic increase in the number of books, magazines, newspapers, and academic papers published each year. In his national bestseller *Megatrends* (1982), business consultant John Naisbitt writes:

> Between 6,000 and 7,000 scientific articles are written each day. Scientific and technical information now increases 13 percent per year, which means it doubles every 5.5 years. But that rate will soon jump to perhaps 40 percent because of new more powerful information systems. . . . That means that [scientific] data will double every twenty months. (24)

Two years following Naisbitt's assessment, Peter Large estimated that, "About 1,000 books are published internationally every day, and the total of all printed knowledge doubles every eight years" (quoted in Wurman 1989: 35). By the end of the 1980s, Richard Wurman had adjusted those figures again, noting that, "The amount of available information now doubles every five years; soon it we be doubling every four" (32). In 2004, "describing the exponential growth of the volume of information, which [today] doubles its value in roughly three years," von Bayer (2004) surmised that, "humans and their machines will create more information in the next three years than in the preceding 300,000 years of history" (4).

The decreasing cost of generating information fueled a second change in the production of information – its *decentering*. Not only is more information being produced today than at any other time in history, but also more people are producing information today than at any other time in history. No longer is the production of information confined exclusively to an elite few (though it may still be dominated by an elite few) – those who own and control the traditional centers of production such as newspapers, book publishers, and radio and television stations. Inexpensive home computers, word-processing and desktop publishing software, as well as affordable video recorders, audio mixing equipment, CD burners, and the internet and World Wide Web have all decentered information production. According to the *New Yorker* columnist John Seabrook (1997), "because more people *can* make content, more do. . . . As a result, the old culture mediators, the people who owned the means of production, have been replaced by the new mediators" (184). While "replaced" is perhaps too strong of word to use in the context of a global entertainment industry that remains highly concentrated, the fact is that ordinary citizens are generating information, much of it online in chatrooms, listservs, and websites, that can reach a mass audience. As early as 1980, Alvin Toffler noted that "video recorders make it possible for any *consumer* to become, in addition, a *producer* of his of her imagery" (180). The full import of Toffler's statement is perhaps most evident in ABC's highly rated and long-running series *America's Funniest Home Videos* (1990–), in which program content is supplied by viewers.

The old adage that "a picture is worth a 1,000 words" highlights precisely why the information explosion is as much a consequence of changes in the format of information as it is changes in the production of information. *Format* refers to the mode in which information is presented for processing. As mass communication professor Mitchell

Stephens explains in his 1998 book *The Rise of the Image the Fall of the Word*, electronic images have steadily come to play a more central and vital role in our lives over the past 30 years. In that same time span, "newspaper readership has been plunging" (Putnam 2000: 218). These trends are significant because while printed text is relatively low density, images are relatively high density and thus contain more information. This density disparity is most readily apparent when text and images are converted to binary code. A 30-page document containing 10,000 words will constitute a much smaller data file than even a single high-resolution image. Bandwidth limitations in the early years of the internet and World Wide Web made transmitting images both cumbersome and challenging. Television is, of course, even higher density than still images such as photographs, which is why we do not yet regularly watch TV online. Because television's moving images, not to mention its sound, contain so much more information than traditional print media do, the rise of electronic technologies has been a central contributor to the growing volume of information we confront in our lives. And while citizens have not stopped reading altogether, even the format of what they read is changing, as books, newspapers, and magazines increasingly utilize pictures, graphics, and other visual material.

Changes in information flow reflect the third key factor contributing to the information explosion. As Wurman (1989) clarifies, "The information explosion didn't occur solely because of an increase in information. Advances in the technology of transmitting and storing information are as much a factor. We are as affected by the flow as by the production of information" (294). *Flow* describes the movement of information, including its distribution (transmission), storage, and retrieval. Digital technologies such as compact discs and networked computers, along with 24-hour cable television, have altered the flow not only of "new" information, but also the flow of "old" or previously existing information. While CDs and the internet allow for the quick and easy retrieval of old information, the emergence of television and radio networks dedicated to repeating or replaying old favorites, contribute significantly to the endless recirculation of old information. So, in addition to more people producing more new, high-density information than ever before, preexisting information is both easier to retrieve and circulates more widely. Changes in the flow of information are also evident in "the widespread reformulation of what constitutes an archive, and just as importantly what constitutes an archivist" (Collins 1995: 25). Recent digital technologies allow individuals to easily manipulate information, thereby creating data collections reflective of their own personal tastes. The low cost of CD technology – not to mention the development of digital audio players such as the Apple iPod – allows individuals to create their own "greatest hits" collection and makes owning the complete works of virtually any musical artist, regardless of obscurity, possible.

But perhaps the most significant change in information flow concerns the collapse of the temporal-spatial relationship between the three stages in the communication process, production, transmission, and processing (Naisbitt 1982: 22). For roughly 100,000 years, communication has been predominantly either asynchronous or synchronous (Shenk 1997: 28). In asynchronous communication, there is a time gap separating the production of information and its reception. Historically, this gap has existed because the sender and receiver were separated geographically, and the channel relied upon the prevailing modes of transportation. The current US Postal Service continues to operate under this model, and a handwritten letter still travels by plane, train, or automobile. In synchronous communication, there is no time gap. Information is processed *as* it is produced, such as conversing with a friend by telephone. Computers, television, and satellites, however, allow for the possibility of faster-than-synchronous communication, meaning that information can be transmitted more quickly than it can be processed. In a few minutes, one can download a library-worth of information from across the globe. Even CNN Headline News, with it graphics, scrolling text, and talking heads, offers information more rapidly than it can be received by the typical viewer.

Society through the Lens of Technocapitalism

As we have seen, the information explosion – arguably the most salient and influential characteristic of contemporary life – is a consequence of changes in the production, format, and flow of information. But what caused those changes? And how have those changes, in turn, transformed our society economically, politically, and culturally? To answer such questions, I utilize Douglas Kellner's notion of *technocapitalism*. "A theory of techno-capitalism," Kellner (1989) explains, "would

combine analysis of new technologies with investigations of the dia-
lectical interrelationships between technology and economy and the
impact of new technologies on economics, politics, society, culture and
everyday life" (190). Following this approach, my aim in this section
is to identify what is meant by the new information technologies,
chart the three key social trends in the rise of these technologies, and
map the changing contours of capitalism in contemporary society.

The phrase "new information technologies," sometimes alternatively referred to as the new electronic or digital media, describes a
coterie of technologies widely adopted by the public since the 1960s
and engineered for creating, manipulating, and moving information
more quickly and easily. The category includes, but is not limited to,
computers, scanners, digital cameras, fax machines, compact disc play-
ers/recorders, videocassette players/recorders, digital video devices,
personal data assistants, cell phones, video games, remote control
devices, satellite dishes, and television. Collectively, the new information technologies have exerted tremendous influence on our society.
In fact, as communication scholar Robert Cathcart (1993) explains,
"Technology is not something distinct from the environment or just
another tool in our environment. Technology *is* our environment"
(289–90). Sociologist Manuel Castells (2000) concurs, noting that
"technology *is* society, and society cannot be understood or represented without its technological tools" (5). To put it another way,
technological innovation is the most fundamental force in triggering
social change (see Castells 2001a: 155; Taylor 2001: 19). Given technology's vital role in shaping society, Ava Collins (1994) maintains that
"talking about popular culture in the 1990s necessarily involves talking
about the new mass communication and information technologies"
(57). As such, it is worth examining the prevailing trends of technological innovation during and leading up to the 1990s.

Trend 1: The rapid *development and adoption of information
technologies*

Unlike the printing press, which emerged slowly and took hundreds of
years to broadly penetrate and reconfigure society, the new information technologies have been developed and adopted at an unprecedented rate. Notes one observer, "Since 1987 we've added over 130
million information receptacles. Americans now [in 1994] possess

148.6 million email addresses, cellular phones, pagers, fax machines, voice mailboxes, and answering machines – up 365 percent, from 40.7 million in 1987" (Tetzeli 1994: 60). Because technology is such a central and powerful force of social change, the rate at which it evolves and is implemented influences the "*rate* of change, [which] has implications quite apart from, and sometimes more important than, the *direction* of change" (Toffler 1970: 4). Since the rapid adoption of television has already been explored in chapter 1, this section focuses on other information technologies. I begin by surveying the penetration rates of what I call "ancillary technologies" because they are used in conjunction with television; then, I examine the development and adoption of computers – a technology of nearly equal influence to television in the 1990s. The following statistics suggest the swiftness with which an array of ancillary technologies were adopted:

- Ownership of videocassette recorders (VCRs) went from 175,000 units in 1978 to 5 million in 1982 to 11 million in 1985. By 1991, nearly three-quarters of American households were equipped with a VCR (Signorielli 1991: 126).
- Prerecorded videocassette sales rose from only three million in 1980 to 220 million in 1990 – an increase of 6,500 percent (Schatz 1992: 25).
- In 1998, 82 percent of TV households had at least one videocassette recorder (Croteau & Hoynes 2003: 4–5).
- In 1996, remote control devices (RCDs) were in over 90 percent of US households – up significantly from 29 percent in 1985. Nearly 300 million RCDs were estimated to be used with broadcast television, VCRs, cable services, or audio CD players in 1995. This figure was expected to grow to nearly 400 million by 1997, as more consumer electronic devices were sold with RCDs as standard equipment (Bellamy & Walker 1996: 1–2).
- In 1998, the electronic-games industry posted sales of $5.5 billion in the US, making it the second-most popular form of home entertainment after TV. According to one survey, 90 percent of US households with children have rented or owned a video or computer game (Quittner 1999: 50).

As important as these ancillary technologies are, it is computers, contends Wurman (1989), that "have become a ubiquitous symbol of a new age, mascots of the information era and of a new way of thinking" (84). Excessively slow, bulky, awkward, and expensive when they first appeared, computers developed at a remarkable pace. ENIAC, the first modern computer, was constructed in 1944. It was larger than a tractor-trailer, weighed more than 15 automobiles, used a whopping 140,000 watts of electricity, and could perform only about 5,000 arithmetic operations per second. The 486 microprocessor typical of computers in the early-1990s, by contrast, was about the size of a dime, weighed less than a packet of Sweet 'N Low, required less than 2 watts of electricity, and could execute 54 million instructions per second (Pritchett 1994: 24). Although the world's first commercial microprocessor introduced in 1971, the 4-bit Intel 4004, performed about 60,000 calculations per second, the introduction of the Intel Pentium Pro in 1995 increased performance to roughly 250 million calculations per second (Swerdlow 1995: 15). So rapid have been the advances in computing power that in 1994 the typical person wore more computing power on his or her wrist than existed in the world before 1961 (Morrison & Schmid 1994: 171). With the cost of computing power decreasing roughly 30 percent every year, it "is now 8,000 times less expensive than it was 30 years ago" (Pritchett 1994: 25, 31). In the mid-90s, when microchips were doubling in performance power every 18 months, Randall Tobias, the Vice Chairperson of AT&T, offered this analogy, "If we had [experienced] similar progress in automotive technology, today you could buy a Lexus for about $2. It would travel the speed of sound, and go about 600 miles on a thimble of gas" (quoted in Pritchett 1994: 41)

The rapid pace of computer development is closely paralleled by the rapid pace of computer adoption and internet use. *Time* columnist Thomas McCarroll (1991) reports that, "During the 1980s, Corporate America spent about $98 billion on 57 million personal computers" (45). During that same time period, the US Defense Department, which had been developing the internet (under the name ARPANET) for military reasons since the 1960s, pushed to commercialize it by financing US computer manufacturers to included network protocols (Castells 2001b: 12). Hence, most computers in the US had networking capabilities by 1990. As computers became connected through the internet, the total number of US email addresses grew by more than 26 million between 1987 and 1994

(Tetzeli 1994: 62). The first version of the hypertext system known as the World Wide Web was developed by Tim Berners-Lee in 1990, but it was University of Illinois student Marc Andreessen's introduction of Mosaic, a free user-friendly web browser, in 1993 that began to popularize the web (Castells 2001b: 16). The first commercial web browser, Netscape Navigator, was introduced in 1994, and a year later Microsoft developed its own browser, Internet Explorer, which it released in conjunction with the Windows 95 operating system. As computing technology increased in power and decreased in cost, computers increasingly became standard fixtures in the home as well as at work.

With the objective of "connect[ing] all Americans to the information infrastructure," the US Department of Commerce's National Telecommunication and Information Administration (NTIA) studied telephone penetration, personal computer (PC) ownership, and internet use in American households in a series of four reports (1995, 1998, 1999, and 2000) titled "Falling Through the Net." Table 2.1 summarizes the findings of these reports.

The data in table 2.1 suggest just how rapidly American households adopted personal computers and began using the internet during the 1990s. Between 1994 and 1997, the personal computer penetration rate grew substantially, increasing by 51.9 percent, while email access expanded by 391.1 percent in that same three-year period (Falling Through the Net 1998). By the turn of the decade, 53.7 million American households (or 51.0 percent of all households) had personal computers and 43.6 million (or 41.5 percent of all households) had internet access. From 1997 to 2000, US households with computers rose by nearly 40 percent, while internet use skyrocketed by 123 percent (Falling Through the Net 2000: 2). In 1999, nearly 85 million Americans were going online at some location, and 5.6 million of

Table 2.1: Percentage of US households with a telephone, personal computer, and internet

	1994	1997	Dec. 1998	Aug. 2000
Telephone	93.8%	93.8%	94.1%	94.6%
Personal computer	24.1%	36.6%	42.1%	51.0%
Internet	< 1%	18.6%	26.2%	41.5%

them – double the number from two years earlier – were teenagers (Okrent 1999: 38). Internet use also showed a prolific increase internationally during the 1990s, jumping from three million users worldwide in 1994 to more than 147 million users by year-end 1998. In 1999, traffic on the internet was doubling every 100 days (Meares & Sargent 1999: 5).

Trend 2: The demassification of media

Over the past 30 years, information technologies have exhibited a second key trend, demassification. This trend is animated by the reconceptualization of audiences. During the era of "mass communication," audiences were typically conceptualized and treated as an anonymous, homogenous entity. Thus, they were targeted with *standardized* messages and products that pandered to general and usually popular tastes. As the media and information technologies have matured, however, they have also diversified their content offerings, becoming increasingly specialized and developing niche markets. In 1982, John Naisbitt offered the following analysis of the magazine industry:

> What is happening in America is that the general purpose or umbrella instrumentalities are folding everywhere. An instructive analog was the collapse more than a decade ago of the general-purpose magazines, *Life*, *Look*, and *The Saturday Evening Post*, with their 10 million circulations. The same year those great mass-audience magazines folded, 300 new special-interest magazines were born. Soon there were 600, 800, and more. We now have 4,000 special-interest magazines and no general-purpose magazines. That is the analog for what is happening throughout society. (99–100)

As with the print media, radio and television are moving toward greater specialization and niche marketing. Since the 1950s, "The diversity of [radio] offerings has," explains Toffler (1980), "sharply increased, with different stations appealing to specialized audience segments instead of to the hitherto undifferentiated mass audience" (176). Between 1950 and 1980, the number of radio stations grew from 700 to 9,000 – a rate that far exceeded population growth (Naisbitt 1982: 100–1). As a result, individuals have greater choice today within a single radio market, everything from hard rock, soft rock and punk to rap, country, and folk. Add to that news, talk, and sports radio and the targeting of subcultural tastes becomes even clearer.

Television, too, has shifted its paradigm from a culture of mass taste to more specialized, fragmented taste cultures (Seabrook 1997: 182). It began in the 1980s, first with the introduction of CNN for serious news aficionados and then with the so-called "MTV explosion" for music lovers. But it did not end there. ESPN was launched to target sports fans, Nickelodeon and the Disney Channel to attract children, the History Channel to appease history buffs, and the Sci-Fi channel to reach science fiction fans. Over time, these taste cultures have subdivided even further. In the news arena, for instance, CNN faces competition from Fox News Channel, two C-Spans, CNBC, MSNBC, and Court TV. "Local TV news programming is [also] booming – up to six or seven hours a day on some stations – and 18 regional cable channels offer 24-hour local news. . . . The result is a proliferation of narrowcast and personalized news sources and a decline in traditional broadcast and mass market outlets" (Zoglin 1996: 61).

What print, radio, and television media have begun, the internet has perfected. Although there were less than 50 websites in the world in 1993, at the turn of the twenty-first century, there were by one conservative estimate more than 8 billion pages on the World Wide Web (Biocca 2000: 23). To many internet observers it seems as though there is a website dedicated to every interest, no matter how personal or obscure. The technologies underlying networked computers are ideal for narrowcasting and niche marketing. Each time an individual visits a commercial website, such as Amazon.com, it generates a cookie – a small data file on the user's computer that records the user's interests and preferences and updates them during subsequent visits. By accessing this cookie, websites can display products and advertisements on their webpages that are specifically targeted toward the interests of that visitor. Therefore, even if two people go to the same website, they will receive personalized content. The diversification of content reflected by the demassification of the media should not be confused with diversification in ownership patterns, however. At the same time that media *content* has become more specialized and thus diverse, media *ownership* has become increasingly concentrated (see Croteau & Hoynes 2003: 34–5). Today, the vast majority of media are owned and controlled by a few multinational conglomerates, such as Time Warner, Viacom, and News Corporation.

Trend 3: An altered sense of time and space

The proliferation of the new information technologies has profoundly modified our sense – our felt experience – of time and space (Harvey 1991: 77; see also Croteau & Hoynes 2003: 304–5; Grenz 1996: 35; Sarup 1996: 98–104). Prior to the widespread adoption of electronic media, time and space were viewed as relatively fixed, immutable concepts. Time, it seemed, elapsed in steady, predictable increments. But today, we speak of "losing time," "time shortages," and "a lack of time." In their book *Time for Life: The Surprising Ways Americans Use Their Time*, John P. Robinson and Geoffrey Godbey (1997) note that "American society is starving ... for the ultimate scarcity of the post-modern world, time" (34). Given the perception of "time-famine," it is not surprising that we fill our lives with "time-saving" devices and strategies, as though time is mysteriously vanishing or passing more quickly than it once did (Gleick 1999: 9–13). In our daily lives, we may impatiently hit the "close door button" on the elevator a second or even third time in the hopes that the door will close faster. The sense that time is in short supply is related to the faster-than-synchronous communication capabilities of the new information technologies. In an environment that delivers information more quickly than it can be processed, we feel a shortness of time. What is shortened, of course, is not time itself, but the length of time between the sending of a message and its reception. John Naisbitt (1982) describes this time that a message is in transit as "information float." Since the 1980s, the new information technologies have steadily collapsed information float, creating an environment where information no longer seems to travel at all (Naisbitt 1982: 22–3; see also Davis & Meyer 1998: 6). Rather it is immediately available. The *immediacy* of information fosters the sense that we are forever out of time. One indication of the public's changing sense of time has been the use of the colloquialism *snail* mail to refer to standard postal mail.

Not only does time feel less abundant today, but it also feels less rigid. In a society once dominated by print consciousness, time appeared to unfold in a highly sequential, predictable, and linear manner. Messages, particularly stories, tended to follow a "straight line" with a clear beginning, middle, and end. Television and cinema, however, have been key forces in disrupting this sense of temporal regularity and linearity (Harvey 1990: 308–23; see also Lash 2002: 18–19). The reason has to do with the "arrangement" or editing of visual media. Depending upon how two scenes are edited together, time on television can pass more slowly than, more quickly than, or at the same speed as "real" time (see Kozloff 1992: 87–8). With a slow dissolve between two scenes, for instance, several days of narrative time can pass in a matter of seconds. Moreover, through the use of flashback, time can seemingly reverse direction. Add to that the highly fragmentary nature of television – with its disconnected sound bites, brief news capsules, and endless commercial interruptions – and time begins to feel less like a continuous thread and more like a patchwork of moments or instances. Moreover, remote control devices, VCRs, and TiVo all allow viewers to manipulate the temporality of messages by speeding them up, rewinding them, and skipping through them. Cumulatively, these technologies have fueled our sense that time is fluid and malleable.

Our sense of space, like our sense of time, has noticeably been altered by the rise of the new information technologies. For generations, as social historian Michel Foucault (1980) explains, "space was treated [by theorists] as the dead, the fixed, the undialectical, the immobile" (70). But technology has forced a rethinking of this view. Perhaps the most noticeable shift in the way we experience space is related to *compression* (Harvey 1990: 240). The near instantaneous nature of communication in the *global village* has collapsed the sense of distance associated with geography. Television beams images from around the globe into our homes on a nightly basis, allowing us to visit and see other places "virtually" first hand. Meanwhile, according to Peter Large, "Computer networks have grown so sophisticated as to stretch our conceptions of space and time. Getting credit card approval to use your American Express card in Paris involves a 46,000-mile journey over phones and computers that can be completed in five seconds" (quoted in Wurman 1989: 305). The internet has, in fact, introduced a whole new lexicon of spatial terms, including cyberspace, hyperspace, electronic ether, and virtual reality. We now speak of internet users "going" online, "visiting" websites, and "meeting" people in chatrooms even though there is no physical travel involved. Such "postmodern hyper-space can be invented and with equal ease commanded to vanish," according to political scientist Pauline Rosenau (1992), and "[it] is dramatically at odds with the philosophical material world of conventional science, where concrete objects, located in an objective geographical space, are charted in terms of latitude and longitude" (69).

The rapid adoption of the new information technologies, the demassification of media, and the changing sense of time and space fueled by computing and telecommunications have all been key forces in the shift to an information economy. Heather Hudson and Louis Leung (1988) situate this shift within a larger historical context:

> We are living in an era of transition. A century ago, the United States was beginning to shift from a primarily extractive economy to an industrial economy in which a majority of economic activity consisted of the transformation of raw materials into manufactured goods. Today we are witnessing a shift from an industrially based economy to an information-based economy. (36)

It is worth noting that while this most recent transition constitutes a major paradigm shift, or to use a geological metaphor – a series of tectonic plate shifts, both industrial and information economies are modes or *phases* of capitalism. Capitalism is not a stagnant system and therefore must be examined in historical context. A discussion of the shift from an industrial economy to an information economy, then, is really a discussion of the dramatic changes in our capitalist system during the past 30 years (Kellner 1989: 176). Moreover, to describe the current phase of capitalism as an information economy is not to suggest that we did not previously deal in information or that we do not currently deal in industrially manufactured products. This shift from industrialism to informationalism is a matter of emphasis, just as the shift from agrarianism to industrialism was a matter of emphasis. Agriculture, after all, did not abruptly halt following the Industrial Revolution; it simply diminished in economic importance. Hence, "the process of capitalist restructuring undertaken since the 1980s," according to Manuel Castells (2000), "can be adequately characterized as *informational capitalism*" (18). In the next sections, I will argue that informational capitalism reflects three deeply intertwined shifts: the shift from goods producing or industrial manufacturing to information services, from Fordism to flexible accumulation, and from nation-state to globalization.

Shift 1:   From goods production to information services

Throughout the nineteenth and twentieth centuries, much of the US workforce was involved in industrial occupations and assembly-line work. During the 1950s, for instance, fully 65 percent of Americans worked in manufacturing jobs where they were involved in the mass production of durable or hard goods, while only 17 percent worked in information jobs such as accounting, engineering, lawyering, and teaching (Naisbitt 1982: 14, 39). "By the late 1970s, however, only 13 percent of American workers were [still] involved in the manufacture of goods, whereas a full 60 percent were engaged in the 'manufacture' of information" (Grenz 1996: 17). During the decade of the 1990s, the services sector, and in particular the information technology (IT) services sector, became an increasingly central and vital component of the US economy (The Technological Reshaping 1995). From 1977 to 1998, information technology's share of the US economy nearly doubled, and between 1995 and 1997, IT reflected more than a third of US economic growth (Meares & Sargent 1999: 5). In 1991 alone, information rather than durable goods was already generating more than a third of the nation's $5.5 trillion gross national product (McCarroll 1991: 44). Although two-thirds of US Americans were working in the services sector by the mid-1990s (Pritchett 1994: 1), the shift began in the 1970s with the creation of 20 million new jobs, 90 percent of which were information, knowledge, and service jobs as opposed to only 5 percent in manufacturing (Naisbitt 1982: 21).

The service economy is an admittedly diverse sector that includes "traditional services" related to food (cooks), education (teachers), transportation (airline pilots), health (doctors) and housing (architects and realtors), "system facilitation services" related to the social infrastructure (economists, bankers, and insurance agents), and the "new information services" related to communication and entertainment (advertisers, marketers, journalists, intellectuals, and computer programmers) (Barber 2001: 78–9). What these seemingly unrelated services have in common, among other things, is a concern with soft goods as opposed to hard goods. Like an industrial economy, an informational economy is concerned with the production and marketing of commodities. But in the new economy, unlike the old, information has superceded hard goods as the principal commodity (Lyotard 1984: 18). During the Industrial Age, factory workers mass-produced durable goods aimed at the body such as clothing, furniture, and automobiles. Today, machines largely produce such goods, so the job of workers has become the production of soft goods, which are aimed at the mind and spirit. The modern workforce manufactures *desires* for goods through marketing, advertising, spin, promotion, and packaging, rather than the goods themselves (Barber 2001: 5–60; Rifkin 2000: 8–9, 82–91). "Global advertising expenditures," notes Benjamin Barber (2001), "have climbed a third faster than the world economy and three times faster than world population, rising sevenfold from 1950 to 1990 from a modest $39 billion to $256 billion" (62). People no longer make hard goods; they sell images and ideologies, which as intangibles are "soft" goods.

Shift 2: From Fordism to flexible accumulation

The shift from manufacturing-based jobs to more service-based occupations has been accompanied by a related shift in the underlying modes of production and consumption. Fordism describes the mass production of *standardized products* at affordable prices for *mass consumption*. It is based on the practices developed, implemented, and popularized by Henry Ford in the early twentieth century. In 1914, Ford introduced the first moving assembly-line at his Highland Park automobile manufacturing plant in Detroit. This and subsequent large-scale industrial plants divided the production process into a specific sequence of tasks that could be performed by unskilled or semiskilled workers with specialized equipment. Workers engaged in the same strict, limited routines every day. Since the mechanized production line enforced rigid, inflexible rules of production, the end product was highly standardized. Ford was famous for his pronouncement that, "customers could have an automobile in any colour they desired – as long as it was black" (quoted O'Sullivan et al. 1994: 117). By simplifying, centralizing, mechanizing, and standardizing the production process, Ford managed to significantly reduce production costs and manufacture an affordable automobile that lent itself to mass consumption.

An unintended side-effect of Fordism and its highly regimented work conditions at Ford Motors was worker *alienation*. "Beyond repeatedly performing their specific tasks," economist Roger Alcaly (2004) explains, "assembly-line workers had no role in the operation.... Workers were [even] discouraged from offering suggestions for making their jobs more efficient" (123). To combat alienating work conditions, Ford offered workers what he called "profit sharing" bonuses that potentially boosted workers' pay to $5 per day. This "good salary" encouraged workers to keep their jobs and simultaneously increased their buying power, allowing them to purchase a car or other consumer goods. But the homogenization of labor ultimately fueled the success of labor organizers, and the United Automobile Workers (UAW) won the right to bargain on behalf of Ford workers in the 1930s. At the height of industrialism in the 1950s and 1960s, more workers, 32 percent, were unionized than ever would be again (Naisbitt 1982: 39). The emergence of the new information technologies in the late 1960s and early 1970s began to change everything, however. According to David Harvey (1990), "Most close observers of the capitalist scene ... concede that [since 1970 or so] something important has happened to the capitalist organization of production, consumption, and accumulation" (70). That "something" was the onset of deindustrialization, variously referred to as "post-Fordism," "flexible specialization," and "flexible accumulation."

The central principle that each of these concepts emphasize is *flexibility*. In the new informational economy of the 1990s, mass production gave way to individual customization. Slowly, personalized products have come to replace standardized products, and specialized and niche marketing have come to replace mass marketing. Whereas Ford Motors typifies Fordism, Dell Computers typifies flexible accumulation. The Dell business model is a build-to-order system that stresses flexibility at multiple levels. Instead of trying to do everything itself like Ford, Dell develops close partnerships with other companies like Sony and UPS, whom it relies upon for various aspects of its business. Since Sony already produces reliable computer monitors, Dell simply acquires it monitors as needed from Sony, which it then combines with other modular components to be packaged and shipped by UPS. Due to customization, there is also little need for inventory, which reduces overstock and storage costs. This is all made possible because of real-time communication. When a customer places a computer order at Dell's website, Sony is immediately informed that it needs to deliver x number of monitors. And by maintaining electronic records on every computer it builds, Dell technicians are able to identify problems more quickly when complaints arise. By integrating information technologies into the sales process, Dell has effectively made its customers part of the production process.

Shift 3: From nation-state to globalization

International trade is certainly nothing new. For centuries, goods have crossed geographic and national boundaries. But during the industrial societies of the nineteenth and twentieth centuries, the exporting and importing of goods was closely tied to the "God-given" location of natural resources in particular geographic regions (Thurow 1996: 8–9). Bananas were grown where the climate was suitable for banana growing, oil was tapped where oil existed, and coal was mined from coal-rich areas, and the countries that lacked these natural resources were forced to purchase them abroad. The uneven distribution of natural resources posed an economic dilemma for many nations. If you import more than you export – known as a trade deficit – or have alternative resources within your boundaries that would be undercut by importation of other resources, how do you sustain economic viability? For many nations, the answer came in the form of economic policies such as bailouts, tariffs, regulations, embargoes, and price-fixing schemes (Barber 2001: 31). By subsidizing nationally produced goods and greatly taxing foreign goods, governments sought to protect their national economic interests. So, while it is fair to say that there was a "world" economy in the industrial era, where countries exchanged commodities, the specific practices of capital accumulation were principled on the interests of individual nation-states.

Whereas the old *world economy* operated in the interest of nation-states, the new *global economy* operates in the interest of multinational corporations. This shift in economic practices is known as globalization. "The map of globalization is one where separate national economies are becoming part of a new decentered economy" (Hartley 2002: 98; see also Fox 2001: 20; Waters 2001: 88–92). Like the other economic shifts of the 1980s and 1990s, this shift is closely related to information technologies. As technologically advanced nations have increasingly shifted from goods production to information services (see Barber 2001: 75; Lash 2002: 26), the need and ability to impose tariffs, for instance, has diminished. How does a national government tax the near instantaneous and free flow of information and capital across global telecommunications and computing networks (Hartley 2002: 98)? Information technologies have created a new cultural space – the global – that erases and destabilizes traditional national and geographic boundaries (O'Sullivan et al.

1994: 130; see also Davidson & Rees-Mogg 1999: 15–16). Driven by the capitalist desire to maximize profits, since the 1980s corporations have been, in the words of economist Lester Thurow (1996), "making each component and performing each activity at the place on the globe where it can be most cheaply done.... Sentimental attachment to some geographic part of the world is not part of the system" (115).

These changes have led to the rise of powerful multinational or transnational corporations and the fundamental restructuring of economic practices. Today, it hardly makes sense to think of a company like General Motors, for instance, as an American corporation when 40 percent of its cars are produced outside of the US and it "employs more people internationally than live in a number of the world's smaller nations" (Barber 2001: 30, 23–4). In a global economy, the principles of free trade rooted in the capitalist ideology of *laissez-faire* – the idea that the market should be left alone – have replaced the principles of protectionism implemented by nation-states. "Globalism," notes political scientist Benjamin Barber (2001), "is mandated by profit not citizenship" (24). Indeed, economic policies motivated by nationalism are largely banned today, bans that are enforced by international agencies such as the World Trade Organization (WTO) and the International Monetary Fund. While some nations, such as China, resisted this shift at first, the force of globalization was too powerful, and China reluctantly joined the WTO in 2001.

The economic trend toward globalization has had two important consequences on the US workforce. First, it significantly undercut the effectiveness of labor unions as bargaining agents, whose political power relies upon the principles of nationalism and economic sovereignty to be effective. An abundance of cheap labor in the "developing world" enables companies to employ "geographic mobility" as a threat in bargaining sessions, telling their employees, "Settle for lower wages and fewer benefits or we will go overseas" (Harvey 1991: 67–8; see also Rifkin 2000: 44–50; Thurow 1996: 17). Many corporations have improved their bottom line simply by decreasing employee benefits such as costly pension packages and health care. Under the threat of outsourcing, workers have little choice but to accept these terms. Second, globalization has fueled corporate downsizing. The new business model, which utilizes information technologies to do the work of many employees, operates on the principle of "lean and mean" (Barber 2001: 27). According to Thurow (1996),

"Announced downsizing soared to 600,000 in 1993, [and] set a one-month all-time record of 104,000 in January 1994" (26). Ultimately, downsizing simply reflects the larger strategy of profit maximization, which includes reducing the number of full-time and long-term employees, who expect to be paid more and have more benefits.

Social Anxieties in the Information Age

The information explosion, rise of the new information technologies, and fundamental restructuring of our capitalist economic system are all evidence of a dramatic social paradigm shift from the Industrial Age to the Information Age. Such rapid and axiomatic change is bound to be disruptive to the human psyche. As the business and international affairs analyst Michael Mazarr (2001) explains in *Global Trends 2005*:

> It should be abundantly clear by now that the advent of a knowledge era [the Information Age], and the associated social and economic transform-ations implied in that transition, will place individuals under immense strain. Coping with change is never easy; coping with the sort of acceler-ated, comprehensive change that we face today could turn out to be the severest test that history has ever imposed on human psychology. (237)

Business consultant and best-selling author, Harry Dent, Jr. (1998), agrees, suggesting that:

> We are in the midst of a huge transition from an old economy to a new one. Human beings accept change grudgingly under the best of cir-cumstances and, since we are facing such massive change today, it is even harder to swallow.... An old economy of products, technologies, and methods of work has reached its maturity. To remain competitive, this economy is struggling to re-engineer itself, to change its time-honored practices and philosophies. Though this is a good move in the long run, right now it only adds to the confusion and anxiety. (95)

Thus, the aim of this section is to chart the psychological strains or social concerns associated with life in the Information Age. Specifically, I contend that the rise of informationalism has resulted in five principal anxieties: feeling overwhelmed, feeling placeless, feeling frenzied, feeling guilty, and feeling fragmented.

Information overload

By 1984, changes in the production, format, and flow of information had generated such a large volume of information at such an alarming rate that John Naisbitt (1982) declared, "This level of information is clearly impossible to handle by present means" (24). Despite his warning, society continued to churn out more and more information throughout the 1980s and 1990s, until we found ourselves overwhelmed by and drowning in a vast sea of semiotic excess. Although information *can* be a good thing, apparently the old axiom that "one can have too much of a good thing" is also accurate. There is a critical point at which the volume and rate of information goes from being useful and instructive to being damaging and debilitating. As individuals were and continue to be flooded by an unending torrent of information from the moment they awake in the morning until the time they fall asleep at night, information overload and information anxiety have begun to exact a serious toll on the human psyche. The feeling of being inundated by too much information can specifically lead to both *decision paralysis* and *information fatigue syndrome* (Edmunds & Morris 2000: 18).

Analysis or decision paralysis arises when one is confronted with so much information that one is literally paralyzed – unable to act on it. Anyone who has traveled to the grocery store and stood in an aisle starring vacantly at the vast assortment of product choices unable to select one has experienced a mild version of this problem. Or perhaps your town has so many restaurants that it has actually become a chore to decide where to eat. Often today, individuals are besieged by so much information that they do not know *where* or *how* to begin processing it. So, in many cases, they simply stop trying. As *Time* columnist Richard Zoglin (1996) explains, "the information explosion hides a paradox. At the same time that people are being inundated with the news as never before, their interest in the news seems to be shrinking. They are just . . . too overwhelmed by all the choices" (61). Too much information often produces apathy – a fact that may account for declining voter participation (see Pelton 1992: 62). In 1960, 62.8 percent of eligible voters went to the polls; but in 1996, following a campaign that inundated citizens with sound bites for months on end, voter turnout had dropped to 48.9 percent (Putnam 2000: 31–2).

Information fatigue syndrome refers to the feeling of tiredness that can accompany too much information. Increasingly, employees report a sense of exhaustion associated with the enormous amount of information they receive and are expected to read and respond to. Email has contributed significantly to this problem by making it easy to disseminate information, as has the internet, which has greatly simplified the task of locating information on virtually any subject. Add to this the mental energy required to process the overwhelming volume of, often unsolicited, information one receives, and it is not hard to understand why caffeine is the most popular drug in the US and drug companies are now creating designer drugs and specialty beverages to help individuals stay alert, focused, and energized.

Identity drift

Although identity formation is a complex process, most scholars agree that the creation and maintenance of a meaningful sense of identity depends upon self-location – the ability to *locate* one's self in time and space (Collins 1995: 31). Traditionally, one defined oneself in terms of national and geographic boundaries, declaring "I'm an American" or "I'm a Texan" (Kellner 1995: 231–2). History, too, was an important marker of identity. Were you born before or after the Second World War? Are you part of the Baby Boom? These spatial and temporal reference points assisted people in creating a stable, meaningful sense of self. But the rise of the information technologies and flexible, global economy have drastically disrupted our understandings of time and space, and in the process fostered a sense of placelessness and a feeling of drift. Joshua Meyrowitz (1985) offered an early account of this phenomenon:

[E]lectronic media, especially television, have had a tremendous impact on Americans' sense of place. Electronic media have combined previously distinct social settings, moved the dividing line between private and public behavior toward the private, and weakened the relationship between social situations and physical places. The logic underlying situational patterns of behavior in a print-oriented society, therefore, has been radically subverted. Many Americans may no longer seem to "know their place" because the traditionally interlocking components of "place" have been split apart by electronic media. Wherever one is now – at home, at work, or in a car – one may be in touch and tuned-in.... Our world may suddenly seem senseless to many people because, for the first time in modern history, it is relatively placeless. (308)

This sense of placelessness should not be confused with the anomie or alienation often associated with modernity. Rather, it describes the feeling of being "un-tethered" even when one is "at home." Today, the once fixed boundaries of time and space are crossed with equal ease on television and the internet. One can be "witness to" events across the globe *as they occur*, or travel to virtual electronic worlds – or nowheres – and interact with and even fall in love with other people.

The rise of the image and corresponding culture of simulacra has resulted in a *flattening* of History. One can seemingly experience the ancient world of the dinosaurs through a film like *Jurassic Park* (1993) or the horrors of the Holocaust through *Schindler's List* (1993). These realer-than-real images have had "a momentous effect on what used to be historical time," by creating a sense of the "past" rooted in pseudohistorical depth, pop history, and the history of aesthetic styles (Jameson 1991: 18–25). It is not uncommon today to hear individuals talk about historical films as experiences rather than as re-presentations of the past. Several years ago, I had a student in a public-speaking class giving a speech on the assassination of John F. Kennedy. As part of his persuasive attempt to convince students of a government conspiracy to cover up the President's assassination, he showed a video clip from Oliver Stone's fictional film *JFK* (1991) as historical evidence. None of the students in the class questioned the evidence, as though "reel" history were "real" history. This lack of historicity intensifies the postmodern feeling of identity drift.

Acceleration

The rapid adoption of the new information technologies along with the collapse of "information float" brought on by those technologies has left many people feeling rushed, frenzied, and "short of time" (Gleick 1999: 9; see also Davidson & Rees-Mogg 1999: 17; Gitlin 2001: 85–6). In fact, in 1994, 51 percent of Americans reported that they did not have enough time to do all that they wanted to (Tetzeli 1994: 62). As a result, individuals were perpetually in a hurry (and often in a huff as well). Given this frenetic state, it hardly surprising that America witnessed the emergence of a whole new psychological condition on its streets and highways in the 1990s – a condition dubbed "road rage." People feel so rushed and hurried in the Information Age that their patience and basic civility seems to be waning. They feel as though they lack the time to "wait" in lines or in traffic, or to engage in "idle" chat. After all, when they do get to their offices, they are likely to be told that they need to be "brought up to speed." For some, the very technologies designed to help us do things more quickly are themselves too slow. A common practice of web surfers in the 1990s using "slow" dial-up modems was to hit the back button on their browser if it seemed as though a webpage was taking too long to load. And who among us does not use the seemingly ridiculous length of time it takes our computers to boot up every morning to undertake another task?

In some ways, the "sense of acceleration is not just a vague and spotted impression," explains Nancy Gibbs (1989); "According to a Harris survey, the amount of leisure time enjoyed by the average American has shrunk [by] 37 percent since 1973. Over that same period of time, the average workweek, including commuting, has jumped from under 41 hours to nearly 47 hours" (58). Again, the new information technologies have been a key force in this shift. Email and cell phones have created the anywhere, anytime workplace, and increasingly US Americans are performing work-related activities even when they are not at work. Many Americans feel like they have to work longer hours in the new informational economy. Under the ever-present threat of outsourcing in a global economy, workers often feel compelled to put in more work-time. Finally, Americans must work longer hours just to stay abreast of the latest technological innovations. Never before in history has the workforce been required to retrain so frequently just to keep the jobs they already have (Naisbitt 1982: 37). According to Michael Verespej (1995) of *Industry Week*, by the mid-1990s technology-induced stress became the leading cause of job disability claims (48). Even when people are not at work and not working, there is still no escape from the relentless stream of electronic images and information. Our inability to escape the rapid information flow, whether at work or at home, has only added to the stress of feeling rushed (McIntyre 1995: E14; see also Borgman 1995: B01).

Not knowing much

Feelings of guilt arise whenever one violates a prevailing social hierarchy. Our society, for instance, values "hard work" over "laziness." Therefore, when one procrastinates to avoid work, he or she often feels a sense of guilt. In the Information Age, few things are more socially valued than knowledge and technical knowledge in particular. Hence, when persons lack knowledge, such as knowledge of or proficiency with the latest technology, they are violating a social hierarchy and often feel guilty. "The information explosion along with the ubiquity and increasing complexity of technology," note communication scholars Timothy Thompson and Anthony Palmeri (1993), "leave most people dwarfed by technology's superiority, ever more guilty of not keeping up with what is 'new'... [– ever more guilty] of *not knowing much* in an information-saturated society" (274–5).

In *The Employee Handbook of New Work Habits for a Radically Changing World* (1994), internationally renowned business consultant Price Pritchett provides an example of how modern "business discourse" fosters guilt about not keeping up with the latest technological innovations. In the book's introduction, Pritchett (1994) writes:

> New Technologies – especially computers and telecommunications – have already created intense, worldwide competition for business. Soon, competition for your own job could come from practically anywhere on earth. Careers have already quit working like they used to. That's not really *anybody's* fault. But employees and organizations are very much at fault if they, too, don't change in order to adapt. It does us no good whatsoever to complain or be bitter about what's happening. In fact, such behavior can only do us harm. . . . We jeopardize our future if we cling to old assumptions and expectations about how careers should operate. Frankly, the world doesn't care about our opinions. Or our feelings. The world rewards only those of us who catch on to what's happening, who invest our energy in finding and seizing the opportunities brought about by change.

From a rhetorical perspective, Pritchett's statement does three things. First, it locates new technologies, "especially computers and telecommunications," at the center of recent changes in the business world.

Second, it characterizes these changes as both *inevitable* ("does us no good whatsoever to complain" and "the world doesn't care about our opinions") and *vital* to career success ("We jeopardize our future if we cling to old assumptions"). Finally, it suggests that it is our "fault" if we do not "adapt" to these changes. Since change is equated with new technologies in Pritchett's discourse, adaptation is really about learning to use computer technologies. In short, Pritchett's message is if you fail to keep up with technological innovation, then it is your fault if you lose your job. Given the pervasiveness of such discourses in business, education, science, and government, it is hardly surprising that a lack of computer skills or literacy would be a significant source of guilt in US society.

Such feelings of guilt are particularly widespread among older workers. In an article for the *Centre Daily Times*, Reid Kanaley (1997) reports:

> Advances in desktop computing, publishing and design and, now, the rise of the internet, intranets and extranets represent "radical, almost revolutionary change" in the workplace, said David V. Day, who teaches work-related psychology at Penn State's main campus. For many workers, he said, the choice is to keep up, or "find yourself in the dust." "For those kids who've grown up with this stuff, they can easily integrate new technology, new advances into their repertoire," Day said. "But for some ... this is radical stuff." ... "Many people feel they've been left behind, they're worthless, because they just don't have an affinity for it," Beacham, 49, said in an interview. "To read the stuff today, you'd think everybody would have to be a master at the computer, or they'd be a failure."

The guilt of not knowing much in the Information Age is further exaggerated by the way that many Americans spend their ever-dwindling leisure time. As noted in chapter 1, television viewing is a significant source of leisure. But in our society, television viewing is valued less than virtually any other leisure activity, and in particular reading. Reading is taught, encouraged, and rewarded in our educational system, and literacy continues to be defined by teachers almost exclusively as a textual practice. Television, by contrast, is defined as "mindless entertainment," "simple-minded," and "flat stupid" (Morrow 1991: 65; 1992: 50). Its unique visual logic is largely dismissed in a society that continues to judge intellect by the traditional standards of print consciousness. Watching TV, then, can be a significant source of guilt for viewers, who feel like they should be doing something "more intellectual." Television viewing is further associated with guilt by blaming it for social ills such as violence and the dissolution of traditional community (Swerdlow 1995: 6).

Fragmentation

In his landmark study of social life in "late capitalism," Fredric Jameson (1991) argues that the central cultural pathology of modernity, namely alienation of the subject, has been replaced in the Information Age by *fragmentation* of the subject (14). What has been termed *fragmentia* by David Shenk (1997) is "A relatively new cognitive disorder where one feels cut off from a sense of wholeness because of common exposure to only incomplete parts of things and ideas" (37). A feeling of incompleteness today arises from both the endless proliferation of media outlets and the very structure of those media (Schement & Curtis 1995: 120). We move through a multimedia environment involving radio, television, newspapers, junk mail, and magazines. Individual technologies such as television are themselves also characterized by a high degree of fragmentation, heterogeneity, and interruption (Connor 1997: 191; Fiske 1991: 58, 60; O'Day 1999: 117). The internet, too, delivers information in bits or packets, and displays information, at least on the World Wide Web, in a decentered, multimedia, hypertextual format. But more than a decade before the web was even developed, Alvin Toffler (1980) had alerted us to the expanding culture of fragmentation:

> On a personal level, we are all besieged and blitzed by fragments of imagery, contradictory or unrelated, that shake up our old ideas and come shooting at us in the form of broken or disembodied 'blips.' We live, in fact, in a 'blip culture.' . . . Instead of receiving long, related 'strings' of ideas, organized or synthesized for us [as in a print-based culture], we are increasingly exposed to short modular blips of information – ads, commands, theories, shreds of news, truncated blips and blobs that refuse to fit neatly into our pre-existing mental files. (181–2)

The feeling of fragmentation is fueled not only by the array and format of the new information technologies, but also by the economic and global consequences of those technologies.

International telecommunications and a global economy have exposed us to *pluralism*, or the co-existence of difference, as never before. Paradoxically, we feel fragmented by being part of a global community, where cultural, national, ethnic, and religious differences appear to be so immediate (Mazarr 2001: 175). The Information Age is also one of fragmentation, then, because "of over exposure to otherness – because, in traveling, you put yourself into a different reality; because as a result of immigration, a different reality comes to you; because, with no physical movement at all, only the relentless and ever-increasing flow of information, cultures interpenetrate" (Anderson 1995: 7). Whereas one once found homogeneity and unity in an appeal to national identity, one now finds heterogeneity and difference. This has divided the subject, split one's sense of self. The feeling of fragmentation is intensified still further by the rise of narrowcasting, niche marketing, and mass customization. As Richard Zoglin (1996) explains:

> People have an easier time of getting information that interests them personally, but it comes at the expense of [traditional notions of] community: they are less likely to share a common pool of information. . . . The audience is being further fragmented by the boom in news outlets catering to special interests. . . . In this fragmented environment, [the] news is no longer a common experience. (61, 62; see also Mazarr 2001: 175)

Like all social anxieties, the feelings of overload, placelessness, acceleration, guilt of not knowing much, and fragmentation brought on by the transition to the Information Age constitute a serious challenge to the human psyche. "But it is . . . wrong," explains Francis Fukuyama (1999), "to conclude that we are incapable of adapting to the tech nological and economic conditions of an age of information" (8). As noted in chapter 1, individuals learn how to adapt to dramatic social change and the anxieties it generates through public discourse. They simply must seek out, as Fredric Jameson (1991) explains, new cultural forms that allow them to "cognitively map" a sense of place and hence a sense of self in this new social landscape (54). Fortunately, a wide range of media texts address themselves to the social anxieties of life in the Information Age, offering an array of symbolic resources for confronting and resolving those anxieties (Collins 1995: 34). In the following two chapters, we turn to the symbolic equipments, to the stylistic medicines, found in primetime 1990s television. We begin with Hyperconscious Television – a cultural form that openly accepted the changes taking place around us, and thus, furnished persons with symbolic tools for "embracing" and "living in" the new social paradigm.

Chapter 3

Hyperconscious Television

A prevalent means of responding to the lack of consensus and image-orgy characteristic of the postmodern condition is that of irony. (Ellin 1999: 139)

The Simpsons *shapes the way Americans think, particularly the younger generation. (Cantor 2003: 67)*

Oh, Marge, cartoons don't have any deep meaning. They're just stupid drawings that give you a cheap laugh. (Homer J. Simpson 1991)

Embracing 'the Future': The Attitude of Yes

Hyperconscious television describes a category of television shows that share an overall attitude or orientation toward the Information Age and the corresponding information explosion. Thus far, I have described that attitude as one of "yes." Hyperconscious television reflects a "yes" attitude to the extent that it recognizes and embraces the new social paradigm. Above all, hyperconscious television displays an awareness of and playfulness with our semiotic-saturated culture. It seems to recognize that every story has already been told, that every plot device has already been tried, and that every character type has already been conceived. Operating as it does, then, in this world of the "already-said" (see Eco 1984: 67–8) – where originality and authenticity no longer seem possible – hyperconscious television abandons the pretense to be telling stories for the first time. It opts, instead, to playfully and often ironically comment on existing cultural forms and genres, plot devices and character types, and its own status as television. Hyperconscious television is specifically hyper*conscious* or aware in three senses. It is aware of the prevailing formulas and formats of media culture, which it endlessly recombines. It is aware of previous stories, televisual and otherwise, to which it continuously alludes. And it is aware of itself, upon which it comments routinely. Hence, the three cardinal characteristics of hyperconscious television are eclecticism, intertextuality, and self-reflexivity.

Not every television program I investigate in this chapter displays these three elements in equal proportion. Some shows, for instance, may make aggressive use of eclecticism, while only occasionally employing intertextuality and self-reflexivity. Despite the sometimes uneven adoption and use of these stylistic devices, the shows examined in this chapter are, nevertheless, best classified as hyperconscious television based on their general "yes" orientation toward the new social paradigm of the Information Age. Since that paradigm has been gradually emerging since the late 1960s, many of the traits explored in this chapter began to be seen in shows prior to the 1990s. What distinguishes the television of the 1990s from previous decades, however, is the frequency, intensity, and centrality of these conventions. Where appropriate, I highlight programs from earlier decades that were important antecedents for hyperconscious TV. The aim of this chapter is threefold: to define and illustrate the chief characteristics of hyperconscious TV through reference to 1990s programming, to undertake a sustained, close analysis of an exemplar, *The Simpsons*, and to examine the specific symbolic equipments this genre provides viewers for confronting the anxieties of living in the Information Age.

Eclecticism: generic hybridity and stylistic pastiche

Eclecticism describes a stylistic device in which a cultural text creatively mixes, blends, or recombines preexisting and relatively discrete cultural forms, formulas, and techniques. On television, eclecticism may involve interweaving well-known historical TV genres to create new generic hybrids, blending high and low artistic styles (Strinati 1995: 226), or even blurring the distinction between image and reality. Richard Campbell and Rosanne Freed (1993) explain that "television is certainly a fertile breeding ground for genre confusion. Categories once chiseled in granite melt in a swirl of crossover jargon: docudrama, infotainment, infomercial, dramedy" (77). One particularly clear predecessor of the trend toward generic hybridity was the ABC series *Moonlighting* (1985–9), starring Cybill Shepherd and Bruce Willis as the unlikely detective duo Maddie Hayes and David Addison. *Moonlighting* was equal parts drama and situation comedy (e.g., dramedy), and to a lesser extent part night-time soap opera, detective series, and even musical variety show (Thompson 1996: 113). So profound was the program's blurring of historical TV genres that the Directors Guild of America nominated one episode for best drama and another episode for best comedy in the same year, an occurrence unprecedented in the 50-year history of the guild (Horowitz 1986: 26). Similarly, the Writers Guild of American awarded the show best episodic comedy in 1985 and then best episodic drama in 1986. In its fusing dramatic elements with comedic syntax, Leah Vande Berg (1989) contends that *Moonlighting* made the familiar generic features of drama and comedy seem strange (26).

The traditional features of drama and situation comedy were made stranger still through the use of advanced digital technologies on David E. Kelley's hit series *Ally McBeal* (1997–2002), which *Entertainment Weekly* columnist Dan Snierson (2000) described as "FOX's provocative lawyer dramedy... famous for its off-kilter plot devices" (31). The show featured Calista Flockhart playing Ally McBeal – a single, neurotic lawyer living in Boston and looking for love. Kelley, concerned that voiceover had become a trite plot device for getting inside a character's head, decided to convey Ally's thoughts as visual fantasies. This led to scenes with magically inflating breasts, floor dragging tongues, foot-in-mouth gags, shrinking heads, dancing babies, and images of Ally being catapulted into a dumpster. But *Ally McBeal* was more than just a dramedy with digitally enhanced fantasies. It was, observes freelance television critic Tim Appelo (1999), a "perverse mixture [of]... sensitive emotions and slapstick fantasy, sharp courtroom drama and madcap song-and-dance routines" (6). Upon learning that her ex-lover's wife may be pregnant in the episode "Being There" (05/04/98), for instance, Ally attempts to trivialize the pain by concentrating on a silly melody. As she does this, the entire office staff breaks into a choreographed dance-routine to a song that exists only in Ally's mind.

As a televisual practice, eclecticism describes more than simply generic hybridity, however. In the world of television, it often involves combining strange and different camera shots, editing techniques, and plot devices. Perhaps no show better illustrates the full range of stylistic pastiche – the patchworking of various styles (see Hoesterey 2001) – than *Twin Peaks* (1990–1), ABC's short-lived surrealistic series about the murder of 17-year-old Laura Palmer (Hendler 2000: 181–2). Written and directed by offbeat filmmaker David Lynch, the series teased and confounded audiences with an unusually large, eccentric cast of characters, as well as a virtually endless array of intricate details, baffling non-sequitors, and nonlinear plot lines. Abandoning the traditional patterns of storytelling, *Twin Peaks* combined long, unbroken camera takes, often lasting from one commercial break to another, with subliminal montages such as the series' finale in which a terrified Laura Palmer is intercut with images of the evil Windom Earl. *Twin Peaks*' lingering camera shots of cherry pie, ceiling fans, doughnuts, chocolate bunnies, Douglas firs, owls, and a changing stoplight, explains David Bianculli (1996), "gave as much emphasis to visual images and lighting, and to the musical score and sound effects, as it did to the script and performances" (348). Two side-effects of hyperconscious television's eclectic impulse have been its conflation of high art and mass entertainment and its elevation of surface over depth, style and image over narrative.

Twin Peaks, perhaps more than any television series before or since, called into question the traditional distinction between high art and mass culture. One of the ways it accomplished this was by forsaking entertainment television's most fundamental convention – the idea of an ongoing series. In its two seasons, *Twin Peaks* portrayed only 32 days in the life of the small Washington town with the same name. Defying the "series" orientation of television by focusing on the murder of Laura Palmer, the show essentially wrote itself out of existence when it solved her murder (Thompson 1996: 158). In focusing on a single, finite story, *Twin Peaks* was stylistically more like literature and cinema than television – two art forms historically perceived as more artistic than television. Indeed, *Twin Peaks* set itself apart from standard television fare by pretending not to be television. By the mid-1990s, the show was airing in syndication on Bravo, the exclusive art-house cable channel, whose motto was "TV too good for TV."

Twin Peaks' importance in the history of 1990s television is also a product of its influence on the visual artistry of subsequent programs such as FOX's single-season *VR.5* (1995) and its more popular series

The X-Files (1993–2002).[1] It was not, however, the only or even the first series to radically supplant narrative with style and image. Several years earlier, the NBC cop-drama, *Miami Vice* (1984–9) had consciously opted in favor of decorative flourishes and dazzling cinematography over narrative and character depth. "In *Miami Vice*," explains Douglas Kellner (1995), "images are detached from narrative and seem to take on a life of their own.... Image frequently takes precedence over narrative and the look and feel become primary, often relegating story-line and narrative meanings to the background" (238–9; see also Hendler 2000: 179; Strinati 1995: 231–2). Music, too, was requisite to creating the show's unique look and feel; elaborates Bianculli (1996),

> This rock-driven, fashion-conscious, Uzi-filled cop show did a lot in the mid-eighties to popularize, in no particular order, pastels, TV violence, and Don Johnson. The synthesized drums of Jan Hammer's pulsating theme song set the mood, and the fast cars, flashy women, and furious gunfire did the rest. To *Miami Vice* and executive producer Michael Mann, style and look was more important than substance and plot, and the sound was an integral part of that style. (198)

The visual and audio explosiveness of *Miami Vice* – articulated through a grammar of fast-paced edits, rock-and-roll music, and creative montage involving neon lights and city landscapes – worked to displace the centrality of linear narrative. Ironically, the program visually glorified a criminal lifestyle with its images of extravagant clothing and expensive cars even as it presented anticrime and antidrug stories. Despite frequent criticism on these grounds, the show was intensely popular among youth for whom identity had already been associated with image, style, and tempo in music videos (see Campbell & Freed 1993: 84).

The music-video-like character of *Miami Vice* suggests the show's debt to the MTV network, whose broadcasting history began August 1, 1981, with the appropriately titled music video, "Video Killed the Radio Star." Designed to target an elusive youth audience of 12- to 14-year-olds and to reanimate a stagnant record industry (Doherty 1987: 352–3), MTV invented a whole new television grammar. Challenging the old logics of continuity, linearity, and unity, the network's programming obliterated a wide array of traditional cultural boundaries. According to Campbell and Freed (1993), "MTV...holds the pole position where pastiche is concerned. This network virtually defines visual disorder; a ceaseless succession of disconnected 3-minute musicals celebrate a sense of fragmentation and incompleteness" (79; see also Kaplan 1985: 146). MTV's influence on culture, dubbed the MTV "revolution," was indeed a revolution of sorts. With surprising speed, this network aided in challenging models of identity that privileged an innate, static sense of self. If the seemingly endless reinvention of popular 1980s icons Madonna and Michael Jackson taught audiences anything, it was that identity was about image and style.

Over time, the programming on MTV has diversified greatly, and today music videos reflect only a small segment of the network's total programming. But even its non-music-video programming employs a fast-paced, nonlinear grammar that privileges image fragments and quick sound bites. As further evidence of its nod to stylistic pastiche, self-promotional ads for MTV in the early 1990s, much like the series *Twin Peaks*, subverted the distinction between high art and mass culture by featuring "everything from avant-garde European animation to actors reading selections from Kafka" (Campbell & Freed 1993: 77). This odd blending of cultural forms was also evident on the animated MTV series *Beavis and Butt-head* (1993–7), created by Mike Judge. In an episode revealingly titled, "Butt is It Art?" (05/09/94), the show's featured adolescent duo, Beavis and Butt-head, evaluate high art using their sexual and scatological vocabulary while on a field trip to an art museum. This blending of high/low culture is also evident in "For Better or Verse" (06/17/93), in which Butt-head composes a haiku for his English class about killing a frog. For his literary efforts (That was cool huh huh/when we killed that frog. Huh. Huh./It won't croak again), he earns an "A" (Rosen 1993: 1E). The series itself was an interesting intersection of cultural forms, in which stories about Beavis and Butt-head were intercut with the two watching and critiquing music videos. Their lowbrow and inane critiques served to reinforce the juxtaposition between art in the form of music videos and low culture in the form of animation and toilet humor. "Beavis and Butt-Head," writes Kellner (1995), "react viscerally to the videos, snickering at the images, finding representations of violence and sex 'cool,' while anything complex which requires interpretation 'sucks' " (143).

Another MTV program to traverse traditional generic boundaries is *The Real World* (1992–). Created by Mary-Ellis Bunim and

Jonathan Murray, *The Real World* was MTV's first "reality-based" series. The program, which is shot in a pseudodocumentary style intercut with taped confessionals reminiscent of cinema verité, is, according to the opening credits, "the story of seven strangers, picked to live in a house, and have their lives taped, to see what happens when people stop being polite, and start being real." Each season a new cast is selected from the thousands of young twentysomething applicants and a new location is chosen. *The Real World* problematizes the traditional categories of reality and fiction on multiple levels. On the one hand, viewers appear to be watching the uncensored, everyday lives of noncelebrities. On the other hand, the show creates a context that is far from everyday by placing the strangers in glamorous locales, finding them pseudowork, editing approximately 180,000 minutes of video down to the 440 minutes that will compose a season, and in some cases, transforming them into celebrities (Moody 2000: 181). On shows such as *The Real World*, it no longer makes sense to distinguish between fake and authentic or image and reality, as it is simultaneously both – a hyperreality. The comparatively low production costs of reality-based television have heightened its attractiveness for networks, and MTV followed *The Real World* with a host of other reality series including *Road Rules* (1995–) and the crossover adventure/gameshow/reality series *The Real World/Road Rules Challenge* (1998–).

MTV did not, however, launch the reality television craze. It first began to become a popular alternative to fictional programming with the introduction of reality-based crime and emergency shows such as NBC's *Unsolved Mysteries* (1987–), CBS's *Rescue 911* (1989–96), and FOX's *America's Most Wanted* (1988–), *Cops* (1989–), and *Code 3* (1992–3). Each of these programs blurs fact and fiction by combining real though heavily edited footage with staged, dramatic reenactments. The popularity of these programs is evidenced by the fact that three of them, which were launched in the late 1980s, are still on the air. The success of these shows has had two consequences on viewers' perceptions of crime and medical crisis. First, since "large portions of tape containing no real action" are edited out, these shows suggest that crime and emergencies are rampant and entail nonstop action (Consalvo 2000: 183). Second, in emphasizing the rationalistic powers of the television camera itself to capture and control crisis, the programs narrate "the authority of technology to solve crises of violent crime or domestic emergency that each of us is likely to confront in everyday life" (Rowe 1994: 116). In short, they depict a world that is chaotic, yet manageable through technology. These perceptions have, in turn, altered the character of fictional shows such as Steven Bochco's crime drama *NYPD Blue* (ABC, 1993–5) and Michael Crichton's medical drama *ER* (NBC, 1994–), both of which were hit series in the 1990s. *NYPD Blue* and *ER*, in many ways, copied the fictional reality of reality-based shows, exaggerating reality TV's conventions to appear even "realer."

When *ER* premiered on September 19, 1994, it broke nearly all the rules and formulas of conventional dramatic structure (Pourroy 1995: 1–2). In fact, that seemed to be the point. As the show's creator and former Harvard medical student Michael Crichton recalls in an interview, "I wanted to write something that was based in reality. Something that would have a fast pace and treat medicine in a realistic way. The screenplay was very unusual. . . . People yelled paragraphs of drug dosages at each other. It was *very* technical, almost a quasi-documentary. But what interested me was breaking standard dramatic structure" (quoted in Pourroy 1995: 2). Crichton did just that by populating the show with hundreds of speaking parts, up to 90 scenes per episode, advanced medical terminology, and the absence of a single, central plot. In the words of writer and producer John Wells, "there wasn't a beginning, middle, and end – it was really just a series of small scenes. It had multiple storylines, and many stories that were just one beat and didn't go anywhere else. There was very little dramatic through line" (quoted in Pourroy 1995: 4). Despite being an hour-long dramatic series, *ER* reflected the fragmented and the highly compelling quick-paced visuals of MTV and reality-based programming.

Through generic hybridity, stylistic pastiche, and hyperreal images, hyperconscious TV deconstructs television's traditional formal categories. In so doing, it promotes eclecticism over unity and celebrates style over substance. This approach functions to distinguish hyperconscious television from nostalgia television and closely associates identity with image. Visuals, be they hyperstylized as in *Ally McBeal*, hypermanufactured as in *The Real World*, or hyperreal as in *ER*, come to supplant narrative in importance and centrality. The next section turns to the ways in which hyperconscious TV not only (re)combines cultural forms, but also how it alludes to and appropriates them.

Intertextuality: allusion and appropriation

Intertextuality describes a stylistic device in which a cultural text gestures to one or more preexisting, and usually pop-cultural, text(s) – its story, plot devices, or characters. Such gestures can operate in an array of modes, including explicit reference, direct appropriation, and parodic allusion (Ott & Walter 2000; see also Eco 2004: 212–35). The first mode, explicit reference, is the simplest, but often the most subtle. It typically involves a character explicitly commenting on some other media text, and often in a manner that is ironic. Direct appropriation or creative inclusion describes an intertextual mode in which a television show literally reproduces a portion of another media artifact. For copyright reasons, this is the least common mode of intertextuality on broadcast television. But it was made famous by the HBO series *Dream On* (1990–6), which depicted the innermost thoughts and feelings of the show's central character, Martin Tupper (Brian Benben), with snippets from old television dramas, comedies, and variety shows (Bianculli 1996: 95; McNeil 1996: 238). The third mode, parodic allusion, describes the caricaturing of memorable or representative features from another cultural text. What each of these modes share in common is an awareness of the larger media landscape and a determination to allude to it.

NBC's *St. Elsewhere* (1982–8) was a clear antecedent to the growing intertextuality of 1990s television, and indeed, meaningful viewing often "depended upon how many of the obscure media references one could find" (Thompson 1996: 84; see also Bianculli 1996: 273–4). The program provided an arena where highly teleliterate viewers could flaunt their vast knowledge of popular culture at a time – the mid-1980s – when young people in the US were frequently being reminded of how uneducated they were. Bestselling books such as Allan Bloom's *The Closing of the American Mind* (1987) and E. D. Hirsch's *Cultural Literacy* (1987) argued that students were being filled with unimportant, irrelevant information. The most stunning example of the extent to which intertextual gestures can be woven throughout the narrative occurs in the episode "Close Encounters" (11/20/85) when an amnesiac patient is admitted to St. Eligius's psychiatric ward. Unable to recall anything about himself, "John Doe #6," played by Oliver Clark, turns to television to find his new identity. After watching an episode of *The Mary Tyler Moore Show*,

John Doe becomes convinced that he is Mary Richards. Robert Thompson (1996) chronicles the intertextual references that litter this episode:

- Oliver Clark plays John Doe #6 playing Mary Tyler Moore playing Mary Richards.
- Also in the psych ward is Jack Riley playing Mr. Carlin, the same neurotic character he played in *MTM*'s *The Bob Newhart Show*, but Clark/Doe/Moore/Richards instead recognizes him as Rhoda (Valerie Harper), Mary's best friend *on The Mary Tyler Moore Show* and the subject of her own spin-off series. So Jack Riley is playing Mr. Carlin who is being mistaken for Valerie Harper playing Rhoda Morganstern.
- Betty White also has a role in this episode as a US Navy doctor. John Doe #6, of course, recognizes her as "Happy Homemaker" Sue Ann Nivens, the character Betty White played in *The Mary Tyler Moore Show*, but she doesn't know what he's talking about, because she's now in a different role. Betty White's character is not, however, completely out of the TV loop. She refers to her boss at NASA as Commander Healy, whom we can assume was once NASA's major Healy on *I Dream of Jeannie*, a character played by Bill Daly, who also starred in *The Bob Newhart Show* in which Mr. Carlin was a character but who John Doe #6 recognizes as a character from another *MTM* series, *Rhoda*, even though Jack Riley *is*, unlike Betty White, playing his original *MTM* role in this episode, complete with Mr. Carlin's old red cardigan sweater. The presence in the episode of Mr. Carlin and the mention by a sane character of Commander Healy imply that the world of *The Bob Newhart Show* and the world of *I Dream of Jeannie* are both part of *St. Elsewhere*'s "real" world, which would mean that Bill Daily exists simultaneously as both Commander Healy *and* Howard Borden from *The Bob Newhart Show*. (87–9)

St. Elsewhere's intertextual gestures to the minutiae of television history, and especially *MTM*, provided both amusement and a sense of "in-group" superiority for the viewers who "got" them. The allusions were, in a sense, a reward for years of active, faithful viewing. The vast web of references also suggested that television had a distinct tradition, one to which *St. Elsewhere* belonged. To the extent that paying homage to the unique history of a cultural form is a practice generally associated with high art, the show challenged the popular perception of television as simple, flat, and inartistic.

In the semiotic-saturated landscape of the Information Age, intertextuality is by no means limited to television references. Many episodes of *Moonlighting* were constructed, for instance, around the narrative premises of other cultural texts such as films, novels, and music. Episodes such as "It's a Wonderful Job" and "The Dream Sequence Always Rings Twice" paid homage to the 1946 film *It's a Wonderful Life* and the 1944 noir film, *The Postman Always Rings Twice*, while the episodes "Atlas Belched" and "The Man Who Cried Wife" were send-ups of literary texts as diverse as Ayn Rand's 1957 novel *Atlas Shrugged* and the popular Aesop fable, "The Boy Who Cried Wolf." But the allusions ran deeper than simply the titles alone. *Moonlighting* did not just refer to classic or familiar texts; it reworked them as part of its very substance. At the narrative climax of "Lady in the Iron Mask" (10/01/85), David and Maddie – both wearing black masks – pursue a murderer through the halls, kitchen, and dining area of an upscale hotel to the soundtrack from the ABC series *The Lone Ranger* (1949–57). Wearing masks and staging a dramatic chase scene to the theme from an old western suggests an awareness of the banality of good vs. evil as a narrative convention. Similarly, in the episode "Atomic Shakespeare" (11/25/86), a full-dress version of Shakespeare's *The Taming of the Shrew*, Elizabethan idioms, iambic pentameter, and double-entendres are combined with contemporary dialogue to create a novel, eclectic form that highlights the timelessness of the story. At one point, Maddie (read: Katherine) responds to a suggestive comment by David (read: Petruchio) with the statement, "If you tryest to plow this acre, your blade may be broken off."

The strange and surreal world of *Twin Peaks* was another television program whose narrative was riddled with intertextual references to classic cultural texts. In fact, *Los Angeles Times* television critic Howard Rosenberg dedicated a series of articles to identifying the show's many allusions. With the aid of his readers, Rosenberg compiled a list of clues that supported popular speculation that Madeleine Ferguson, Laura Palmer's look-alike cousin who appeared in the town of Twin Peaks following Laura's murder, was actually Laura herself.

The numerous intertextual film references to support this point include:

- The 1944 Otto Preminger film, tellingly titled *Laura*, told the story of an apparent murder victim who turns out to be still alive. The man who stalked Laura in the film was named Waldo Lydecker; the veterinarian and myna bird in *Twin Peaks* were named Lydecker and Waldo, respectively.
- The insurance man in another 1944 film, Billy Wilder's *Double Indemnity*, was named Walter Neff. The insurance man in *Twin Peaks* was also named Mr. Neff. The 1981 film *Body Heat* was inspired by *Double Indemnity* and featured a woman – named Maddie! – who faked her own death by assuming the identity of a look-alike friend she arranged to have killed.
- In Alfred Hitchcock's *Vertigo* (1958), a police detective named *Ferguson* falls in love with a girl named *Madeleine*. The girl, who had blonde hair (like Laura Palmer), later is believed to have committed suicide, but she reappears in a new identity with dark hair (like Madeleine Ferguson). (Thompson 1996: 156–7)

With such meticulously buried references, it is little wonder that David Bianculli (1992) would claim of *Twin Peaks* that "never before, in the history of television, had a program inspired so many millions of people to debate and analyze it so deeply and excitedly for so prolonged a period" (271). In weaving intertextual allusions throughout the narrative each week, *Twin Peaks* appealed to a media savvy audience. To the extent that such references served as clues to Laura's "murder," the devoted, attentive viewer was rewarded for obsessing over the text. And to the extent that such allusions were just meaningless non-sequitors, the series further distinguished itself from logical, linear storytelling.

Over the course of the 1990s, intertextuality in hyperconscious television tended to shift away from the sly references typical of *St. Elsewhere* and *Twin Peaks* and toward the parodic allusions characteristic of *Moonlighting*. A central force fueling this shift was the renaissance in primetime animation spurred by the success of *The Simpsons* (1989–) on FOX (Stabile & Harrison 2003: 2). Following ABC's cancellation of *The Flintstones* (1960–6) in 1966, there was a 30-year absence of animation in the networks' primetime lineups

(Hilton-Morrow & McMahan 2003: 74). This is significant because, thanks to its ability to place characters in otherwise impossible situations, adult animation lends itself to social satire. If an animated show wants to comment on a personality in the news, it simply draws a new character that resembles and sounds like that person. If an animated series wishes to comment on a news event or cultural trend, it can easily invent a parallel situation for its primary characters. Live-action programs are, by contrast, more restricted, as the situations they can create are frequently limited by budgetary constraints. Indeed the unusually high production cost of *Moonlighting* was one reason for the show's cancellation. But *The Simpsons* along with the many primetime animated shows that followed – Nickelodeon's *The Ren and Stimpy Show* (1991–5), MTV's *Beavis and Butt-head* (1993–7), *Daria* (1997–2001), and *South Park* (1997–), and FOX's *King of the Hill* (1997–), *The PJs* (1999–2001), and *The Family Guy* (1999–2002) – went where live-action could not, which was anywhere they wanted. They traipsed through the history of media culture, plundering its codes, characters, and conventions.

Beavis and Butt-head was, for instance, according to Douglas Kellner (1995), "purely a product of media culture, with its characters, style, and content almost solely derived from previous TV shows" (145). The characters were themselves a sort of hybridized reworking of Wayne and Garth, who in the late 1980s, commented on everything popular on NBC's *Saturday Night Live* (1975–), and the janitor and two robots who sat around critiquing old B-movies on Comedy Central's *Mystery Science Theater 3000* (1988–99). *Beavis and Butt-head*'s parodic allusions to pop culture fueled nearly every episode, poking fun at fast food culture in the episodes "Burger World," "Customer's Suck," and "Closing Time," Army recruitment advertisements in "Be All You Can Be," and late-night entertainment and stand-up comics in "Late Night with Butt-Head" and "Comedians." Through the trope of comedic exaggeration, *Beavis and Butt-head* satirized the forms, formulas, and techniques of the media and culture industries. In so doing, it appealed to an audience who saw themselves as too "hip" to the marketing strategies of Madison Avenue and Hollywood to blindly be taken in. Like the sly "in-jokes" on *St. Elsewhere*, the parodic allusions to prevailing cultural conventions on *Beavis and Butt-head* rewarded viewers for their knowledge and understanding of the vast media landscape.

In addition to comedic exaggeration, *Beavis and Butt-head* alludes to and comments on media texts through comic inversion. Unlike the idyllic, saccharine-sweet families of television's past from CBS's *Leave It to Beaver* (1957–63) to NBC's *The Cosby Show* (1984–92), *Beavis and Butt-head*, ABC's *Roseanne* (1988–97), the WB's *Unhappily Ever After* (1995–9), USA's *Duckman* (1994–7), and FOX's *Married . . . With Children* (1987–97) privilege the antifamily – rude, dysfunctional, impoverished, and often unattractive. The characters on these shows not only poke fun at TV's all-too-perfect families, but they also frequently make fun of viewers by correlating their own imperfections with media culture and television in particular. Al (Ed O'Neill) and Peg Bundy (Katey Sagal), the central characters on *Married . . . With Children*, for example, spend nearly all of their time on the sofa watching "trashy" adult programming and daytime talk shows. In fact, the Bundy's living room is the show's primary set, with the camera positioned just behind their TV. As we stare at them wasting their pathetic lives on our TVs, they stare back at us doing the same through theirs. Viewers thus become the joke. Guilty of the same sins as the characters, they are invited to laugh at themselves and their own participation in a TV obsessed media culture.

Like the hapless Al Bundy, Duckman (voiced by Jason Alexander), a doltish private detective, stumbles through life unable to earn even the respect of his own children on the 1990s USA animated series *Duckman*. But whereas Al Bundy's life, like Homer Simpson's, is spent watching TV, Duckman's life, like the characters on *South Park*, is spent living the prevailing narratives of media culture. "In the Nam of the Father" (04/24/95), Duckman takes his family on a budget vacation to Vietnam, where he experiences horrible flashbacks from the war. But the flashbacks are not real, as Duckman was never in the war. It turns out that his war memories are simply a collage of Vietnam War films he has seen throughout his life. After saving the President's life in the episode "Papa Oom M.O.W. M.O.W." (03/11/95), Duckman becomes a sleazy tabloid sensation and the subject of his own made-for-TV movie. Episodes such as these reinforce the idea that Duckman's identity, from his memories to his personae, is merely a product of the media culture in which he is immersed. The show was, in the words of one television critic, "[an eclectic] train crash of sight gags, puns, [intertextual] spoofs, and mock-existential ponderings" (Hiltbrand 1994: 15).

Self-reflexivity: irony and cynicism

Self-reflexivity, or simply reflexivity, is a stylistic device in which a cultural text demonstrates an explicit awareness of itself as a cultural text. On television, it is a show that not only knows it is a television show, but also ironically or cynically comments on that fact. One of the more common modes of self-reflexivity is the incorporation of "in-jokes" or "sly references" to the program's production history that only dedicated fans would recognize. In many of the antecedents to hyperconscious television, the self-referential gestures were both subtle and obscure. Although *St. Elsewhere* made frequent references to itself, for instance, the references were always carefully woven *into* the narrative. After the show's lackluster first season, NBC head Grant Tinker – in an effort to make the show seem cheerier – requested that its dingy, urban hospital be made a "lighter, brighter place." When the first episode of season 2 aired, the scaffolding lining the hospital's hallways symbolized the show's makeover. In explaining the construction, Dr. Donald Westphall (Ed Flanders) tells a colleague that the new paint job is a gift from the "Chairman of the Board," who "thinks brighter walls will let the patients live longer." Only the serious *St. Elsewhere* fan would have recognized that "Chairman of the Board" was a reference to Grant Tinker and that the unhealthy patient was the show itself. While the obscurity of such self-references likely promoted a feeling of in-group superiority among fans, such references were lost on many viewers.

In the years following *St. Elsewhere*, other television programs began to incorporate in-jokes and self-reflexive references, but in far less subtle ways. By 1985, *Moonlighting*, which creator Glenn Caron described as "the show that knows it's on television," had transformed self-reflexivity into a central stylistic device (quoted in McNeil 1996: 567; see also Feuer 1992: 157). "It was not uncommon," explains television scholar Robert Thompson (1996), "for the show to open with an introductory scene in which David and Maddie addressed the audience directly. They'd read letters from viewers or they'd discuss the shows slipping ratings, its high incidence of reruns, or its poor showings at the Emmy Awards.... Performed in character by David and Maddie, not Bruce and Cybill, these scenes established the fact that this was a series about two detectives who *knew* they were characters in a TV show" (113; see also Horowitz 1986: 24).[2] Although these introductory scenes were designed originally as padding for episodes that were too short, the knowing jabs at television became a regular feature of the show. Before long, *Moonlighting*'s characters were referring to writers, upcoming commercial breaks, and the need to solve the mystery before the final credits (Vande Berg 1989: 23). In one episode, the show ended with the actors walking off the set, getting in their cars, and driving off the studio lot, reminding viewers they are just actors on a TV show.

Thus, *Moonlighting*'s self-reflexivity was not limited to in-jokes about its production history. Rather, the program drew attention to the well-worn formulas of network television by repeatedly violating them. Although self-reflexivity interrupts viewers' willing "suspension of disbelief" by highlighting the constructed, fabricated nature of the world seen on television, it is nonetheless pleasurable according to Campbell and Freed (1993), "because it tweaks our anticipation and cynicism by adding a whole new level of self-centered amusement" (80). This new level of self-amusement functions to reinforce viewers' connection with the show by fostering the sense that the characters and the audience are sharing a joke (J. Williams 1988: 92). As Michael Dunne (1992) elaborates,

> By referring directly and ironically to generic conventions, the series [*Moonlighting*] exploited the audience's familiarity rather than being restricted by it. The producers thus had access to all the devices of conventional production techniques without seeming conventional, and the viewers could relish familiar forms of escapist entertainment without seeming to watch the same old kind of TV show. As is often the case with self-referentiality, then, the parties involved could have their cake and eat it. (38)

Instead of laughing *at* the characters, the audience is now laughing *with* the characters. Writing in *American Film*, Jack Curry (1986) explains that *Moonlighting* is "just plain fun" because "it's self-aware . . . [and] challenges the audience's expectations while congratulating them for getting the joke" (49). As ABC program executive producer Gus Lucas put it, "It's very irreverent, yet it respects the viewer" (quoted in Curry 1986: 49). The rise of self-reflexivity on primetime network television emerged, in part, to combat the predictability of television's formulas, which increasingly seemed tired and clichéd.

The FOX series *Parker Can't Lose* (1990–3) continued the convention of self-awareness early in the 1990s by having the show's cocky young high-school protagonist break the fourth wall and speak directly to the camera in every episode. This stylistic device, which was popularized among teens by the film *Ferris Bueller's Day Off* (1986), was also evident on NBC's Saturday morning series *Saved By the Bell* (1989–93) and Nickelodeon's afternoon program *Clarissa Explains It All* (1991–3). As with Ally McBeal's digitized fantasies, Parker's voiceovers and asides to the audience were both central to narrative development and reminded viewers that they were watching television. The show's recognition of its own "fictionality" was further reinforced by Parker's close friend, Jerry Steiner, who wore a long coat from which he would retrieve items such as frozen yogurt, computer printouts, a glazed ham, and even a live Doberman. Each item Jerry removed from his coat was accompanied by the sound effect of velcro ripping. At the close of one episode, Parker tells his love interest to hurry up and kiss him or they'll miss the start of *In Living Color* (1990–4) – the show that followed *Parker Lewis Can't Lose* on FOX affiliates (Campbell & Freed 1993: 80). Such devices had the effect of saying to audiences, "we know that you know that this is TV." The shared understanding between the show and its audience that it was, indeed, a show appealed to media-savvy viewers, fostering a sense of connection without requiring highly specialized viewer knowledge.

Self-reflexivity was also a regular feature of the "antifamily" shows *Unhappily Ever After* and *Roseanne*. The father of the Malloy family and main protagonist on *Unhappily Ever After*, Jack (Geoffrey Piersen), along with his stuffed bunny, Mr. Floppy (voiced by Bobcat Goldthwait), regularly talked to the camera, often lamenting the poor ratings of Warner Brothers Programs. In addition to self-reflexive comments about its poor ratings, *Unhappily Ever After* commented on casting decisions, such as in the episode "Tiffany's Rival" (09/ 08/96), when first-time character Sable (Kristanna Loken) informs Tiffany Malloy (Nikki Cox) that she will be a regular character, having signed a contract to appear in upcoming episodes. Similarly, when the actress who played Becky (Lecy Goranson) on *Roseanne* departed the show in the fifth season, other characters repeatedly commented on how different Becky (Sarah Chalke) looked the next season (see Owen 1997: 45–6).[3] While such self-references were central to the show, "What *Roseanne* is likely to be remembered for most though," notes

Bianculli (1996), "are the clever closing-credit sequences that step outside the show's self-imposed 'reality' " (268). In the first episode of season 8, "Shower the People You Love with Stuff" (09/19/95), for instance, Lecy Goranson returns briefly as Becky for half the season. In the closing credits, both Beckys (Goranson and Chalke) dance as though they were each other's reflection. The scene, filmed in black-and-white, is an allusion to *The Patty Duke Show* (1963–6), in which Patty Duke played identical cousins. Goranson and Chalke are dancing to the tune of *The Patty Duke Show*, but its lyrics have been altered to comment on the multiple Beckys:

> Meet Lecy the one you used to see
> From eighty-eight to ninety-three
> But Sarah came and took her place
> Because she had a similar face
> That's life on TV

> But they're Beckys
> Nearly identical Beckys all the way
> One pair of matching actors
> But only one part to play

In some instances, entire episodes or series – rather than just a few select scenes – of a 1990s television program were self-referential. The most obvious and famous example is the NBC hit *Seinfeld* (1990–2002). Though frequently touted as a show about nothing, it was in fact a show about itself (Hendler 2000: 180). The premise involved real-life stand-up comic Jerry Seinfeld playing a stand-up comic named Jerry Seinfeld who is working to get his own television series on NBC. When the "fictional NBC" on the NBC show is preparing the pilot for the show *Jerry*, Jerry Seinfeld plays himself playing himself. The casting of the other characters for *Jerry* is based on the characters on *Seinfeld*, who were themselves cast based on friends of Jerry Seinfeld. Another highly self-reflexive show is MTV's *Beavis and Butt-head*. This series satirizes the MTV viewer by portraying the dead-end lives of two heavy-metal-heads who spend most of their time watching MTV. In the episode "Lightning Strikes" (02/16/95), Beavis and Butt-head get struck by lightning while imitating the actions of someone on TV. This episode was likely a reference to the 5-year-old in Ohio who supposedly started a fire that burned down his house after watching Beavis and Butt-head playing with fire (McNeil 1996: 83). It is an instance of art imitating life that is imitating art.

When rumors of cancellation began to circulate about the FOX series *The Family Guy*, the show spoofed its own demise in the episode "If I'm Dyin' I'm Lyin'" (04/04/00) by featuring Peter Griffin (voiced by Seth MacFarlane) and his son, Chris (voiced by Seth Green), trying to prevent their favorite TV show from being cancelled. Likewise, *Duckman* featured an episode, "Clip Job" (05/08/95), in which Duckman was forced by a crazed media critic and self-appointed sponsor to watch humiliating scenes of his life compiled from the television series about his life. In another episode, "American Dick" (05/28/94), Duckman is profiled in a *Cops*-like reality TV show. In the *Beavis and Butt-head* episode "Generation in Crisis" (07/14/94), Beavis and Butt-head become the subjects of an amateur filmmaker's documentary on American youth culture. In gesturing to their own status as television programs, hyperconscious shows actually distance themselves from television. By highlighting their relationship to production and technical conventions, these programs suggest that they are more sophisticated than nonreflexive television.

Self-reflexivity is certainly not new to the medium of television. Many television genres have long recognized their televisuality: talk shows, news programs, and late-night programs. But the "new" self-awareness is unique on at least two counts. First, it has found its way into genres that historically have been silent about their constructedness: dramas, situation comedies, and soap operas. In the past, the device of self-reflexivity would have destroyed the illusion of reality that these programs work so hard to create. Second, hyperconscious television highlights its status as television in an ironic manner. In laughing at itself, hyperconscious television invites viewers to laugh at themselves watching television – a medium that has long been viewed as uncritical. While Johnny Carson knew he was on TV on NBC's *The Tonight Show* (1954–), David Letterman mocks the fact that he is on TV on CBS's *Late Night with David Letterman* (1993–). Letterman satirizes network television, shooting plastic darts at the camera, trekking backstage, and just generally "taunting the shabby enterprise of show biz and [his] own involvement in it" (Campbell & Freed 1993: 80). Through self-reflexivity, hyperconscious television seeks to elevate itself above traditional television.

Taken together, the three characteristics of hyperconscious television – eclecticism, intertextuality, and self-reflexivity – describe a program that is hyperaware of the prevailing stylistic codes of culture, other cultural texts, and its own status as television. This awareness often operates in an ironic mode, as television contributes to the very cultural trends on which it comments. Hyperconscious television celebrates the centrality of image and montage, often at the expense of narrative substance and linear storytelling, and it consistently privileges and even rewards viewers for media literacy. Although none of the devices it employs are entirely new, the resulting formula is "new" in its intensity, its prevalence in prime time, and its appropriation and reworking of traditional generic categories. From antecedents such as *St. Elsewhere*, *Miami Vice*, and *Moonlighting*, hyperconscious television exploded onto the screen over the course of the 1990s, first in shows like *Twin Peaks*, *Parker Lewis Can't Loose*, *Unhappily Ever After*, and *Roseanne*, and later in programs such as *Ally McBeal*, *Seinfeld*, *ER*, *Duckman*, *Beavis and Butt-head*, and *The Family Guy*. But it has perhaps reached its fullest expression in the FOX series *The Simpsons* – to which we now turn.

The Simpsons as Exemplar

The history of the FOX series *The Simpsons* has become something of a legend among fans and TV executives alike. The creation of "Life in Hell" cartoonist Matt Groening, *The Simpsons* began its life as a series of animated shorts on FOX's entertainment-variety program, *The Tracey Ullman Show* (1987–90). Although crudely animated, the original 48 shorts served to introduce many Americans to the Simpson family, which still includes Homer (voiced by Dan Castellaneta), the dim-witted, beer-loving father who works at the local nuclear power plant; Marge (voiced by Julie Kavner), the nurturing mother who sports a blue beehive hairdo; Bart (voiced by Lisa Cartwright), the bratty, wise-cracking and proud underachieving 10-year-old; Lisa (voiced by Yeardley Smith), the socially conscious and musically gifted 8-year-old; and Maggie, the pacifier-sucking baby. The first full-length, stand-alone episode of *The Simpsons* – a holiday special titled, "Simpsons Roasting on an Open Fire" – aired December 17, 1989. With no money to purchase Christmas gifts for his family, Homer takes a part-time job as a mall Santa. When he loses this job, he winds up at the Springfield dog track, where viewers witness their first "glimpse of the dizzying spiral of self-referential metahumor to come" (Turner 2004: 17). Begging his father to place a bet, Bart says to Homer, "Aw, come on, Dad, this can be the miracle that saves the Simpsons' Christmas. If TV has taught me anything, it's that miracles always happen to poor kids at Christmas. It happened to Tiny Tim, it happened to Charlie Brown, it happened to the Smurfs, and it's going to happen to us."

As it turns out, Bart's comments were prophetic, and not just for the Simpson family. The special ended up being a sort of Christmas miracle for the fledgling FOX network, garnering surprisingly strong ratings and finishing first in its time slot among adults aged 18 to 49, despite the fact that FOX was only available in 88 percent of US households at the time (Turner 2004: 17). Shortly after beginning its regular prime-time run in January 1990, *The Simpsons* became the FOX network's highest rated show, consistently winning its Sunday evening time slot. After its first season, which included only 13 episodes, FOX executives made the bold decision to move *The Simpsons* from Sunday nights to Thursday nights, where it would compete head-to-head against television's highest rated program four years running, NBC's *The Cosby Show* (Kimmel 2004: 95; see also Brooks & Earle 2003: 1467–8). The contrast could not have been starker. Whereas the Huxtables were a model family, the Simpsons were clearly dysfunctional. Thanks, however, to the juxtaposition of the all-too-perfect Huxtables with the all-too-human Simpsons, it was, in the words of sociologist Todd Gitlin, "becoming harder to get an audience to believe in family fairyland" (quoted in Elm 1990: 8). By *The Simpsons'* third season (1991–2), *The Cosby Show* had slipped to eighteenth in the Nielsen ratings, where it ended its 8-year run (Brooks & Marsh 2003: 1469). *The Simpsons*, by contrast, was just warming up. And although *The Simpsons* never actually beat *The Cosby Show* in overall ratings, it "bested this powerful competitor in key male demographic groups" (McAllister 1994: 1495; see also Kimmel 2004: 96–7).

Over the course of its 18 (and counting) seasons, *The Simpsons* has surpassed several key cultural milestones and earned numerous accolades. In February of 1997, for instance, *The Simpsons* became the longest-running primetime animated series ever (Scott 2001: 44), claiming the three-decade-old record held previously by ABC's *The Flintstones* (1960–6). A year later, Bart Simpson was named one of the 20 most important entertainers of the twentieth century, and in 2000 the Simpsons earned their own star on the Hollywood Walk of Fame (Bianculli 2000: 46; Corliss 1998: 204). *The Simpsons* has captured numerous awards, including a Peabody and 15 Emmys, and been described by critics as "one of the smartest and best-written comedies on television," "the greatest show in the history of television," and "a full blown institution – the smartest and most resonant pop icon of its time" (on awards, see Kimmel 2004: 219; Mason 1998: B7; Pinsky 2001: 34; quotations from Kimmel 2004: 81; Cantor 1997: 34; Turner 2004: 18). As Chris Turner explains in his 2004 book *Planet Simpson*, "*The Simpsons* was not just a show you watched but a language you spoke, a worldview you adopted.... the touchstone of its age" (8, 10). *The Simpsons'* "worldview" is, I argue, best classified as hyperconscious, as it revels in quotationalism and hyperironism, relying upon "its audience's televisual literacy in largely unprecedented ways" (Matheson 2001: 108–25; see also Gianoulis 2000: 409; Stabile & Harrison 2003: 9). "'The Simpsons,'" explains US poet laureate Robert Pinsky (2000), "is often about television itself, in ways that illuminate the nature of the video medium" (12). To illustrate *The Simpsons'* hyperconscious worldview, I undertake a close textual analysis of one episode from the show's seventh season, "The Simpsons 138th Episode Spectacular" (12/03/95).

The decision to analyze this particular episode was motivated by several factors. Though *The Simpsons* did not surpass *The Flintstones* as the longest running primetime animated series until its 167th episode, "The offbeat show," explains Bill Keveney (2000), "picks its own benchmarks as it did in 1995 with '*The Simpsons* 138th Episode Spectacular'" (11E). It seems appropriate to reflect on the same episode of *The Simpsons* that the series' creators chose to reflect upon itself. In addition to being a sort of self-imposed benchmark, "The Simpsons 138th Episode Spectacular" is also a spoof of television clip shows – of the tendency of long-running series to occasionally produce episodes that consist predominantly of "clips" or "outtakes" from previous episodes. In doing so, the episode both draws attention to prevailing televisual conventions and reminds viewers that *The Simpsons* itself participates actively in that same cultural legacy. Finally, the episode aired during what has been called "*The Simpsons'* Golden Age – roughly, early 1992 to mid-1997," ranking among the 10 most heavily viewed episodes of the seventh season (Turner 2004: 3).

The title sequence of the episode begins with a drum roll, which is followed immediately by a deep, off-camera voice that exclaims, "Live from the Springfield Civic Auditorium – it's the Simpsons 138th Episode Spectacular!" During the voiceover, the audience is whisked inside the Civic Auditorium where they see for the first time the "set" of *The Simpsons*. As an animated cartoon, *The Simpsons*, of course, requires no set. Nevertheless, the audience is shown an image of what the Simpson home would look like if it were a set for a live-action drama or situation-comedy, replete with three fake walls, cameras, stage lighting, and an audience. This image, along with the show's regular practice of animating scenes that mimic camera viewpoints and editing, functions to parody the constructed, fabricated nature of "real" television. As viewers gaze upon the image of the obviously fake Simpson home, TV celebrity Troy McClure (voiced by Phil Hartman) walks onto the stage and announces:

> Hello, I'm Troy McClure. You may remember me from such FOX network specials as "Alien Nose Job" and "Five Fabulous Weeks of 'The Chevy Chase Show.' " Tonight we're here to honor America's favorite nonprehistoric cartoon family. You'll see long lost footage, never-before-seen material from your favorite episode, old favorites you can't see in syndication [clips from episodes MG07, 8F13, 2F20, and 9F03 are quickly shown]. So join me, won't you, for "The Simpsons 138th Episode Spectacular"?

In addition to parodying the practice of live-action series to produce "clip shows," Troy's introduction pokes fun at the whole business of televised entertainment in two ways. The reference to the FOX specials "Alien Nose Job" and the "Five Fabulous Weeks of 'The Chevy Chase Show' " are gestures to *Alien Autopsy* – an actual special that had recently aired on FOX – and *The Chevy Chase Show* (1993) – an actual FOX network program that lasted only five weeks. In highlighting a trashy tabloid special and a disastrous late-night talk show, the references suggest that FOX is a tawdry, flashy network – a critique that includes *The Simpsons*, as it also airs on FOX. The humor of this sequence relies, in part, on the knowledge that FOX and *The Simpsons* had variously been accused of being crude, sleazy, and lacking in any social value (see Kimmel 2004). On a second level, Troy himself satirizes the use of famous personalities to gain ratings and sell products. While Troy McClure is only a "star" in the Simpsons' world,

Phil Hartman (who voices Troy) is a television celebrity outside that fictional world, where he is widely recognized for his role on *Saturday Night Live* and as a spokesman for various companies such as Burger King. In the first few moments of the title sequence, the episode has self-reflexively critiqued the simple formulas and cheap appeals of television, even as it has employed them.

The remainder of the title sequence involves two parts, both of which are regular features on *The Simpsons*.[4] The first is called the "blackboard scene" by fans, and finds Bart scribbling an apology on the school blackboard as punishment for his misdeeds that day. In other episodes, for instance, Bart can be seen writing, "I will not call my teacher 'Hot Cakes' " (03/25/90), "I will not belch the National Anthem" (02/14/91), " I will not conduct my own fire drills" (03/12/92), "I will not sell miracle cures" (04/15/93), and so forth. In this particular episode, though, Bart is writing, "I will only do this once a year." To the casual viewer, the remark will likely be read as a reference to some unnamed misdeed for the day, but to the "serious fan," the comment refers to the "clip show" premise of the episode. Bart is assuring loyal viewers that *The Simpsons* will not air more than one clip show per season. The latter, fan-based interpretation also means that Bart recognizes he is a character on a television series, an awareness that he has demonstrated before. Following a perceived snub at the Emmys in 1993, Bart scribbled on the blackboard, "I will never win an Emmy" (09/30/93). Bart's self-awareness, or more accurately, the producers' self-awareness (as Bart is only an animated character), functions as an "in-joke" for fans familiar with the show's production history.

The second regular feature is known as the "couch gag" and involves several shots of the Simpson family rushing home to watch *The Simpsons* on television. In each gag, an unexpected event occurs as the family approaches or sits on the couch, such as it collapsing (01/21/90), rotating 180 degrees to reveal a secret room (01/08/92), or deflating (11/03/92). The "general" gag of the Simpsons rushing home at the end of the day is an homage to the opening sequence of *The Flintstones*, but the "specific" gag often parodies popular television series, films, or other cultural artifacts. In the spirit of the clip show, this episode plays a series of previous couch gags in rapid succession.[5] To "get" the allusions, the audience is required to read intertextually across media. As such, the show appeals to a televisual and media-savvy audience by rewarding them with in(termedia)-jokes. To the extent that the Simpsons symbolize the typical America family, the couch gag also pokes fun at the program's viewers by parodying their own obsession with television and *The Simpsons* in particular. Despite their dysfunctionality, the Simpson family offers a great deal with which viewers can identify. Writing in *The Christian Century*, Victoria Rebeck (1990) explains that viewers recognize themselves in the Simpsons precisely because they "are not an ideal family" (622). Indeed, the Simpsons have been referred to as "the only real people on TV" (Zehme 1990: 41) and "more 'human' than the cast of most live action sitcoms" (Erickson 1995: 451).

A cartoon family rushing home each week to watch a series about themselves operates in a self-reflexive, "comic frame." In portraying the typical American family to be obsessed with television, the couch gag invites viewers to laugh at the Simpsons' obsession with *The Simpsons*, as well as their own obsession with the series and television in general. Thus, when viewers hit their couches to watch the Simpsons hitting their couch to watch *The Simpsons*, dramatic irony is at work. Viewers are shown that the "guilty pleasure" of television viewing is an unavoidable "sin" of the human condition, at least in the Information Age. In laughing at the Simpsons, viewers are asked to laugh at themselves, a practice that works to assuage the guilt they may have about "wasting time" and being "couch potatoes." But the motive of the comic frame is, according to Barry Brummett (1984b), "to teach the fool – and vicariously the audience – about error so that it may be corrected rather than punished" (219). When the Simpsons are swallowed by their sofa, viewers are made *aware* of their own foibles so that they may find a measure of distance from an ultrasaturated media landscape.

As with most television programs, the title sequence of *The Simpsons* sets in motion the plot(s) that will develop over the course of the episode. But whereas traditional television series craft their plots around the actions of the characters, *The Simpsons* crafts its "plot," if it can be called that given its nonlinear structure, around the appropriation of past cultural stories, forms, and formulas. That "The Simpsons 138th Episode Spectacular" is a "clip show" hardly matters, then, for the series typically structures its plot(s) as a collage, pastiche, or web of popular cultural fragments. In any given episode, the show may combine allusions to as few as 5 or as many as 20 works of literature, music, film, television, and current news items. The series' reliance on popular arts prompted creator Matt Groening to remark on one occasion that "There are jokes you won't get unless you've actually attended a few classes in college" (quoted in Corliss 1994: 77). The literary references range from Allen Ginsberg to Tennessee Williams, while the cinematic gestures include classics such as *Citizen Cane* (1941) along side more recent blockbusters such as *Jurassic Park* (1993). The series further reworks the cultural landscape by featuring celebrity voices from astronaut Buzz Aldrin and physicist Stephen Hawking to singer Cyndi Lauper and actress Liz Taylor. In fact, more celebrities have lent their voices to *The Simpsons* than any other television show in history. Performing on the show is, as Hal Erickson (1995) observes, "a sort of status symbol, in the manner of the 'special guest villains' on the 1960s TV series *Batman*. To quote eminent psychologist Dr. Joyce Brothers: 'There are three ne plus ultras in our culture: Being in the *New York Times* crossword puzzle, being on the cover of *Time*, and being a voice on *The Simpsons*'" (453). Each episode of *The Simpsons* tests the cultural knowledge of its viewers. The show rewards culturally savvy fans with elite "in-jokes," not to mention textual messages that can only be seen by freeze-framing individual scenes on a VCR.

Following the title sequence and first commercial break, viewers return to the Simpson set at the Civic Auditorium where Troy McClure begins to narrate the history of the show. "*The Simpsons*," he announces, "began as the brainchild of cartoonist Matt Groening, the already-famous creator of such comics as 'Damnation,' 'Johnny Reb,' and 'True Murder Stories.'" At the mention of Groening's name, the screen flashes an image of a bald man with an eyepatch saluting in front of an US flag. Appropriating the camera angle, backdrop, and pose from the promotional poster for the film *Patton* (1970), the image comically casts Groening in a menacing light. This perception is then reinforced with grotesque images of the previously mentioned comics – parodies of his actual "Life in Hell" strip. Continuing with historical background, Troy adds, "In 1987, Groening teamed up with award-winning producers James L. Brooks and Sam Simon." The images that accompany these introductions are of the tycoon from Parker Brothers Monopoly surrounded by bags of money and an eccentric-looking Howard Hughes lying naked in bed. Although narratively much of Troy's "history" is factual, the repeated images of popular culture fictionalize the history as well. The line between fact and fiction is discernable to fans, who are invited to laugh each time the line is crossed. To fully appreciate the narrated history of the show, then, requires a strong media and Simpson knowledge.

Preparing viewers for an early clip from the animated shorts, Troy asserts, "And what better place to premiere their creation than on *The Tracey Ullman Show*, the nation's showcase for psychiatrist jokes and musical comedy numbers? On April 19th, 1987, America met *The Simpsons*." At this point, the entire 1:48 short, "Good Night" (04/19/87), airs before returning to Troy who now has a look of disbelief on his face, as though he has never seen the clip before. Covering his expression with an awkward laugh, Troy comments, "They haven't changed a bit, have they?" For fans, the obvious irony of the remark makes it humorous. In several cases, the characters' personalities have changed dramatically since the original shorts, and in all cases the characters' appearances have changed drastically. Unreflective of such changes, Troy introduces several additional vignettes from *The Tracey Ullman Show*, including "The Perfect Crime" (12/13/87), "Space Patrol" (11/08/87), "World War III" (11/22/87), and "Bathtime" (03/19/89). By the time the "camera" returns to Troy, he admits, "Maybe the drawings were a little crude, but all the characters were there: Itchy and Scratchy, Grampa Simpson, and Krusty the Klown." As he names these characters, images of each are shown. But rather than showing actual images from *The Tracey Ullman Show*, the images are childish, crayon drawings. Exaggeration is the primary comic device here, as the images are even cruder than the original animation.

Closing out the first act, Troy promises, "When we return, more classic moments, and, for the first time ever on TV, our private reel of Simpsons outtakes, including alternate endings to 'Who Shot Mr. Burns?' " The (cartoon) audience in the auditorium applauds and Troy walks off the set, where he sighs and lights a cigarette. This segment functions as a satire of the whole "clip show" premise and the business of television generally. Since *The Simpsons* is an animated cartoon, there are no outtakes. In "creating" outtakes, the show pokes fun at other 1990s series such as *Roseanne* and *Home Improvement*, which regularly aired outtakes. Moreover, having the "camera" follow Troy offstage mocks the difference between a star's on-screen and off-screen personas, reinforcing the idea that television is just a make-believe world of images. Reminding viewers that the world of television is a carefully constructed set of images is central to the show itself, as an awareness of TV's formulas is central to the humor. When Homer becomes trapped in space in the episode "Deep Space Homer," for instance, Bart reassures the family who is watching the tragedy unfold at home on television: "Of course he'll make it. It's TV." The humor derives from the recognition that television shows do not kill off major characters.

Just prior to the commercial break, an "off-camera" voice queries, "In the opening credits, what does the cash register say when Maggie is scanned?" The question refers to the show's traditional title sequence in which Marge accidentally has Maggie scanned at the grocery store as she is rushing to get home. The question itself satirizes the use of dramatic cliff hangers just before commercial breaks to keep viewers watching, and *Simpsons* fans' obsession with knowing minutiae about the show. Following the commercial break, Troy responds, "The cash register says, 'NRA4EVER,' just one of the hundreds of radical-right wing messages inserted into every show by creator Matt Groening." The answer given by Troy reflects a very selective in-joke, as only the most serious fans would know that the cash register actually does not say anything when Maggie is scanned, and that while Matt Groening does insert hidden messages, neither he nor the messages are right wing. In lampooning its fans and creator alike, the series heightens the in-group sensibility of the show and strengthens the feeling of exclusivity among fans. Fans are, after all, invited to adopt the same self-reflexive comic frame toward themselves that the show's creator adopts toward himself.

Among the most common characteristics of television is the audience's "suspension of disbelief," which is reinforced narratively by the pretense to be telling a story for the first time, and by the lack of acknowledgment of the camera, the status of the actors as actors, and the audience. But this episode consistently violates this televisual trait. After answering the trivia question, Troy remarks, "Over the six years *The Simpsons* have been on the air, we've received dozens of letters from fans wanting to know more about the show. Tonight, we'll answer some of your questions." Despite being portrayed as a "special guest host," Troy is himself a fictionality that exists only in *The Simpsons'* universe. In light of his own fictional status, that he is "aware" that the show is fictional but not that he too is fictional creates a comic incongruity that reminds viewers once again of television's endlessly constructed character. Turning to the first letter, Troy reads, "Professor Lawrence Pierce of the University of Chicago writes, 'I think Homer gets stupider every year.' That's not a question, Professor, but we'll let the viewers judge for themselves." The humor of this statement operates on two levels. On one level, the author of the letter is atypical of the majority of fan mail the show likely receives. On a second level, it is funny because Troy makes fun of its highly educated author. Among the key ways that *The Simpsons* appeals to its audience, which tends to be younger, is by critiquing authority figures, and in particular educators. In the episode "Separate Vocations" (02/27/92), for instance, the blackboard scene features Bart writing, "I will not expose the ignorance of the faculty."

The reading of Professor Pierce's letter is followed by five short clips of Homer, each one from a different season of the show. In the first clip, "Blood Feud" (07/11/91), Homer, pretending to be his boss, is exposed as a fraud when he does not know his boss's first name. A segment from "Flaming Moe's" (11/21/91) represents Homer engaged in the lollipop dance, while a spot from "Marge vs. the Monorail" (01/14/93) features Homer gleefully singing the theme song from *The Flintstones* until crashing his car into a tree. Clip four from "Deep Space Homer" (02/24/94) finds Homer drifting weightlessly about the Space Shuttle eating ruffled potato chips to the tune of "Blue Danube," and a segment from "Treehouse of Horror V" (10/30/94) depicts Homer making silly noises and chasing Marge. The montage is typical of the series and requires a high degree of media knowledge to appreciate fully. Like the show's regular allusions to popular culture, the shorts are stripped of their original context and recombined toward a new end. In this instance, the message appears to be that Homer has exhibited idiotic behavior across the show's programming history.

Having offered this interpretation, the "camera" returns to Troy reading a second letter, "Dr. Linus Irving of the Sloan-Ketterling Memorial Institute writes, 'How does Matt Groening find the time to write and draw an entire *Simpsons* episode every week?' For the answer to this, we go straight to the source." The "camera," which appears to be filming through a window, then switches to a shot of Matt Groening at his office desk. Upon noticing the camera, Groening shouts, "get out of my off-," raises a gun, and fires several shots at the camera. A fuzzy screen is abruptly replaced with Troy remarking,

"Of course, what Matt *meant* to say, according to his attorneys, is that he couldn't possibly do it alone. And he insisted that we make time to acknowledge the hard work of everyone who makes *The Simpsons* possible." Although brief, the sequence parodies the reclusiveness of many celebrities and their inability to behave in socially acceptable ways without the aid of their lawyers. In addition to lampooning celebrities generally, it further reinforces an unflattering image of Groening, which is humorous to fans because of its incongruity with Groening's actual personality.

Turning to the final viewer letter, Troy begins, "Ambassador Henry Mwebwetumba of the Ivory Coast writes, 'What is the real deal with Mr. Burns's assistant Smithers? You know what I'm talking about.' Ha, ha, ha, of course, we do." The sequence that follows is, again, a collage of clips from past episodes that function as an "answer" to the letter. Clip one, from "Rosebud" (19/21/93), shows Smithers imagining Mr. Burns popping out of a cake naked and singing, "Happy Birthday, Mr. Smithers" in a parody of Marilyn Monroe's famous salute to JFK. A spot from "Dog of Death" (03/12/92) depicts Smithers staring longingly at Mr. Burns, who is asking, "Nonsense! Dogs are idiots. Think about it Smithers. If I came into your house and started sniffing your crotch and slobbering all over your face, what would you say?" A third clip from "Lisa vs. Malibu Stacy" (02/17/94) finds Smithers booting-up his computer, on which a bitmapped picture of Mr. Burns appears, saying, "Hello, Smithers. You're quite good at turning me on," while the fourth clip from "Marge Gets a Job" (11/05/22) represents Smithers, in an allusion to *Peter Pan*, having a reoccurring dream in which Mr. Burns floats in each night through his bedroom window. While all the clips suggest that Smithers is gay and that he fantasizes about Mr. Burns, Troy returns to explain, "As you can see, the real deal with Waylon Smithers is that he's Mr. Burns's assistant. He's in his early forties, is unmarried, and currently resides in Springfield. Thanks for writing! We'll be right back." In the six seasons previous to this episode, the show has regularly alluded to Smithers' homosexuality, but never explicitly confirmed it. In further reinforcing this impression without confirming it, the sequence functions as a reflexive parody of the show's own handling of this topic.

Before cutting to commercial, the announcer poses another series-related trivia question: "Which popular *Simpsons* characters have died in the past year?" Given that two characters had, in fact, died on the show in the past season, the question appears to genuinely be a test of fan knowledge. But viewers are dealt a comic reversal when the announcer returns after the break to declare, "If you said Bleeding Gums Murphy and Dr. Marvin Monroe, you are wrong. They were never popular." As with the first trivia segment, the show's fans are the target of the joke. Rather than asking an impossible question that has no correct answer, the show poses a "trick" question that teases fans for thinking they know the answer. Continuing to mock fans, Troy interjects, "Right now, you're probably saying, 'Troy, I've seen every *Simpsons* episode. You can't show me anything new.' Well, you've got some attitude, Mister. Besides you're wrong! Because sometimes episodes run long and certain scenes never get aired. So, fire up your VCR, because here, for the first time ever, are the cut-out classics." Highlighting the archival (videotaping) practices of obsessive fans and the production constraints of live-action series, Troy's transition simultaneously invites viewers to laugh at television's modes of production and at themselves.

The four "cut-outs" that follow all function as intertextual gestures to prominent popular cultural artifacts. Introducing the first cut-out, which, of course, would not exist for an animated series, from "Krusty Gets Kancelled" (05/13/93), Troy explains, "When Krusty the clown got cancelled, he tried everything to stay on the air. Here's what you didn't see." The segment opens with Krusty delivering a shameless appeal at the conclusion of his children's show: "Watch my show, I'll send you this book featuring me in a variety of sexually explicit positions." A parody of Madonna's coffee-table book titled, *Sex*, the segment implies that Madonna's book, like Krusty's, was merely a marketing scheme designed to rekindle sagging popularity. Moments later, when Krusty is informed that the network has cancelled his show, he begs, "replace me with something as educational and uplifting as I tried to be." As Krusty's show was neither educational nor uplifting, its replacement with a hemorrhoid infomercial starring Claude Atkins critiques the lack of educational value of most children's television programming.

Returning only momentarily, Troy narrates "When Springfield legalized gambling, Homer became a blackjack dealer – and comedy was in the cards." We cut to an "outtake" from "$pringfield" (12/16/93), where viewers observe Homer dealing cards to a Mr. Blofeld and Mr. Bond. The scene, a parody of *Casino Royale* and other James Bond movies, illuminates the "well-worn" formulas of the spy genre through the ensuing dialogue:

BLOFELD: 20. You're move, Mr. Bond.
BOND: I'll take a hit, dealer. [*Homer gives him a card*] Joker! You were supposed to take those out of the deck.
HOMER: Oh, sorry. Here's another one.
BOND: What's this card? Rules for Draw and Stud Poker?
BLOFELD: What a pity, Mr. Bond. [*Two goons grab Bond*]
BOND: But, it's Homer's fault! I didn't lose. I never lose! Well, at least tell me the details of your plot for world domination.
BLOFELD: Ho, ho, ho. I'm not going to fall for *that* one again.

The scene invites viewers to laugh at its violation of the formulaic plot devices in James Bond and other spy films, such as the "good guy always wins" and "the bad guy reveals his sinister plot, allowing the hero's escape." But it is only funny to the extent that viewers posses the media savvy to know those cinematic codes.

The Simpsons' generally playful attitude toward the implosion of image and reality is evident in the third cut-out, which Troy introduces by noting, "Earlier this year, Homer's long-lost mother returned. And so did a long-lost package." In this supposedly "previously unseen footage" from "Mother Simpson" (11/19/95), Homer is seated at the kitchen table in his home with his mother, eating food from the many-years-old care package, when he exclaims, "Hey! Space food sticks. Oh, I wish I had *these* on my space adventure. Did you know I was blasted into space two years ago, Mom?" Mother Simpson's response – "Well, sure. I read all about it. It *was* national news." – suggests that the fictional adventures of the cartoon character Homer Simpson are "real" in the Simpson universe. Furthermore, in the Simpson universe, the media (e.g., the realm of image production) always serves as the reference point for the "real" no matter how outlandish the claim. Mother Simpson knows Homer was an astronaut because she heard about it on the national news.

Introducing the final cut-out scene, this one from "Treehouse of Horror IV" (10/28/93), Troy announces, "When Homer sold his soul for a donut, he found Hell isn't all it's cracked up to be in these never-before broadcast scenes." Searching for an attorney to defend

Homer from Satan's claim on his soul, Marge pages through the telephone directory, ultimately arriving at an advertisement for Lionel Hutz, which reads, "Cases won in 30 minutes or your pizza's free." A parody of the promotional gimmick Domino's Pizza employed in the 1980s, the advertisement relies upon specialized knowledge of popular culture for comedic effect. To fully appreciate the reference, one must first know that Domino's Pizza guaranteed delivery "in 30 minutes or your pizza's free" and, second, that the promotion was discontinued after a Domino's driver caused a serious accident and the company was sued. Thus, the advertisement for attorney Lionel Hutz is humorous, not only because it exaggerates the ridiculous gimmicks that lawyers concoct to gain business, but also because it appropriates a promotional slogan that ultimately led to legal claims against its creator. To fully be "in" on the humor of the four outtakes, then, viewers are required to combine their knowledge of previous episodes and production history with intertextual allusions to popular culture.

When the camera returns to Troy following the fourth outtake, he is shown asleep on the sofa behind the film projector used to show the outtakes. Poked by a cane from off-stage, he quickly awakens to declare, "If that's what they cut out, what they leave in must be pure gold! Let's watch some more of those fabulous *Simpsons* outtakes." The disjunction between Troy's words and his actions functions as another self-reflexive gesture by suggesting that *The Simpsons* itself is simply part of the mindless, sleep-inducing content of television. Like the previous cut-outs, the final three scenes invite viewers to read intertextually. In the first scene – "unseen footage" from Homer and Apu" (02/10/94) – Apu moves in with the Simpsons and shows an Indian film on the family's TV. When Bart declares, "This movie you rented sucks!," Homer retorts, "No it doesn't. It's funny! Their clothes are different from my clothes. [*laughs*] Look at what they're wearing! [*laughs more*]." In addition to parodying Indian films, a reference likely lost on many viewers, the scene stresses the way that TV uses crude stereotypes to signify difference. In this case, stereotypical clothing is the primary signifier of Indian identity. In laughing at Homer's ignorance of and insensitivity toward a foreign culture, viewers are invited to reflect on television's frequent use of stereotypes.

Preparing the audience for unseen "footage" from the episode "Burns's Heir" (01/14/94), Troy recalls, "A few years back, Bart was adopted by Mr. Burns. In this very special outtake, Homer attempts a reconciliation with his estranged son. Watch." When Homer shows up at Mr. Burns's opulent estate to reclaim his son, Mr. Burns unleashes a robot that bears an uncanny likeness to fitness guru Richard Simmons to chase Homer away. As the robot dances to "Shake Your Booty," it commands Homer to "Shake the butter off those buns." As Homer flees in fear, the robot turns to Mr. Burns, who orders his assistant Smithers to shoot it. The subsequent images parody a scene from the film *Terminator 2* (1991), in which a menacing artificial life form heals itself from a massive head wound after being shot. Read intertextually, the scene implies that Richard Simmons is, in his own way, a scary, indestructible alien. Hence, to "get" the joke, the viewer must not only recognize the science-fiction reference, but also integrate it with popular perceptions of 1980s icon Richard Simmons.

At this point in the episode, Troy reappears briefly to introduce the final outtake – this one from the seventh season premiere, "Who Shot Mr. Burns? – Part Two" (09/17/95):

> This past summer, all of America was trying to solve the mystery of who shot Mr. Burns. [*pause*] Then they found out it was a baby. [*long pause, coughs*] To keep this bombshell secret, the producers animated several solutions that were never intended to air. [*scenes of Barney, Tito Puente, Moe, Apu, and Santa's Little Helper each shooting Mr. Burns are shown*] And to keep the show's animators, editors, staff, and hangers-on from leaking the solution, two completely different endings were produced: one real, one phony. Here's the ending you were never meant to see.

As with so many of Troy's comments during this episode, his voiceover accentuates the show's status as a product within a circuit of production and consumption. Satirizing the use of season-ending "cliffhangers" to retain viewers and increase ratings the following season, this scene encourages viewers to laugh at their own complicity in television's strategies of encouraging consumption. Self-awareness of consumerism is a regular feature of *The Simpsons*, which often draws attention to the ways the show itself is marketed.

On another level, Troy's comments refer to America's obsession with two other murder cases: J. R. Ewing and O. J. Simpson. CBS's *Dallas* (1978–91) aired the most famous cliffhanger in television history when it ended the 1979 season leaving the viewers to wonder, "Who Shot J. R.?" Given that Mr. Burns, like J. R., is a wealthy, greedy, deceptive character and that he was only wounded rather than killed, the sixth season cliffhanger of *The Simpsons* is full-fledged parody of *Dallas*. But it also hints at the obsession with the O. J. Simpson case, a reference that is made explicit when the so-called "phony" ending is shown. Commenting on the alternative ending in which Smithers has shot Mr. Burns, Troy remarks, "But of course, for that ending to work, you would have to ignore all the Simpson DNA evidence. [*laughs*] And that would be downright nutty." Interpreted through the lens of the O. J. Simpson trial, Troy's admonition is an indictment of the jurors in that case. To the very end, the episode turns upon viewer knowledge of popular culture for meaning.

In his closing statements, Troy takes a final stab at Matt Groening, TV's producers, and the whole business of television:

> Yes, the Simpsons have come a long way since an old drunk made humans out of rabbit characters to pay off his gambling debts. Who knows what adventures they'll have between now and the time the show becomes unprofitable? I'm Troy McClure, and I'll leave you with what we all came here to see . . . hardcore nudity!

Drawing on knowledge of Matt Groening's early cartoons, specifically his "Life in Hell" comic strip featuring rabbits, the first statement self-reflexively satirizes the show's producer, while the second statement locates the show squarely in the profit-driven entertainment industry. Finally, the last statement exaggerates the popular perception that television programming is trashy. As the final credits roll, "Shake Your Booty" provides background music for clips of "nudity" from 20 different episodes.[6] In combining self-reflexivity with intertextual allusions to previous episodes through rapid montage, the final scene of "The Simpsons 138th Episode Spectacular" is a synecdoche of the show and of hyperconscious TV. The unique symbolic equipments that derive from this mode are explored in the next section.

Symbolic Equipments in Hyperconscious TV

In the 1990s, hyperconscious television emerged as a prominent mode of public discourse. Characterized by the rhetorical devices of eclecticism, intertextuality, and self-reflexivity, its general attitude toward the shift from the Industrial Age to the Information Age was a playful, welcoming one. As noted in chapter 1, modes of discourse function symbolically to assist individuals in confronting, managing, and resolving the actual and perceived difficulties of their sociohistorical context. The remainder of this chapter explores how hyperconscious television equips individuals to address the specific anxieties brought on by the information explosion and thereby adapt to life in the Information Age. This discussion is roughly divided into two parts, ways of being and ways of knowing. Public discourse, whether mediated or nonmediated, furnishes both ontological and epistemological resources. With regard to ontology, public discourse, and television in particular, both offer models of identity – not of who to be, but of *how* to be – and provide specific cultural resources for enactment (Ott 2003a: 58). Public discourse also works on an epistemological level to shape the ways one processes information. The mind is trained, so to speak, to operate in an identifiable fashion.

Few concepts are as complex and contentious as that of identity. Part of the difficulty lies in the fact that the Western understanding of "the self" has been in the making for thousands of years. In traditional premodern societies, the idea of the self was a relatively unquestioned and therefore unproblematic matter. One simply was who one was, an individuated embodiment of an immortal soul. The premoderns, explains Walter Truett Anderson (1997), "knew with . . . certainty who and what they were, because every interaction through the day's activities or through a lifetime recognized and reaffirmed their names, family connections, and social roles" (35). But this all began to change as society transitioned into the modern era. The French philosopher René Descartes, who lived during turbulent times characterized by constant religious and political conflict, was skeptical about whether beliefs about anything were beyond question. As he contemplated the things that it was possible to question, Descartes concluded that the only thing beyond doubt is the existence of a rational, self-aware, individual subject. The Cartesian subject, as it is now known, was grounded in the premise, "I think, therefore I am," and was the center of the knowable world. The German philosopher Immanual Kant later refined the Cartesian view of the subject, noting that it involved the "search" for a substantial, innate essence. But both Descartes and Kant viewed the self as rational, essential, and fundamentally unchanging.

A somewhat more mutable understanding of the self in modernity is evident in the writings of the Danish philosopher and theologian Søren Kierkegaard and the French philosopher Jean-Paul Sartre. For Kierkegaard and Sartre, the self is an existential project for each person in which one forges an identity from available social roles and materials, endlessly combining and recombining resources in an effort to develop a uniquely individual self. Unlike the rationalist view of identity as innate and inherent, writes Douglas Kellner (1995), "The existential self is always fragile and requires commitment, resolve, and action to sustain" (232). The principal difference, therefore, between the rationalist and the existentialist concept of the self is that the former assumes the truth of a unitary self that needs to be *discovered* and the latter aims to *develop* a unitary self by overcoming inner conflict (Anderson 1997: 19, 23–4). The rise of the information technologies has problematized both of these (modernist) conceptions of the self, however. By constantly exposing us to and saturating us with conflicting messages and ideologies, the mass media have dramatically undermined any grounds upon which to base a unitary self, whether discovered or developed. One consequence is the fragmentation of the subject.

Hyperconscious television provides resources for addressing this matter by proffering an alternative model of the self – one that views fragmentation not as an unwelcome threat, but as an opportunity for an expanded and adventurous form of self-expression. Psychologist Kenneth Gergen (2000) terms this conception of the self "multiphrenia," noting that it involves "the acquisition of multiple and disparate potentials for being," the "splitting of the individual into a multiplicity of investments" (69, 73–4). On a formal level, the very character of hyperconscious television itself might be described as multiphrenic given its eclectic mixing of cultural codes and categories. Programs such as *Moonlighting* and *Ally McBeal* have split personalities, juxtaposing dramatic and musical entertainment elements with the situation comedy, while shows like *The Simpsons* and *Twin Peaks* interweave elements of high and popular culture. Above all, eclectic forms value hybridity and simultaneity. They accomplish this, at least in part, by elevating image over narrative. An image is a surface *collage* of signs, whereas a narrative is a developing *sequence* of signs. As such, images favor simultaneity over causality; they allow for fragmented expression. Through the appropriation and mixing of existing images, styles, and looks, one can be – or more accurately, one can perform – many selves at once. One can also readily alter their personae by incorporating different images and looks.

"Postmodern identity, then," argues Kellner (1995), "is constituted theatrically through role-playing and image construction.... postmodern identity revolves around leisure, centered on looks, image and consumption" (242). During the (modernist) Industrial Age, when identity was rooted in the relatively distinct and immutable categories of nation-state, religion, and ethnicity, one was a product of these "substantive" categories. But as the information revolution called the truth of these very categories into question, image, style, and look increasingly became more important resources for performing identity. Close analysis of *The Simpsons* indicates that hyperconscious television models just such a performative notion of the self. By drawing attention to the cultural codes that give shape to any form through self-reflexivity, the programs in this genre indicate that identity, be it a specific character or even the show itself, is based on a carefully managed image. The radical change in Troy McClure's on- and off-"camera" demeanor, the satirizing of creator Matt Groening, and the easy invention of past lives through cultural appropriation (such as Homer being an astronaut) during "The Simpsons 138th Episode Spectacular" all highlight the centrality of image and style to one's personae. This model of identity was apparently not lost on viewers, as soon after *The Simpsons*' debut young teens across the country began wearing Bart Simpson T-shirts with slogans such as "Don't have a cow, man" and "I'm Bart Simpson, who the hell are you?" to perform a designer self. A symbol of rebellion, Bart was a character with whom young boys in particular identified and upon whom they drew to craft their own sense of self (Conrad 2001: 75). A 1999 survey conducted by Children Now – a US national child advocacy organization – found that Bart Simpson ranked second as a television role model for boys ages 10–17 (Huff 1999: 130). The success in appropriating Bart's image to project an antiauthoritarian image is evidenced by the number of high schools who banned Bart Simpson T-shirts.

The Simpsons rushing home each week to watch *The Simpsons* suggests a further link between identity and media consumption. Bart is partially a product of what he watches, which in his case is Krusty the Clown. To communicate this component of his identity, Bart's room is littered with Krusty-related merchandise (Ott 2003a: 63). Since a sense of self in this model is defined and affirmed through consumer choice, being a "fan" of a particular combination of television shows can be used to craft a relatively distinct yet flexible identity (see Kellner 1995: 231–62; Rosenau 1992: 42–61; van Poecke 1996: 183–4). Such an identity is, of course, far more fluid, mobile, and open to revision than modernist views of identity because it is created through images. As one's tastes change, so too does one's identity. Hyperconscious television addresses itself to the matters of fragmentation and identity drift primarily by socially valuing those trends. When one adopts a multiple, fluid identity that is endlessly performed through reference to our consumer culture, "identity anxieties" dissolve, for anxiety is the product of a rational, unitary subject that feels externally threatened. The playing of a persona in relation to the images and styles circulated by the culture industries potentially poses a different problem, however. Since this model of identity is linked to consumption and television consumption in particular, and television is socially constructed as having little cultural value, this model of identity frequently evokes feelings of guilt.

Hyperconscious television provides viewers with stylistic medicines for addressing this guilt in two ways. First, the programs in this genre symbolically elevate themselves over more traditional television programming through self-reflexivity and stylistic pastiche. Speaking to the significance of reflexivity, Jane Feuer (1984) explains, "self-conscious strategies distinguish 'high-art' from the unselfconscious popular arts – such as TV series" (44). By reinscribing itself within the tradition of self-conscious high art, hyperconscious television erects a new cultural hierarchy in which the guilt of television viewing is assuaged. "The Simpsons 138th Episode Spectacular" conveyed its awareness of itself as television by highlighting its own formulas through the clip-show premise, as well as the parody of TV cliffhangers. By ridiculing the forms and formulas of television, hyperconscious television elevates itself above those forms. Moreover, through stylistic pastiche, the programs in this genre work to question the high/low art binarism itself by denaturalizing it. When *The Simpsons* reworks the musical *A Street Car Named Desire* into one of its episodes, with Marge, as Blanche Dubois, singing, "Stella! Can't you hear me yella? You're putting me through hell-a!," it is recoding the original text in much the same way that Andy Warhol's paintings of popular icons do, and exposing the categorical arbitrariness of high and low art.

The use of self-reflexivity generally and critical self-reflexivity in particular appeals to viewers who see themselves as "hip" to media culture and as sophisticated consumers not easily manipulated by televisual (and advertising) gimmicks. Demographically, such viewers tend to be younger, ranging in age from 21 to 32. One explanation for the savvyness of so-called Gen-X viewers is that they, unlike Boomers (born 1946–64) and Matures (born before 1946), have been immersed in media culture since birth, and thus are more likely to recognize its dominant codes. As Margot Hornblower (1997) explains, "Self-mockery is a marker of Xer sophistication, and thus a staple of any show – from David Letterman to Conan O'Brien – seeking twentysomething viewers" (66). The self-awareness of hyperconscious television appeals to viewers who are skeptical of or cynical about media and politics, and helps account for the popularity of the emergence of the anti-ad advertisement in the 1990s. Hyperconscious television does more than simply treat its viewers as media savvy, however; it repositions them as cultural elites.

In addition to creating a new cultural hierarchy in which hyperconscious television is socially valued, this genre of programs creates a new cultural hierarchy in which the interpretive abilities of its viewers are socially valued (at least by it). This is the second means by which hyperconscious television resolves the guilt of too much TV viewing. Traditionally, television viewing has been perceived as "mind-deadening" (Watts 2003: 19). As such, heavy viewers are, as chapter 2 noted, disparagingly referred to as "couch potatoes," "tube heads," and "stupid-box junkies." So pervasive was this sentiment that television was considered for many years a subject unworthy of academic attention and study. While society is frequently telling TV viewers how lazy and dumb they are, hyperconscious television is rewarding them for their vast knowledge of media culture. Through repeated intertextual references, the programs in this genre regularly "test" viewers on matters of popular culture (see Collins 1995: 140). Each episode of *The Simpsons* is, for instance, like a game show in which contestants are quizzed on their ability to recognize allusions to celebrities, films, media events, literature, and other television shows. Within hours of a new episode, dedicated fans meet online to share their individual observations. It is here that they are validated, even heralded as celebrities, by their peers for their ability to "catch" media references. The more obscure the reference one recognizes, the greater the reward and validation (through participation in a more selective in-group) from the community. *The Simpsons* invites its viewers not just to watch it, but to study it intently. The guilt of television viewing is again absolved through the creation of a new social hierarchy. By altering the basis of valued "knowledge," *The Simpsons* locates its viewers at the top of the new hierarchy, where they can see themselves as "smart."

In assessing the symbolic equipments that hyperconscious television furnishes viewers for resolving the guilt of heavy media consumption and television viewing, the programs in this genre reorder what is considered knowledge or, at least, valued knowledge. But programs such as *The Simpsons* do more than simply rearrange various knowledges into a new hierarchy of cultural value; they fundamentally alter the *way* that we process information and *how* we know the world. As Alvin Toffler (1980) explains, "We cannot transform all our media of communication and expect to remain unchanged as a people. A revolution in the media must mean a revolution in the psyche" (405). Unlike print, which is highly sequential and thus privileges a linear way of knowing, hyperconscious television fosters a nonlinear way of knowing. It aids in the cognitive development of an associative, conditional, and constructive epistemology. In his book *Lateral Thinking* (1970), Edward de Bono introduces the term PO to describe this mode of information processing. "PO is a patterning device," according to de Bono (1970), "[and] may also involve depatterning and repatterning" (226; see also de Bono 2005: 62–3). In this section, I maintain that three types of information patterning comprise the PO logic of hyperconscious television: provocation, provisionality, and prosumption.

PO *as provocation*

To understand information patterning through provocation, it is helpful to distinguish between two types of mediated entertainment. First, there are those media messages animated by story and narrative, in which image plays a secondary or supporting role. These messages *follow* a plot that unfolds sequentially, step-by-step, one part formally *leading* to the next – the successive arousal and fulfillment of desires (Burke 1953: 123–4). Such messages are linear to the extent that narrative and editing convey causality. The murder of an individual at the outset of a traditional crime drama, for example, *leads* to the search for a murdered. The story involves following the clues to the guilty party. Second, there are those media messages where image supplants narrative, and visuals are primary. One does not *follow* an MTV video, because there is often no rational sequence. Rather, images – which are themselves composed of thousands of signs processed simultaneously rather than sequentially – favor the devices of juxtaposition and montage, whose meaning is created laterally rather than linearly. By recombining traditional TV formulas through eclecticism and stylistic pastiche, hyperconscious television repatterns data in novel, unexpected ways. PO is provocative, explains de Bono (1970), because it "generates connections that have nothing to do with experience" (227). But precisely what mental function is served by the informational pattern of provocation?

In a cultural landscape where the information explosion has induced feelings of cultural fragmentation, the lateral logic of provocation demonstrates that information, ideas, and people can be meaningfully *connected* by means other than sequence and causality. Whereas narrative-based media generate meaning step-by-step, image-based media generate meaning side-by-side. Hyperconscious television suggests that images and information can be processed associationally and spatially (see Gardner 1983: 170–8), rather than exclusively causally and temporally. This is, as Dennis Cali (2000) notes, the same logic that underlies "hyperlinks" on the World Wide Web (401). Like linked webpages, the individual clips that comprise "The Simpsons 138th Episode Spectacular" do not follow causally from one another. Rather, they are aggregated according to the relations that Troy and viewers assign to them. Nor is the practice of reading laterally or reading by association limited to the "clip show" premise. Through its numerous intertextual references to "external" media texts, *The Simpsons* and other hyperconscious programs invite viewers to continually depart from the storyline to make meaning. One does not simply follow the story, which is often non-sensical and whose conclusion does not follow from its introduction. Rather, the viewer reads the primary text *in relation to* other media texts. The ability to read laterally fostered by the logic of provocation reduces feelings of fragmentation by providing a cognitive tool for repatterning.

PO *as provisionality*

Traditional media texts, from books to films, tend to privilege semiotic closure by leading the reader or viewer to a predetermined conclusion (and thus meaning). This type of textuality is often referred to as a *closed text* because it seeks obedience from its consumers, shutting down the likelihood of multiple, diverse interpretations (see Eco 1979). Hyperconscious television is decidedly more open, however. An *open text* does not impose a clear, singular meaning; indeed, it encourages viewers to actively interpret the text in a plurality of ways. The distinction between closed and open texts suggests that in addition to texts being structured to invite either linear or lateral thinking, media texts can also be structured to promote either finished or provisional thinking. Hyperconscious television programs frequently do not impose a strong and tidy sense of closure or resolution at the end of an episode. Since hyperconscious shows elevate image over narrative, their "endings" often raise more questions than they answer. *Twin Peaks* provides a clear example of this openness, as its images were always multicoded to allow for diverse interpretations. Hyperconscious television programs allow, even encourage, viewers to endlessly discuss and debate their meanings.

In light of its semiotic openness, it is hardly surprising that hyperconscious television attracts significantly larger and more active online communities than does nostalgia television. Rather than telling viewers *what* to think and feel, hyperconscious television simply tells them *to* think and feel. After each new episode of *The Simpsons*, fans gather online to share their unique insights about the episode. They offer commentary of various scenes, messages, and characters. Many of their observations are based on having viewing a videotaped version of the show one frame at a time using a VCR, suggesting that meaning is hidden, complex, and not immediately obvious. The primary *Simpsons* fan-based website, www.snpp.com, is a massive collaboration in which fans compile their individual observations about and reactions to each episode. From a cognitive perspective, hyperconscious television suggests that meaning is neither obvious nor finished. Such provisionality trains the minds of viewers both to be open to revision and to view meaning locally and contextually, rather than universally and absolutely. This is a useful mental tool for a social environment characterized by feelings of acceleration, in which social change is rapid and ubiquitous. By valuing individual impressions and meanings, provisionality provides comfort in the face of a radically changing world in which the grounds for making universalizing claims have been deconstructed.

PO *as prosumption*

Prior to the linguistic turn in the 1970s, the communication process was theorized as a relatively linear affair with three clearly delineated stages, involving a message source (the producer), a unified message (the text), and an end target (the consumer or audience). This model favored the Author-God as the privileged site of meaning, and conceived of audiences as relatively passive receivers, unable to (re)make messages. But the assumptions underlying this model were called into question by poststructuralist theory, which suggested that audiences were active co-creators of both meaning and textuality. Indeed, for the French literary theorist Roland Barthes (1988), "*the Text is experienced only in an activity of production*" (157). Prosumption refers to a way of processing information that is active, creative, and productive. It is less a structural characteristic of texts (as is openness), and more an interpretive practice of viewers. That said, "prosumers" – a term coined by Alvin Toffler (1980: 406) – tend to be drawn to hyperconscious television because the rhetorical devices of eclecticism, intertextuality, and reflexivity all introduce gaps and ruptures into the smooth surface of textuality. These breaks allow viewers to construct their own texts from the fragments of our media culture. Indeed, text construction is the primary task of audiences and readers viewing hyperconscious television (see McGee 1990: 274).

Since prosumption is an interpretive practice of audiences, prosumers will often "read" in this manner regardless of whether or not the text easily lends itself to such interpretive practices. Using remote control devices, for instance, viewers can exercise prosumption:

> [A] viewer might...enjoy watching four to five different television programs at one time. Admittedly, this kind of zapper misses the majority of any one of these programs being transmitted. However, from a creative perspective, the zapper is actually creating a new program (from the combination of other programs), in the sense that the zapper is watching a combination of electronic signals no one else is likely to be watching. In this way, the zapper changes the traditional role of the viewer from passive receiver to active programmer of the array of video signals transmitted by producers. (Chesebro & Bertelsen 1996: 134–5)

Given that prosumption is a mode of reading exercised by some but certainly not all television viewers, one way of learning more about prosumers is by examining the literature on remote control device (RCD) use. According to Robert V. Bellamy, Jr. and James R. Walker (1996), the most accurate demographic predictor of remote control device use is age. Specifically, they found that RCD use is the highest among younger viewers (106). Having grown up in a media culture of 30-second news capsules and quick-cutting MTV videos, younger audiences have been taught to combine fragments of information quickly and meaningfully. Indeed, the nature of RCD use is as telling as the frequency of use. While older viewers tend to use the remote control device for switching the TV on and off or changing stations between programs (activities that preserve the privileged status of the Author-God), younger viewers use RCDs to watch multiple programs simultaneously, to prevent boredom with TV's well-worn formulas, and to avoid the commercials (Bellamy & Walker 1996: 107–15).

Prosumption is not exclusively an interpretive activity, however. In some cases, viewers and fans literally produce their own cultural products to be consumed by other fans. As I have noted elsewhere, "Episode guides, character biographies, production schedules, fanzines, fiction, and artwork represent just a few of [fans'] varied products" (Ott 2003b: 227). These cultural products frequently reflect high production values and develop their own cult followings. The creators of "Babylon Park," for instance, have transformed the principal characters on the syndicated series *Babylon 5* (1992–7) into cartoons that appropriate the animation style and scatological humor of the characters on *South Park*. "Babylon Park" videos – "the ultimate crossover epic, blending the labyrinthine story lines of *Babylon 5* and the limitless fart jokes of *South Park*" – are sold online for as much as $24.95. The apparent homology between hyperconscious television and fan art would suggest that fans are learning techniques of cultural production from the shows in this genre. The self-reflexivity of hyperconscious television operates as a sort of tutor for fans who want to produce their own art, be it images or fiction. In a landscape of semiotic excess, it is easy to feel overwhelmed by the endless bombardment of signs. In fostering a logic of prosumption, however, hyperconscious television collapses the distance and distinction between producer and consumer. The thunderous downpour of images and information that make consumption impossible is thus reinvented as a bottomless lake of resources for prosumption and for cultural production.

Hyperconscious television's playful "yes" attitude toward the burgeoning Information Age functions symbolically to transform social threats into opportunities. From its eclectic blending of styles to its self-conscious use of images, it models a way of being that is rooted in performance and personae. It suggests that identity can be fluid and multiplicitous. Further, it celebrates knowledge of the popular cultural landscape, reducing the guilt associated with a postmodern consumer culture. Through the logic of PO, hyperconscious television rewires the human brain, preparing it for the unique challenges of a social environment characterized by rapid, never-ending change and semiotic excess. This mind is highly adaptive and creative, unconfined by the strictures of linear, rational thought. But as the next chapter illustrates, the attitude of "yes" is only one possible response to the epochal changes of the 1990s. Nostalgia television responds differently and therefore offers a different set of resources for negotiating life in the Information Age.

Notes

1 *The X-Files* is, I argue, probably best classified as a hyperconscious program given its highly open-ended narrative, cynical characters, portrayal of information technologies, and critique of the nation-state. For an excellent analysis of *The X-Files*, especially its delegitimation of the nation-state, see Cantor 2003: 111–98.

2 David and Maddie read viewer mail in "Every Daughter's Father is a Virgin" (02/18/86), they discuss losing an Emmy award in "The Son Also Rises" (09/23/86), and they plead for viewers to continue watching the show in "Take My Wife, for Example" (02/07/89). Vande Berg (1989) describes another instance of self-reflexivity in the episode, "Twas the Episode before Christmas" (23).

3 In "Terms of Estrangement, Part 2" (09/22/92), the character of Becky (originally played by Lecy Goranson) moves from Landford, Illinois, to Minnesota. Although she is no longer a regular character on the show, she makes brief (phone) appearances from her Minneapolis apartment in "The Dark Ages" (09/29/92) and "Good Girls, Bad Girls" (11/24/92). When Becky returns to Landford and as a regular character in "Homecoming" (11/16/93), she is played by Sarah Chalke. Chalke is later replaced by the original Becky (Lecy Goranson) in the Fall of 1995. The two appear together in the season premiere's closing credits.

4   *The Simpsons'* title sequence typically entails three components: the blackboard scene, Lisa playing a saxophone solo, and the Simpsons rushing home for the couch gag. Due to the extended introduction with Troy McClure, Lisa has no saxophone solo in this episode, though her playing provides background music during a portion of the couch gag. For a complete list of blackboard scenes with Bart, visit "The Simpsons Archive" at http://www.snpp.com/guides/chalkboard.openings.html

5   The 12 couch gags include the sofa transforming into a giant brown slug and swallowing the family (8F18), the family running off the edge of the film (9F02), the entire town of Springfield arriving to watch *The Simpsons* (9F10), the Simpsons shrinking (9F09), the dog growling at the family from the sofa (8F09), a large Monty Python foot squashing the family (1F02), the size of each family member being inverted (2F31), Escher relativity (2F09), the Simpsons chasing the sofa down an infinite hallway (2F06), the family swimming to the sofa (1F17), the Simpsons as parodies of early Mickey Mouse cartoons (2F11), and the family forming a chorus line (9F08). For a complete list of couch gags, visit "The Simpsons Archive" at http://www.snpp.com/guides/couch.opening.html

6   The clips include Barney's diaper coming off in "Lisa the Beauty Queen" (10/15/92), Nelson removing Martin's swim trunks in "Bark of Darkness" (09/04/94), Homer's impression of Mr. Burns in "Rosebud" (10/28/93), Bart as Dr. Cheeks in "Round Springfield" (04/30/95), Willie's kilt rising in "Bart's Girlfriend" (11/06/94), Homer's clown pants getting caught in his mini-bicycle in "Homie the Clown" (02/12/95), Bart flashing "don't tread on me" in "Bart vs. Australia" (02/19/95), Homer's robe blowing open in "Homer, Bad Man" (11/27/94), Bart as a baby swinging on a clothesline in "Lisa's First Word" (12/03/92), Marge's glimpse of Mr. Burns in the bathroom in "Brush with Greatness" (04/11/91), Bart interrupting Homer and Marge in the bedroom in "Grandpa vs. Sexual Inadequacy" (12/04/94), Homer getting out of the shower in "Homer, Bad Man" (11/27/94), a photo of Bart riding Snowball in "And Maggie Makes Three" (01/22/95), Homer running from a Krusty doll in "Treehouse of Horror III" (10/29/92), Bart on the toilet in "Sweet Seymour Skinner's Baadasssss Song" (04/28/94), Homer dragging a stone chained to him in "Homer the Great" (01/08/95), Rabbis in the sauna in "Like Father, Like Clown" (10/24/91), Bart doing a Nixon impersonation in "I Love Lisa" (02/11/93), Homer naked in the forest in "Call of the Simpsons" (02/18/90), and Homer throwing his hat over the camera in "Colonel Homer" (03/26/92).

Chapter 4
Nostalgia Television

With the transition to a post-industrial society, the sense of insecurity seems to have grown along with the intensity of the nostalgic impulse.... In its collective manifestation, the nostalgic impulse might be understood as a response to rapid change. (Ellin 1999: 124)

Common sense tells us that nostalgia is especially appealing in troubling or confusing times. A number of theorists of postmodern culture have discussed the emergence of nostalgia as a cultural strategy, arguing that, in many cases, the use of nostalgia is an antidote to the perceived instability and incoherence of [the Information Age]. (Dow 1996: 171)

Nostalgia realigns cognition and emotion to produce comfort and security. (Wilson 2005: 23)

Celebrating 'the Past': The Attitude of No

The genre of nostalgia television is, in many ways, rooted in fear – the fear of social change, the fear of new technology, and perhaps most of all the fear of loss, loss of innocence, harmony, and safety. Its general attitude or orientation toward the Information Age and attendant information explosion, then, is principally one of rejection. Nostalgia television says "no" to the ever-changing social, political, and economic landscape and endeavors, instead, to recover and restore "traditional" values, beliefs, and social relationships. As Thomas Doherty elaborates, "The urge for nostalgia, to reach back for the past, grows stronger the faster we rush into the future" (quoted in Maurstad 1997: C1). But nostalgia television is no less postmodern than is hyperconscious television, for it does not affirm a set of conditions or truths that ever actually existed. Rather, it pines for an idealized, romanticized past – a sentimentalized memory of a better time and/or place. Since it longs for something that never was, nostalgia television does not have to be set in the past, though it often is. Nostalgia television is animated not by history, but by story. It stories a return to innocence by fostering a sense of simplicity and spirituality. It stories harmony and wholeness through the devices of narrative and community. And it stories a world of safety and comfort through appeals to authenticity and sincerity. The three key traits of nostalgia television, then, are purity, unity, and security.

An examination of the generic elements of nostalgia television warrants the same qualifications as did the discussion of hyperconscious television in chapter 3. Not all of the programs in this genre, and especially the genre's precursors, exhibit all three generic traits with equal intensity. What they do share is a common outlook. Nostalgia television shows are united, first and foremost, by their implicit mourning over and explicit attempt to recuperate what they perceive to have been lost in the transition to the Information Age. These losses are, of course, fictions, as we have never been innocent, harmonious, and safe. But prior to the rise of the new information technologies, which exposed us to difference and otherness on a daily basis, these fictions were easier to sustain. The transition to the Information Age beginning in the 1960s did not destroy these values and concepts; rather, it demystified them, exposed them as illusions. Nostalgia television (re)mystifies these values as a mode of escape from the perceived threats of contemporary life. In contrast to hyperconscious television, whose attitude is articulated chiefly through images, the basic attitude of nostalgia television finds its greatest resonance at the level of storytelling. The goals of this chapter are: to define and illuminate the three generic properties of nostalgia television during the decade of the 1990s; to engage in a close textual investigation of one particularly representative example, *Dr. Quinn, Medicine Woman*; and to highlight the symbolic equipments this genre provides for living in the Information Age.

Purity: simplicity and spirituality

Purity is a rhetorical mode that operates on the level of both form and content to affirm a feeling of innocence and a world of uncorrupted states. At a formal level, it accomplishes this through generic simplicity. Nostalgia television *seemingly* does not mix, blend, or otherwise pollute the discrete cultural codes and formulas of television. It operates, instead, almost exclusively "in bounds" or in accordance with the traditional television genres of drama and to a lesser extent situation comedy. On the level of content, it purifies the social world by invoking wholesomeness and spirituality. Such spirituality comes in many forms, ranging from faith in mystical forces to the belief in a benevolent almighty.

Through generic hybridity and stylistic pastiche, the eclectic forms of hyperconscious television, like much of the rest of our contemporary cultural landscape, represent the pollution, disorder, defilement, and corruption of "pure" forms, and therefore chaos and danger. As Mary Douglas (2002) explains in *Purity and Danger*, "Dirt offends against order. Eliminating it is . . . a[n] effort to organize the environment" (2–3). Dirt refers here not simply to uncleanliness, but to the mixing of categories, to social disorder, and to dis(semiotic)array (see Stallybrass & White 1986: 23). What nostalgia television does, alternatively, is go about "separating, tidying, and purifying" cultural forms, of making them "clean" in the biblical sense of proper, suitable, and fitting to their class (Douglas 2002: xiv, 3). The symbolic function of classification generally, and genre purification in particular, is to restore a sense of order to a world that "feels" turbulent, chaotic, and otherwise threatening. One way of assessing the extent to which nostalgia television participates in this process is by examining *how* popular critics name and describe certain programs.

One of the key precursors to nostalgia television in the 1990s is the NBC series *Cheers* (1982–93). "A generation from now," writes David Bianculli (1996), "*Cheers* will be regarded with the same reverent affection we now feel for such classic sitcoms as *The Honeymooners*, *The Dick Van Dyke Show*, and *M*A*S*H*. It is to the eighties what those shows were, respectively, to the fifties, sixties, and seventies" (67). Bianculli not only locates *Cheers* squarely within the recognized boundaries of the situation comedy by comparing it to the "classic sitcoms" of earlier decades, but he also suggests that such classics (read: categorical exemplars) warrant "reverent affection." In other words, *Cheers* is praiseworthy precisely because it enacts the very televisual codes and formulas that make a sitcom a "classic." Writer Kurt Vonnegut goes even further than Bianculli, suggesting that

Cheers is *the* classic sitcom: "I would say that television has produced one comic masterpiece, which is *Cheers*. I wish I'd written that instead of everything I *had* written" (quoted in Bianculli 1992: 266). The term "masterpiece" is used to describe art works that best exemplify the characteristics of a particular artistic tradition or style. Although *Cheers* was a Nielsen top 5 series for six seasons, it did not start there, and, indeed, was almost cancelled after its first season (McNeil 1996: 158). *Cheers'* survival and ultimate success is due, at least in part, to another forerunner of nostalgia television, *The Cosby Show* (NBC, 1984–92).

When *The Cosby Show* joined *Cheers* on Thursday nights in 1984, NBC suddenly had a profitable powerhouse lineup that would continue into the early 1990s. Importantly, just before the introduction of *The Cosby Show*, "some analysts predicted that the age of the sitcom had passed" (McNeil 1996: 180; see also Bianculli 1996: 76). Serial dramas such as *Dallas* (CBS, 1978–91) and *Dynasty* (ABC, 1981–9) were, after all, consistently outperforming network sitcoms. But the announced "death" of the situation comedy was premature, for *The Cosby Show* "finished second in the ratings in 1984–1985, and topped the charts (sometimes by huge margins) for the next four seasons" (McNeil 1996: 180). In the 1970s, sitcoms had increasingly mutated into irreverent "kids-know best" shows. *The Cosby Show*, by contrast, was gentler and sought to recover the traditional (read: nuclear, wholesome, simpler, and stable) "family values" of earlier sitcoms such as *The Adventures of Ozzie & Harriet* (ABC, 1952–66), *Father Knows Best* (CBS, 1954–5 and 1958–62; NBC, 1955–8; ABC, 1962–3), and *Leave It to Beaver* (CBS, 1957–8; ABC, 1958–63) (Bianculli 1996: 76–8; see also Brooks & Marsh 2003: 247). In doing so, *The Cosby Show* "ushered in a new era of sitcoms, many of them based on the traditional family; by the end of the [1980s] decade there were more sitcoms on the network primetime schedules than at any other time in television history" (McNeil 1996: 180). *The Cosby Show*, then, was viewed as having, quite literally, renewed (read: purified) the genre of the situation comedy.

At the same time that the situation comedy was returning to (and reinventing) its roots, many dramatic series were undergoing a similar "purification." In addition to generic hybridity, hyperconscious television utilizes stylistic pastiche. Through this device, shows such as *Miami Vice* and *Twin Peaks* were transforming (and some would say corrupting) the category of drama by elevating image and style over story and narration. Nostalgia television counters this trend and returns the tradition of storytelling to the center of dramatic series. While numerous nostalgia television shows illustrate this process, I would like to single out three in particular. The same season that NBC premiered *Miami Vice* on Friday nights, it introduced the nostalgic *Highway to Heaven* (1984–8), starring Michael Landon as angel Jonathan Smith, on Wednesday nights. According to Alex McNeil (1996), "Few people expected the series to do well, given its lack of car chases and beautiful women" (378). But the show was successful, ultimately knocking ABC's hit series *The Fall Guy* (1981–6), starring Lee Majors as Hollywood stuntman and bounty hunter Colt Seavers, out of the Nielsen top 20 and into another time slot. *Highway to Heaven* rejected the increasingly fast-paced, image-obsessed character of dramas such as *Miami Vice* and *The Fall Guy*, and instead privileged "Tender, emotional *stories* about the value of kindness in life" (emphasis added, Brooks & Marsh 2003: 534).

Highway to Heaven was, many believe, the inspiration or at least the model for the 1990s CBS hit series *Touched by an Angel* (1994–2003). This hour-long dramatic series concerned an angel named Monica (Roma Downey), who was sent from heaven to inspire and to assist mortals who were at a crossroads in their lives. Monica received advice and occasional assistance from her superior and fellow angel, Tess (Della Reese). Like *Highway to Heaven*, *Touched by an Angel* downplayed image in favor of good storytelling. The second-highest rated dramatic series during the 1990s behind *ER*, it was successful for different reasons. Whereas the hyperconscious *ER* "oozed adrenaline, projecting the breathless, high-pressure environment in which a group of young doctors struggled to save lives" (Brooks & Marsh 2003: 348), *Touched by an Angel*'s "wholesome, edge-free scripts offer[ed] viewers a respite from urban grit and gripe" (Jacobs 1996: 38). In this statement by *Entertainment Weekly* writer A. J. Jacobs, he explicitly locates *Angel*'s sense of wholesomeness and purity in its scripts, in its stories. Further, these stories offer respite and escape from "urban grit and gripe" (read: disorder and pollution of the postmodern city) – the very *image* of chaos that animated *ER*. In 1995, CBS moved *Touched by an Angel* from its original Wednesday night time-slot to Saturday evening, where it was sandwiched between the western dramas *Dr. Quinn, Medicine Woman* (1993–8) and *Walker, Texas Ranger*

(1993–2001) – a lineup marketed by CBS as "America's Night of Television."

Walker, Texas Ranger may not have featured any angels, but it was no less grounded in traditional values (or storytelling) than *Highway to Heaven* or *Touched by an Angel*. *Walker* was an hour-long drama about modern-day Texas Ranger Cordell Walker (played by martial artist Chuck Norris), whose independent approach to crime-solving was rooted in the traditions of the Old West. Despite the fact that Walker "believed in dealing with criminals the old-fashioned way – by beating them up" (Brooks & Marsh 2003: 1276), the show had, according to Richard von Busack (1996), "a certain softness to it, a warmth and fuzziness." The show's "warmth" emanated from its weekly assurance that "good" would triumph over "evil." *Walker* was not a show about subtleties or blurred moral boundaries. Rather it was, in the words of Ed Robertson (2006), "a classic morality play." Reinforcing this perception, a promotional statement for the series intones:

> In a time when heroes are scarce, truth and justice ring through Norris' character and contribute to his believability. As a result of these values, *Walker, Texas Ranger* has dominated its time slot since its inception. The series continues to appeal to the mass population by providing a true American hero and bringing television audiences back to the tradition of the good guys beating the bad guys. (Columbia Tri-Star Television 2006)

The language of this statement explicitly indicates that *Walker, Texas Ranger* seeks to restore a lost purity by taking viewers "*back to* the tradition" of clear morality and the values of truth and justice.

The impulse of nostalgia television to recapture an elemental simplicity and lost purity occurs at the level of content as well as at the more formal level of genre purification. Nostalgia television quite literally seeks to "purify" society by offering spiritual redemption from the twin sins of technology and science (see Ellin 1997: 26). One especially clear example of this process is provided by the quirky, but deeply spiritual, CBS series *Northern Exposure* (1990–5). This hour drama centered on recent Columbia University Medical School graduate Joel Fleischman (Rob Morrow), who despite his numerous protests finds himself assigned to practice medicine in the remote town of Cicely, Alaska. Although frequently compared to the equally quirky but much darker *Twin Peaks*, "*Northern Exposure*," explains Bianculli

(1996), "was almost all sweetness and light...and spent most episodes exploring some aspect of spirituality" (231). As Robert Thompson (1996) elaborates, "The real cornerstone of *Northern Exposure*...was its spirituality. Represented most prominently by [local radio] deejay Chris, a mail-order minister who preached... every major world faith and then some, and the community of Native American townsfolk and visitors, the spiritual life played a crucial role in the daily operations of Cicely" (166). This "spiritual life" was consistently depicted on the series as a rejection of technology and a triumph of faith over modern-day science.

The premiere episode of the second season, "Goodbye to All That" (04/08/91) affords an example of the show's general antitechnology sentiment. After Holling Vincoeur (John Cullum), proprietor of a local saloon, installs a satellite dish that receives 200 channels, his girlfriend Shelly Tambo (Cynthia Gear) becomes obsessed with the televisual extravaganza. Cultural critic Jim Collins (1992) recounts the narrative development of Shelly's relationship with television over the course of this episode:

> Shelly quickly becomes a television addict, her entire life suddenly controlled by the new technology. She becomes maniacal in the process, and we see her calling the shopping channel to order thousands of dollars of kitsch items. The determination of her character by television programs is stressed repeatedly, as she dances to music videos or dresses up as a Vanna White wannabe to watch *Wheel of Fortune*. But by the end of the program she has confessed her television sins, in a mock confessional to the disk jockey-priest, and resolves to watch selectively. (323)

In this episode, Shelly's image-centered identity is critiqued, as her obsession with technology and television in particular is portrayed as a sin. In contrast to hyperconscious television, which resolves the guilt of too much TV viewing comically by suggesting that it is an unavoidable part of the human condition or through transcendence by valuing televisual knowledge, *Northern Exposure* resolves it tragically through mortification. After being shown the error of her ways in the form of public castigation over the radio, Shelly "corrects" her behavior and vows to watch less television.

According to Richard Campbell and Rosanne Freed (1993), at the heart of *Northern Exposure's* demonizing of technology lies an implicit critique of modern science.

"[P]ostmodernism" celebrates the recovered ideals of a downsized, multicultural community/tribe and the mythic beliefs discarded by modern science. Paraphrasing Chris the DJ on *Northern Exposure*, rationalism nailed magic to the cross of modern science – and it's time for a resurrection. . . . Weekly, the hapless modern man – in the guise of cosmopolitan Jewish doctor, Joel Fleischman – fights the power of the pre-modern philosophies. When Fleischman's medical miracles typically fail, a pungent native potion cures the local flu epidemic and a hip tribal medicine man correctly diagnoses a problem patient. (82)

Such plot devices function, at once, to reaffirm the importance of mysticism and spiritual forces in the structuring of everyday life, and to indict science and technology as poor substitutes, or if one prefers, false Gods. Apparently, *Northern Exposure*'s spiritual undercurrent resonated with many viewers, and by its third season, it was among the Nielsen top 10 programs. "An inclusion of the spiritual and the sacred was very unusual for a prime-time series at the time," explains Thompson (1996), "but it wouldn't be for long" (167). *Northern Exposure* had demonstrated a public desire, even need, for a spiritual (re)turn.

Many of shows that followed, particularly on CBS, responded to this need, including *Walker, Texas Ranger, Touched by an Angel*, and *Promised Land* (1996–9). On *Walker*, spiritualism came, first, in the form of Cordell's martial arts skills. Not only did these skills allow him to fight crime largely without the tools and technology of a (post)-modern society, but they also encoded him with an ancient eastern mysticism. This sense of spiritual mysticism was further reinforced by the fact that Walker, himself half-Indian, frequently sought advice from his stereotypically wise Native American uncle, Raymond Firewalker. Two episodes, in particular, that feature this relationship are "Rainbow Warrior" (11/05/94) and "On Sacred Ground" (03/11/95). By the mid-1990s, the spiritual undertones of shows like *Northern Exposure* and *Walker, Texas Ranger* were rapidly becoming overtones. Columnists Mark Lasswell and Ed Weiner (1997), writing for *TV Guide*, observed that, "If TV is beginning to experience a spiritual revival, then CBS's *Touched by an Angel* and its spin-off, *Promised Land*, are devout evangelists" (38). Although religion and God were central to both of these shows, *Angel's* staffers claimed that "The series is *spiritual*, not religious . . . a show for Jews, Muslims, and Buddhists as well as Christians" (Jacobs 1996: 38). What was important, intriguing, and compelling about these programs was not that they advocated a specific set of religious values or doctrines, but that they articulated a renewed sense of faith in universals and absolute truths.

At a time when the very foundations of knowledge and truth were being challenged and questioned, many viewers simply wanted to "believe" in something. Indeed, a 1997 *TV Guide* poll found that 56 percent of Americans think that religion does not get enough attention on primetime TV (Kaufman 1997: 33). Through their narratives of God's grace and love, *Touched by and Angel* and *Promised Land* reassured viewers on a weekly basis that despite the chaos and confusion of contemporary life, there were still certain constants and certainties in the world. These series also narrated that such spiritual foundations were not always immediately evident, but commonly involved some sort of personal soul searching, self-journey, or spiritual quest. Purity was not something that came easily, but something that had to be (re)discovered beneath the surface of images endlessly circulating in society. In contrast to hyperconscious television, which privileges surface over depth, nostalgia television seeks to recover an elemental purity that has been obscured by the array of signs and styles that intermingle in our media landscape. No show narrated the message of an uncorrupted core more successfully than *Touched by an Angel*, which 66 percent of respondents described as "the most spiritually rich primetime program" on television (Kaufman 1997: 35). In the next section, I demonstrate that nostalgia TV not only invites a turning inward to find clarity, but also to find unity.

Unity: narrative and community

Unity is a rhetorical mode the functions to create a sense of wholeness, totality, and most of all harmony. On a formal level, this sense is fostered through traditional storytelling, which according to film and literary scholar Seymour Chatman (1978) entails events and existents connected in a linear sequence and ending in narrative resolution (21). Unlike intertextual allusions, which continually radiate outward in multiple directions, classical narratives are "self-contained" stories whose meanings arise from the relationships among internal elements. On a second level, unity is fostered through the depiction of community, be it social or familial. Within nostalgia television, community is almost always figured in traditional terms involving shared values and common geography. As such, community is represented as relatively stable and fixed.

If – given its intertextual arrangement of eclectic and decentered images – the central metaphor for the structure of hyperconscious television is a "web," then the central metaphor for the structure of nostalgia television would be a "line," and more specifically a line that possesses a clear beginning and ending. Like all narratives, nostalgia television is comprised of events (actions or happenings) and existents (characters and setting). In classical narrative, events are not arranged randomly in a chance compilation, but "are radically correlative, enchaining, entailing" (Chatman 1978: 45). "Their sequence," explains Chatman "is not simply linear but causative. The causation may be overt, that is, explicit, or covert, implicit". The individual events that comprise a story are arranged to form a narrative thread, each event inviting subsequent events. A ringing telephone, for instance, invites someone to answer it. The ensuing conversation reveals details that, in turn, advance the plot. According to Kenneth Burke (1953), narrative *form* may be defined as "an arousing and fulfillment of desires. A work has form in so far as one part of it leads a reader to anticipate another part, to be gratified by the sequence" (124). As stories unfold, events raise questions and expectations that later events in the narrative answer and fulfill. Thus, the line reaches its predetermined end when the central questions and expectations aroused at the outset are resolved in the conclusion. To the extent that a story does this well, it is said to have psychological unity. This is perhaps the defining formal characteristic of nostalgia television.

It is readily apparent in murder mystery series such as *Matlock* (NBC, 1986–92; ABC, 1993–5) and *Murder, She Wrote* (CBS, 1984–96), whose plots are inevitably set in motion by a crime that will ultimately be solved by Benjamin Matlock (Andy Griffith) or Jessica Fletcher (Angela Lansbury) by narrative's end. Despite what Karen E. Riggs (2006) has called "the formulaic nature of the program," *Murder, She Wrote* was a highly successful series, consistently ranking in the Nielsen top 20. "The secret to the show's success," explains Bianculli (1996), was due in part to "the neatly resolved mystery plots" (217). Whether consciously or not, the assurance that justice will be served and order restored at the end of every episode is profoundly appealing for viewers who feel threatened by a fragmented, chaotic world. This sense of closure and unity is not limited to murder mysteries, however, and animates other nostalgia television programs such as Fox's *Beverly Hills 90210* (1990–2000) and NBC's *Friends* (1994–2002). At first glance, these programs may appear to be unlikely candidates for inclusion in the category of nostalgia television. But both series rely upon traditional plot structures, in which characters confront challenges – typically serious in the case of *Beverly Hills 90210* and humorous in the case of *Friends* – that must be resolved, either within that episode or a subsequent episode.

The precise texture and feel of a narrative is a product of its existents as well as its events. Existents refer to a narrative's setting and its characters. In its search for a lost unity, nostalgia television often escapes into the past in search of a less fragmented, more harmonious time. Describing this trend, Virginia Mann (1991) writes:

> When times get tough, the tough go back in time. That's the conventional wisdom on TV this fall [1991]. In addition to programming a flurry of forget-your-troubles comedies, the beleaguered networks are harking back to eras remembered as kinder and gentler. ABC's "Homefront" is set in 1945, as a small Ohio town welcomes home its war heroes. CBS's "Brooklyn Bridge" begins in 1956, shortly before the Dodgers deserted. NBC's "I'll Fly Away" . . . has winged it back to late-Fifties Georgia. The common thread is nostalgia. (E01)

In retreating to the past, these shows are able to depict a downsized, elemental folk culture that celebrates family, community, and traditional values. Significantly, *Homefront* (1991–3), *Brooklyn Bridge* (1991–3), and *I'll Fly Away* (1991–3) are all set shortly before the turbulent sixties, when issues of difference and otherness began to garner substantial attention on both a national and international stage.

But even ABC's *The Wonder Years* (1988–93), which was set *during* the 1960s when racial tensions, Vietnam, political assassinations, and the "space race" dominated the news, was about simpler times. A half-hour situation comedy, this show was not about the political and social issues of the era; rather, it was a nostalgic look at "growing up" in the American suburbs. Its sentimental gaze was accomplished by exploring life through the eyes of 12-year-old Kevin Arnold, played by Fred Savage (see Brooks & Marsh 2003: 1320; Haithman 1988: 8G).

In the opening sequence of the show's pilot episode, a grown-up Kevin (voiced By Daniel Stern) nostalgically recalls his childhood:

> 1968. I was twelve years old. A lot happened that year. Denni McLain won 31 games, the Mod Squad hit the air, and I graduated from Hillcrest Elementary and entered junior high school – but we'll get to that. There's no pretty way to put this: I grew up in the suburbs. I guess most people think of the suburbs as a place with all the disadvantages of the city, and none of the advantages of the country, and vice versa. But, in a way, those really were the wonder years for us there in the suburbs. It was a kind of golden age for kids. ("Pilot" [01/21/88])

With the very first word, the audience is transported to the past – not just to any past, but to a past of child-like simplicity and wonder. Even though an adult Kevin narrates the show, the images are of 12-year-old "Kevin's little world" (Haithman 1988: 8G). This world, the audience is told, was a "golden age for kids." And it functions as a "golden age" for viewers, who in recalling childhood memories are returned not to a demanding, adult sixties of social pressures, but to a sentimentalized, child-like sixties of pure wish fulfillment.

Since contemporary places can also be coded in sentimental ways, nostalgia television does not have to be set in the past to celebrate the ideals of tightly knit family and community. TV can, in the words of Campbell and Freed (1993), "reinvent a nostalgic community that's either explicitly in the past (the 1950s extended family of *Brooklyn Bridge*, and the 1960s adolescent entanglements of *The Wonder Years*) or feels like it should be . . . with playfully unabashed portrayals of places as we might like them to be" (82). The depiction of a "nostalgic present" is evident in the settings of many nostalgia television programs, which are frequently set in rural communities, small (often southern) towns, or wide-open frontiers. In his analysis of "nostalgia films," Fredric Jameson (1983) argues that "the small town setting has a crucial strategic function: it allows the film to do without most of the signals and references which we might associate with the contemporary world, with consumer society – the appliances and artifacts, the high rises, the object world of late capitalism. . . . It seems to me exceedingly symptomatic to find the very style of nostalgia films invading and colonizing even those movies today which have contemporary settings" (117).

Murder, She Wrote takes place, for instance, in the tiny fictional seaside village of Cabot Cove, Maine. Although the legal drama *Matlock* was set in modern day Atlanta, "When a case bogged down Ben [Andy Griffith] would repair [*sic*] to his handsome, 100-year-old stone house in Willow Springs, Georgia, where he would strum his banjo and ponder clues. Mayberry was not far away, in spirit at least" (Brooks & Marsh 2003: 752). Another series to actively appeal to a nostalgic present was *Northern Exposure*, whose executive producers, Joshua Brand and John Falsey, were concurrently producing the nostalgia programs *Brooklyn Bridge* and *I'll Fly Away*. Set in the fictional city of Cicely, Alaska, *Northern Exposure* prominently featured a "frontier" setting.

In the popular imagination, the "frontier" represents remoteness, simplicity, and nature in its uncorrupted state. It reflects an idealized imaginary that is both physically distant from the modern city and psychologically distant from "civilization" and the bustling pace of city life. At the same time, the frontier is closer, at least psychologically, to nature. Its depiction of spacious skies and a vast, barren landscape function to create a space where one can "find" a meaningful sense of self. According to Bonnie Dow (1996),

> [T]he frontier performs a leveling function; it strips life to its essence in a context that has few institutional pressures . . . The West is a world in which every person, supposedly, is measured and valued by what s/he does and what s/he can contribute. . . . [Through a frontier-motif], Westerns, then, offer the ultimate context for discovering the authentic self. . . . Westerns return us to a simpler locale, where the stakes are clear and the autonomy of the self is given. (173, 177)

As the nation's "last frontier," Alaska provided an ideal setting for the spiritual soul-searching at work in *Northern Exposure*. Such inward reflection was aided not just by the landscape, but also by the frequent depiction of Native American culture. The emphasis in these depictions is not on the actions of specific Native Americans, but on what Native American culture represents – harmony with nature. As Ed (Darren E. Burrows) seeks to learn about his parents and thus himself in "The Big Kiss" (04/15/91) and "Duets" (01/18/93), he consults the 256-year-old Indian spirit of One-Who-Waits; similarly, when Maggie (Janine Turner) develops concerns about aging, she undergoes an ancient Indian ritual in "Northwest Passage" (09/28/92). These particular episodes, as well as *Northern Exposure* more generally, suggested that identity is an inward process of searching, not an outward process of bringing together image fragments from our media-saturated culture.

Whereas hyperconscious television relies upon viewers' knowledge of media culture to (re)create a sense of belonging and self, nostalgia television eschews consumer culture in favor of a simpler time *or* place, which it constructs either through depictions of a downsized, elemental folk culture or an uncontaminated natural landscape. Robert Thompson (1996) evinces this distinction through his comparison of *Northern Exposure* to other popular dramatic series:

> Sly [intertextual] allusions to and inside jokes about television...were less important in *Northern Exposure* than they had been in some of the earlier quality dramas [such as *St. Elsewhere* and *Moonlighting*]....
> *Northern Exposure* came to depend less and less upon "inside" jokes for its hipness. "Outside" was more what this show was all about. Shot mostly near Seattle, the show's physical distance from Hollywood was reflected in its style and attitude. The scenery was different from most TV...Rather than making fun of popular culture, which *St. Elsewhere* had done so adeptly, *Northern Exposure* seemed more concerned with ignoring it. (165)

Nor was *Northern Exposure* alone in its use of a frontier motif. Other nostalgia television shows to utilize a barren, uncorrupted landscape in an attempt to recover a missing harmony included ABC's *The Young Riders* (1989–92), an hour-long drama about six young recruits for the Pony Express, and *Walker, Texas Ranger*, which was "the first network-TV show to film exclusively in Texas...and reek[ed] atmosphere" (von Busack 1996).

As the characters on nostalgia television seek to confront the problems of (post)modern living and to recover a missing harmony – where everything works in unison – they are aided as much by community as by setting. According to television scholar Ella Taylor (1989):

> If we understand the television narrative as a commentary on, and resolution of, our troubles rather than a reflection of the real conditions of our lives, it becomes possible to read the television work-family as...an affirmation of the possibility of community and cooperation amid the loose and fragmentary ties of association. (153)

The centrality of community within nostalgia series is readily apparent in many of their theme songs. From *Cheers'* "Where Everybody Knows Your Name" and *The Golden Girls'* (NBC, 1985–92) "Thank You for Being a Friend" to *The Wonder Years'* "With a Little Help from My Friends" and *Friends'* "I'll Be There for You," the theme music of these series stresses the unwavering reliability of community. Community is, of course, always defined by exclusion and by absence. The sense of unity and wholeness communicated by community in these programs is further reinforced by the near homogeneity of the communities themselves. In other words, these communities overcome cultural fragmentation by expelling racial, class, and ethnic difference. The so-called *Friends* "gang" provides a good example. Not only are they always (or, at least, an impossible amount of the time) with one another – either in the idealized coffee shop, Central Perk, or their respective Greenwich Village apartments – but those places also reflect a "totally sanitized Bohemia . . . without a single writer or artist, or person with an unconventional lifestyle (except for Ross's [David Schwimmer] wife and her lover) or radical politics. Similarly, their New York is without any poor, or the ethnic and racial tensions that plague the city" (Auster 1996: 5).

Thus, as the characters on nostalgia television struggle to "discover" themselves and to confront the seemingly daily romantic crises in their lives, they can always count on support from their friends – friends who think, act, and look like them (e.g., they are equally beautiful and wealthy). The characters on nostalgia television are able to resolve their personal identity crises so quickly and easily (usually by the end of an episode) because they rarely have to confront difference and otherness. "This romanticized world of relationships bears a striking resemblance," observes Albert Auster (1996), "to the appeal of escapist Hollywood musicals of the thirties and forties. It provides a certain amount of relief from the emotional and economic anxieties of the real world" (6). Like *Friends*, *Beverly Hills 90210* consists of a group of wealthy, White youth, who assist each other with life's challenges. In the first episode and much of the first season, "life's challenges" were explicitly linked to a fast-paced consumer culture. The initial premise of the one-hour drama was that the Walsh twins Brandon (Jason Priestly) and Brenda (Shannen Doherty) have just moved from Minnesota to Beverly Hills, where their "down-home values stand out in the flashy, trendy, fast-car suburb" (Blumenfeld 1992: D5). That the Walsh children ultimately manage to "fit in" is due in equal parts to the show's nostalgic depiction of community,[1] and as the next section illustrates, its melodramatic mode of storytelling.

Security: authenticity and sincerity

Security is a rhetorical mode that functions to create a mood of safety, warmth, and comfort. Like purity and unity, it too brings together form and content. Formally, nostalgia television fosters a sense of security by providing psychological escape from the threatening "real world" into a safe "reality fiction." Its narratives invite viewers to forget that they are watching television by (pre)tending to be entirely unaware of their own constructedness or participation in a media culture and circuit of production, transmission, and reception. Whereas hyperconscious TV repeatedly foregrounds its status *as television* through self-reflexivity, nostalgia television is utterly silent about its status as television. The characters display no awareness of themselves as characters and the story demonstrates no awareness of itself as a story. The resulting "illusion of reality" is accomplished and sustained through specific narrational strategies – strategies rooted in appeals to authenticity and sincerity.

In his landmark essay "Introduction to the Structural Analysis of Narratives," Roland Barthes (1988) argues that narration is as important to storytelling as events and existents; at its most basic level, narration implies communication: "there is a donor of the narrative and a receiver of the narrative" (109). This arrangement, though seemingly simplistic, raises several important and complex questions. What is the nature of the narrator? What is the narrator's relationship to the story-world? How does the narrator conceptualize the audience? What is the relationship between the donor of the narrative and the receiver? As an initial answer to these questions, it is helpful to contrast the narration of nostalgia television with that of hyperconscious television. Whereas the hyperconscious narrator is reflexive, reminding the audience that this is merely a fiction, the nostalgic narrator is concealed, obscuring the fact that a story is even being told. Hyperconscious TV narrates with an ironic "wink," while nostalgia TV narrates with a sincere but subtle "smile." The wink directly and explicitly acknowledges viewers, and it asks for their knowing participation. The smile acknowledges the audience only indirectly and implicitly; it creates participation unknowingly. Thus, when nostalgia television is working ideally, the audience forgets, at least for a time, that this is a story (read: fiction). Or seen from another angle, they forget everything *outside* the story. Their (post)modern worries disappear as they lose themselves in, escape into, the story.

To better understand this process and the ways in which it fosters a sense of security, it is helpful to examine a few specific examples. *The Wonder Years* utilizes a homodiegetic narrator, meaning that the narrator is also a character in the story-world (i.e., the diegesis) that s/he is describing. Typically, homodiegetic or "character narrators are considered less objective and less authoritative than heterodiegetic narrators [who exist unacknowledged and outside of the story-world]" (Kozloff 1992: 82). *The Wonder Years* overcomes this difficulty by modifying its use of the character narrator. To alter the perception that the narrator is less objective and authoritative because he is involved in the action, the narrator in *The Wonder Years* is represented as the adult version of story's central character, 12-year-old Kevin Arnold. The rhetorical effect of this narrational age gap is to legitimize the story being told. If young Kevin Arnold narrated the story, it might appear childish, embellished, and unreliable. The adult voice, by contrast, conveys maturity and objectivity, as an adult has greater experience and perspective from which to tell the story. This functions to assure the audience of the story's veracity and fidelity. This process is evident near the conclusion of the pilot episode, as the adult Kevin ruminates on one especially memorable evening from his childhood:

> That night I decided to go for a walk. The days were still long and back then kids could still go for walks at dusk without the fear of ending up on a milk carton. I went down to the big climbing tree in Harper's Woods. I didn't admit it to myself until years later, but in my mind was the shadow of a thought that Winnie might be there.

The phrase "I didn't admit it to myself until years later" conveys a sense of raw earnestness by suggesting that only over time has the narrator gained the sufficient historical and emotional perspective to tell this story accurately and honestly. In combining the perception of first-hand knowledge with personal reflection and sincerity, the audience has little reason to doubt the character's claim that it was safer for kids "back then." Hence, the narration of grown-up Kevin creates, according to Kathryn Baker (1988), "a warm . . . evocative homage to that hazy, long-lost world that was suburban America in the late

1960s" (7C). Although the setting of *The Wonder Years* may transport viewers to the past, it is the narration that both creates and guarantees the comfort and safety of that past.

The Wonder Years' use of homodiegetic narration to reinforce its nostalgic point of view is the exception on television generally and on nostalgic television in particular. Most nostalgia television programs adopt a heterodiegetic narrational strategy, in which the narrator is unseen and unknown. The narrator in this model is, in effect, an anonymous, omniscient Author-God, who is infallible. Instead of hearing and seeing a story through one person's eyes, viewers themselves are made observers and interpreters of events and actions. Heterodiegetic narration is compelling because it appears to be completely unmediated and un-narrated. Viewers are simply *witnesses* to the "reality fiction." As Denis Wood (1992) explains:

> As long as the author – and the interest he or she unfailingly embodies – is in plain view, it is hard to overlook him, hard to see around her, to the world described, hard to see it ... *as the world.* Instead it is seen as no more than a *version* of the world, as a *story* about it, as a *fiction*: no matter how good it is, not something to be taken seriously. As author – and interest – become marginalized (or done away with altogether), the represented world is enabled to ... *fill our vision.* Soon enough we have forgotten this is a picture someone has arranged for us (chopped and manipulated, selected and coded). Soon enough ... it is the world, it is real, it is ... *reality.* (70)

It is much easier to suspend one's disbelief in a story when that story is quite literally unfolding before one's eyes. Sarah Kozloff (1992) describes the process this way:

> The vast majority of television narrators strive for neutrality and self-effacement, as if viewers are supposed to overlook the fact that the story is coming through a mediator and instead believe that they are looking in on reality. Other styles are possible, however. Some shows – I'm thinking of *Moonlighting* – convey an "arch" tonality and an assertive self-consciousness, deliberately flouting conventions of realism. (83)

The specific "other style" that Kozloff mentions in this statement corresponds to the narrational strategy of hyperconscious television, which as noted in the previous chapter works to destroy viewers' "suspension of disbelief." The nonreflexive narrational style of nostalgia television, by contrast, appeals to authenticity, saying to viewers, in effect, "this is 'really' happening."

Nostalgia television frequently combines its use of a heterodiegetic narrator with the more general narrational *style* of melodrama. Originally, melodrama was used to describe nineteenth-century stage plays that were "characterized by sensational and romantic plots, strong and often emotional appeals to the audience's emotions, extravagant staging, exaggerated characters and happy endings with virtue triumphant" (Watson & Hill 1997: 140). Today, melodrama has become one of the prevailing narrational styles of TV. According to Lynn Joyrich (1992), melodrama is especially comforting in a society characterized by simulation, fragmentation, and semiotic excess because it reaffirms the possibility of universals:

> Melodrama might at first appear to be an odd form in which to search for signs of the real. But as Peter Brooks has argued, the melodramatic mode, above all, expresses the desire to find true stakes of meaning, morality, and truth. It thus emerges in times of doubt and uncertainty, employing signs which may seem overdetermined and excessive in order to mark out values left cloudy by a disintegrating sacred system. Combating the anxiety produced by a new order which can no longer assure us of the operation, or even existence, of fundamental social, moral, or "natural" truths, melodrama "arises to demonstrate that it is still possible to find and to show the operation of basic ethical imperatives, to define, in conflictual opposition to the space of their play. That they can be staged 'proves' that they exist." ... As the political, social and aesthetic representations of modern society lose their legitimacy, we are forced once again to find new stakes of meaning, and melodrama is the form to which we turn. In a simulated society which typically stages reality in order to "prove" its existence, melodrama offers a way to assert the "actual" drama of life. (235–6)

While melodrama's insistence upon fundamental, natural truths offers psychological comfort and reassurance in uncertain and unsettling times, it is melodrama's fascination with the everyday – the actual drama of life – that underlies its appeal to "authenticity." Its narratives possess fidelity for viewers because they reflect experiences with which audiences can easily identify. Consider *Beverly Hills 90210*, about which *The Washington Post* observes, "Each week, the [Walsh] twins and their beautiful-people friends navigate their way out of some universal teen-age crisis" (Blumenfeld 1992: D5). In describing her personal affection for the series, 16-year-old fan Silke Wolf explains, "It deals with stuff that we [teens] care about" (quoted in Blumenfeld 1992: D5).

In addition to sustaining the illusion of reality through identifica-tion, the conventional traits of the melodramatic style – including mood-enhancing music, intimate close-ups, and familial spaces – all rely upon widely shared cultural codes for meaning making. Whereas hyperconscious television's intertextual allusions to specific "external texts" require specialized viewer knowledge, nostalgia television's dra-matic "overcodings" require only general cultural knowledge. In this narrational style, interpretation is not a self-conscious "game" or "quiz," but an unconscious process that seemingly occurs "naturally." In other words, the melodramatic style makes the interpretive process invisible. The more invisible this process, the more it "feels" as though meaning is universal and given, rather than local and constructed. Joyrich (1992) describes this relationship in the following manner:

> Melodrama is then a privileged forum for contemporary television, promising the certainty of clearly marked conflict and legible mean-ing...Melodrama allows us both closeness and certainty through its appeal to a pre-linguistic system of gesture and tableaux that aims beyond language to immediate understanding. In its attempt to render meaning visible and recapture the ineffable, melodrama emphasizes gestures, postures, frozen moments and expressions....[T]hus, [it] tends to deny the complex processes of signification and to collapse representation onto the real, assuring its audience of firm stakes of meaning....Melodrama's promise of universally legible meaning seems to be particularly compelling in the postmodern era, experienced by many as desperately in need of some kind of grounding. (245)

Programs such as *Highway to Heaven*, *Beverly Hills 90210*, *Walker, Texas Ranger*, *Touched by an Angel*, and *Promised Land* all employ a melodramatic narrational style. In doing so, they affirm that life's problems, be they romantic, economic, or spiritual, are universal, and that there are moral and experiential truths upon which one can act to address those problems. And even if the "beliefs" narrated by these series have little practicality or utility for the "real world" of the Information Age, they nevertheless furnish comfort by providing escape into a "fictional reality," a nostalgic world of both elemental purity and social harmony. Perhaps no series in the 1990s better illustrates the incorporation and integration of nostalgia television's generic characteristics of purity, unity, and security than CBS's *Dr. Quinn, Medicine Woman*.

Dr. Quinn, Medicine Woman as Exemplar

When *Dr. Quinn, Medicine Woman* premiered on January 1, 1993, as a mid-season replacement for the unpopular *Frannie's Turn* (CBS, 1992), it was an unlikely candidate for success. In addition to its Saturday evening time slot, which is historically weak for network shows, it was greeted by less than enthusiastic reviews in the popular press. Commentators were especially critical of the show's depiction of the past, which included numerous historical inaccuracies (see Kilday 1993: 108; Stein 1993: 43). In the words of one critic, the show was pure "frontier hooey" (quoted in Schindehette 1993: 74). In spite of these criticisms and its poor time slot, *Dr. Quinn, Medicine Woman* "was an immediate success, boasting the highest 'TvQ' rating of any television program in recent history" (Dow 1996: 164). A show's TvQ rating is calculated by dividing the percentage of persons who indicate that they like a show by the percentage of persons who are familiar with it. *Dr. Quinn*'s first-place TvQ rating of 45 in early 1993 was, according to industry experts, all the more impressive given the small percentage of people who were familiar with the program at the time (Mandese 1993: 61). Following its introduction, *Dr. Quinn* consistently won its Saturday evening time slot and it finished as a Nielsen top 25 series each of its first two seasons (Brooks & Marsh 2003: 1469).

But why – especially given criticism over its historical accuracy – was *Dr. Quinn, Medicine Woman* so popular? The series resonated with a large number of viewers because, despite being set in a fictional past, it was relevant to audiences in the 1990s. In the words of the show's producers:

> While the headstrong Michaela can be tough, Beacon Hill never prepared her for such a rugged world where the people are as coarse as the climate and their ideas seem from another time. By having Dr. Quinn's sophisticated values clash with the considerably cruder mindset of her Western neighbors, the series is able to explore situations and issues that are very much a part of life today. Whether championing the cause of

gun control, exposing environmental polluters, battling disease or sexist cowboys, or liberating oppressed frontier women, Dr. Mike, at great personal risk, bucks the conventional wisdom of the Old West and emerges as more than just a pioneering feminist. In the tradition of "Little House on the Prairie," DR. QUINN, MEDICINE WOMAN is steeped in traditional family values and an understanding of the spirit and strength that built America. (Dr. Quinn Medicine Woman 2006)

On one level, this statement suggests that the series was appealing to contemporary audiences because it addressed modern-day issues such as gun control, environmental pollution, and gender discrimination in a simplified, frontier context. On a second level, it hints at an even more fundamental social relevance – the creation of a meaningful self from competing, even opposing cultural fragments. According to the show's producers, *Dr. Quinn* simultaneously "bucks the conventional wisdom" *and* celebrates "traditional family values." What appears, at first, to be an impossible composite of progressive feminist values and traditional maternal, familial values achieves coherence in the character of Dr. Mike, who "emerges as *more* than just a pioneering feminist" (emphasis added).

Through its nostalgic construction of the Old West, *Dr. Quinn, Medicine Woman* constructs a space to resolve (post)modern-day anxieties associated with informationalism. To more fully understand this process and the symbolic equipments that accompany it, this section reviews the basic narrative premise and essential characters of the show, and conducts a close textual analysis of the episode titled "Woman of the Year" (05/06/96). In addition to being one of the 10 most popular episodes aired during the fourth season, this episode affords a particularly clear example of the how the elements of purity, unity, and security address the unique challenges of living in the Information Age.

Dr. Quinn, Medicine Woman is the story of an independent young woman doctor who leaves Boston following the death of her father and medical partner to establish a private medical practice in Colorado Springs, Colorado in the 1860s. Having anticipated a male doctor, the local townspeople initially greet Michaela (Jane Seymour), or "Dr. Mike" as she is later called, with a combination of hostility and skepticism. Only Charlotte Cooper (Diane Ladd), the owner of the town boarding-house, and Byron Sully (Joe Lando), a mysterious mountain man, befriend Michaela from the outset. Shortly after Michaela's arrival, Charlotte becomes deathly ill from a rattlesnake bite, and asks Dr. Mike to care for her three children, 10-year-old Brian (Shawn Toovey), 12-year-old Colleen (Erika Flores/Jessica Bowman), and 17-year-old Matthew (Chad Allen). Michaela adopts the children and then moves them into a homestead owned by Sully, whom she marries at the conclusion of the third season. The show's six seasons more or less reflect six years, a time period over which the community gradually accepts Dr. Mike. At its base, what the show narrates is Michaela's continuous reconciliation of her multiple, conflicting identities as a devoted wife and mother, professional doctor, feminist, and humanitarian.

The episode "Woman of the Year" consists of three relatively independent stories. The primary story revolves around Dr. Quinn's nomination as Colorado Territory's "Woman of the Year." The second story focuses on Hank Lawson/Hans (William Shockley), the local saloon owner, and his attempt to hide his profession and lifestyle from his grandmother, who makes a surprise visit to the town. The third story concerns Sully's actions as the "Indian Agent" within the area. Each of the three stories deals centrally with questions of identity; the dramatic tension in the first two storylines arises because of inconsistencies between who the characters are and how they behave. The tension in the story relating to Sully, by contrast, is a product of the fact that his behavior and self-identity are highly consistent.

As is typical of the melodramatic mode, the episode's central storylines are set in motion during the introductory sequence, which takes place at the town's train depot. Moments after the train's arrival, Sully and Michaela reach the station in a horse-drawn buggy. As Dr. Mike moves off to inspect the medical supplies she ordered, Horace Bing (Frank Collison) presents Sully with a letter from the government. Although Sully does not open letter, the camera's lingering gaze on his expression of dismay as he crumples the letter in his hand signals that it is "bad news." Sully hastily tucks the letter away in his pocket and turns to help Michaela, when an elderly woman disembarking the train approaches him. She asks Sully if he can direct her to the town tailor, an inquiry that befuddles him since the town has no tailor. Overhearing this conversation from across the platform, Hank scurries behind several crates where he hides until the elderly woman turns her back, at which point he dashes out of sight almost knocking Sully down in the process. When Sully finally reaches Michaela, a second, unfamiliar woman has departed the train and interrupts them. The woman identifies herself as Beatrice Cartwright (Bibi Besch) and ultimately announces the purpose of her visit:

BEATRICE: Excuse me, are you Dr. Quinn? Dr. Michaela Quinn?
DR. MIKE: Yes, yes I am.
BEATRICE: Oh, I'm so very honored to meet you. I'm Beatrice Cartwright of the Denver Chapter of the Women's Suffrage League.
DR. MIKE: Pleased to meet you. And this is my husband Byron Sully.
BEATRICE: Yes, of course, the mountain man. May I be the first to offer your wife my personal congratulations?
SULLY: [*confused*] Sure.
BEATRICE: Do you mean no one has notified you?
DR. MIKE: Notified us of what?
[*A man calls out for help and Dr. Mike leaves momentarily to examine a young girl who has fallen on the train tracks. She then returns to Sully and Beatrice.*]
DR. MIKE: Well, if you're staying in town perhaps we can visit later.
BEATRICE: I do hope so. You're precisely the reason I'm here – to observe you for a few days.
DR. MIKE: Observe me? I don't understand.
BEATRICE: Dr. Quinn, you are one of our nominees for Colorado Territory's "Woman of the Year."

This interaction is important not only because it introduces the character of Beatrice along with her narrative purpose, but also because it serves to reinforce the general coding of both Sully and Michaela. Beatrice refers to Sully as "the mountain man," a statement that reaffirms his link to nature. Sully's woodsman attire, wolf companion in early episodes, and friendship with the Cheyenne Indians are other indices of his close relationship with nature. Likewise, Dr. Quinn's gentle care of the young girl who has fallen establishes her dual professional and maternal traits.

In addition to associating Sully with nature, defining Michaela as doctor and mother, and coding Hank as shifty and bizarre, the opening sequence raises three questions. Why is Sully upset by the letter he received? Why did Hank behave so strangely when he saw the elderly woman? And will Beatrice recommend Michaela as Colorado Territory's "Woman of the Year"? In creating a desire to know the answer to these questions, the show formally promises to answer them over the course of the episode. The manner in which those questions are answered along with their contemporary relevance is the focus of the remainder of this section. The introductory sequence is followed immediately by the opening credits, which foreshadow the importance of a western landscape in resolving the questions raised in the opening sequence. Back-to-back images of a locomotive and a stagecoach cutting across the open frontier establish the uncorrupted terrain upon which the action occurs. The camera cuts to a close-up image of a stagecoach and Dr. Quinn peering out from its interior. The movement of the stagecoach across the frontier symbolizes both her journey from Boston to Colorado Springs, and her inner journey to find herself. In subsequent frames, Michaela hangs the sign "M. Quinn M.D." on her clinic door, rushes to help people in medical need, and looks after her children. Her multiple identities are represented in the montage of images which are intercut with panoramic views of valleys and mountains. The barren landscape functions symbolically as the "thread" that holds Michaela's numerous identities together.

In the episode's second sequence, Sully and Beatrice wait outside the medical clinic as Dr. Quinn stitches the knee of the young girl who had fallen on the train tracks. When Michaela emerges, the young girl's father thanks her and apologizes for not being able to pay her. Dr. Mike assures him that the jar of plums she recently received from his wife is "payment enough," a statement that signifies the centrality of community to *Dr. Quinn*. That Beatrice is witness to this interaction and reacts positively suggests to viewers that Dr. Quinn has made a good first impression. As the young girl and her father leave, Colleen approaches, joining Beatrice and her mother (Dr. Mike) in conversation:

> BEATRICE: I apologize for my unannounced arrival, Dr. Quinn. Perhaps the committee thought a spontaneous visit would allow me a more candid observation.
>
> DR. MIKE: This is all so very flattering. But my life feels quite ordinary. As you can see my practice is mostly fevers and scraped knees.
>
> COLLEEN: Ma's done so much more. She's treated epidemics and done all kinds of surgeries.

Colleen's statement expresses pride in her mother, highlights the professional competence of her mother, and draw's attention to the modesty of her mother's statement. That Dr. Mike engenders such respect from her daughter fosters the impression that she is an excellent mother as well as an accomplished physician. Within minutes of learning the news of her nomination, then, Dr. Quinn has been heavily coded as a deserving candidate. This brief exchange is also important because it privileges candidness over insincerity. That Dr. Mike was unaware of the nomination suggests that Beatrice will observe the real Dr. Quinn as opposed to a performance.

Beatrice, Michaela, Colleen, and Sully saunter over to the town cafe for lunch where Beatrice describes the criterion by which the committee will select its "Woman of the Year." As in the introductory sequence, the conversation is interrupted by an action that further reinforces how deserving a recipient Dr. Quinn is. In this instance, the interruption descends "from on high" as the local pastor, Reverend Timothy Johnson (Geoffrey Lower), practically deifies Michaela in offering his congratulations:

BEATRICE:	The Suffrage League recognizes the woman pursuing excellence in all aspects of her life, raising a family while working her career, building the rich fiber of her community.
DR. MIKE:	Ms. Cartwright, the fact that your chapter would consider me is overwhelming to say the least. There must be so many deserving women.
REV. JOHNSON:	Dr. Mike, this is wonderful news. [*to Beatrice*] You couldn't have made a better choice.
DR. MIKE:	Thank you Reverend, but I . . . this is just a nomination.
REV. JOHNSON:	[*to Beatrice*] She's modest too. If you want to hear about the miracles that this woman works I hope that you will seek me out. [*to Dr. Mike*] We're so proud of you.

Dr. Quinn's actions to help the little girl and her continued modesty suggest her worthiness for the award, while the testimony of Colleen and Rev. Johnson (a representative of God no less) reinforce this perception. At this point, it is virtually inconceivable that Dr. Mike would not earn Beatrice's recommendation for Colorado's "Woman of the Year."

Meanwhile, Hank has continued to behave strangely since returning from the train depot. Upon seeing the elderly woman in town, he rushes into his saloon and pleads with his patrons to pretend that they do not know him. A short time later, Hank gathers with his friends at the local cafe and explains that he has lied about his life in the letters that he sent to his grandmother. He confesses, "A ways back I had some letters written and I kinda told this person a few things. Like I had a wife and kids. Ya know. I was respectable." Not wanting to disappoint his grandmother, Hank then requests that his friends "play along" while his nanna is in town. Though his friends are skeptical – particularly Horace, who must "loan" Hank his wife Myra (Helene Udy), their baby girl, and his job at the telegraph office – they reluctantly agree to participate in the charade. Since the town has no tailor, when Hank finally greets his nanna, he informs her that he stopped tailoring to operate the telegraph office – covering his previous lie with another one. Thus, Hank takes on an entirely new identity based solely on appearances and images. As Hank and his nanna begin to reminisce, she mysteriously collapses.

The third sequence begins with Dr. Mike reviving Hank's grandmother at the medical clinic. Michaela asks Hank's nanna if she has fainted before and she assures Dr. Mike that she has not. Based on this information, Dr. Mike diagnoses her condition as fatigue brought on by her recent trip and releases her. The episode returns to the principal storyline later that evening, as Beatrice joins Michaela, Sully, and their children at their home for dinner. During the meal, Michaela discusses Sully's role as the "Indian Agent" in the region, remarking that, "These have been terrible times for the tribes here. They can have no better friend than Sully." The conversation once again reaffirms Sully's connection to nature and spirituality.

At various points throughout the conversation, Colleen interjects with comments rather obviously intended to make her mother look good. She first compliments her mother's cooking (despite the fact that she does most of it) and then she requests her mother's help with a science project concerning electricity, noting Michaela's impressive knowledge of a variety of subjects. With these remarks, Colleen becomes the first in a series of people who will attempt to convey a "perfect image" of Michaela.

The following day, Horace and Hank swap occupations so that Hank's nanna will not learn that he is really the town saloon owner. When nanna visits her grandson at the telegraph office, he must hide pictures of Horace and Myra, and lie about what he does to maintain the appearance of respectability. In the meantime, Beatrice interviews various townsfolk about Dr. Michaela Quinn. She speaks first with Dorothy Jennings (Barbara Babcock), the local newspaper editor, who credits Michaela for her career success and her life: "I wouldn't be a writer today if it weren't for her. Truth is Michaela saved my life." Then, Beatrice speaks with Michaela's oldest son, Matthew, who is the town sheriff. He explains that becoming sheriff was motivated by his desire "to help people," a trait he learned from his mother. The third person Beatrice interviews is Loren Bray (Orson Bean), the owner of the general store, who informs her, "I even let her cut into me once. Fact is Dr. Mike saved my life." As true as the claims may be, their gravity and uniformity suggest that the community is lobbying for Michaela. Music and extreme close-ups hint that Beatrice is now becoming skeptical about Dr. Quinn's true identity.

When Sully arrives home that evening, he finds Michaela sitting by the fire reading a book on electricity. As the two begin to talk, the audience learns both are struggling to reconcile their sense of self with the demands placed upon them by others:

DR. MIKE: I could never follow this type of science in school.
SULLY: Why don't you just tell her [Colleen] you don't know about electricity?
DR. MIKE: I can't do that. She and Becky [Colleen's friend] are counting on me. I'll figure this out. [*long pause*] Something troubling you? [*Sully retrieves some letters from the government*]
SULLY: This one says I gotta make the men cut their hair. This one, medicine men gotta stop their ceremonies. This one says gotta take down the teepees and build log houses, and a church. Government don't want me helping them rebuild their tribes. They want me making 'em white.
DR. MIKE: Hazen [the government official] doesn't know you've been ignoring these [letters]. What are you gonna do?
SULLY: What I've been doing. [*Sully throws the letters in the fire*]

This interaction suggests that the two differ sharply in the means by which they address the tension between who they are and what others expect them to be. While Dr. Mike apparently has no natural affinity for electrical science, she feels compelled, much like Hank, to perform a "false" image of herself. By contrast, Sully appears intent on acting on his convictions (e.g., being true to himself), despite the potential negative ramifications. As the episode develops, one of these identity-based models is clearly privileged over the other. During church service the next morning, Rev. Johnson takes a moment to introduce the town's visitors: Hank's nanna and Beatrice Cartwright. The Reverend participates in the lie about Hank's identity by publicly treating Myra as though she were really Hank's wife. That Rev. Johnson is now perpetuating this fiction seriously calls into question the trustworthiness of the townsfolk. Thus, when Colleen's friend Becky (Haylie Johnson) approaches Beatrice following the church service and begins heaping praise on Michaela, including the all too familiar, "Truth is Dr. Mike saved my life," it sounds decidedly rehearsed. Indeed, the interaction invites the audience to wonder whether Beatrice will believe the positive stories everyone has told her about Michaela up to this point or will view them as attempts by the town to create a false image. As the congregation begins to exit the church, Hank's grandmother collapses a second time.

The fourth sequence opens with Michaela coming out of the clinic to advise Hank of his grandmother's status. She informs him that his nanna now admits to fainting like this for several months, and that she has detected an irregular heartbeat. Given these findings, Dr. Mike has prescribed digitalis, which she believes will stabilize nanna's heart. Much like her grandson, Hank's nanna has been perpetuating a false image of herself, acting healthy even though she was not. In this instance, the image she fosters endangers her life, suggesting the danger of creating false appearances. As Hank leaves, Sully invites Michaela to accompany him on a relaxing buggy ride, but she declines, having previously promised to help Colleen with her science project. Throughout the afternoon, Hank and Myra spend time with nanna, and in the process shun Horace. By that evening, Horace – angered by how close Hank and Myra have become – confronts them, expressing his distaste for the charade. Meanwhile, at the homestead, Michaela tries to demonstrate the properties of electricity to Colleen and Becky. The experiment she has them try fails, however, and it is becoming obvious she is not very adept at this type of science. Just as they are about to repeat the experiment, Rev. Johnson arrives at the house to inform Dr. Mike that Hank's nanna has collapsed a third time, and is at the clinic.

Upon arriving at the clinic, Hank begins to angrily criticize Michaela's doctoring. In front of Sully and Beatrice, he accuses her of being too stubborn to admit that she does not know what is wrong with his grandmother:

DR. MIKE: I'm sorry this has been so trying for you. But I did believe that her condition would stabilize with this medicine. Now clearly, it hasn't, but I'm certain that with more time –

HANK: What's more time gotta do with it? You don't even know what's wrong. You're just too bull-headed to admit it.

DR. MIKE: I –

HANK: Admit it! [*brief pause*] You can't, can you? Because the great Michaela Quinn has gotta have all the answers.

DR. MIKE: I'd like to see my patient now, if you don't mind.

HANK: Go ahead. I wouldn't want you to lose your big award.

Through this exchange, the central storyline achieves its dramatic climax. As the scene fades to commercial, viewers are left wondering whether or not Hank is correct. Has Dr. Mike's desire to appear knowledgeable compromised the safety of her patient? And will Beatrice recommend Michaela for the "Woman of the Year" award in light of this development?

The first scene of the fifth and final sequence takes place later that same evening in the medical clinic. Michaela is studying her medical books in an attempt to understand why the digitalis failed to correct nanna's heart problem when Sully enters. Their interaction highlights the pressure individuals sometimes feel to be something other than themselves. In closing on Sully's advice, the scene validates his approach to this tension. To the extent that Sully has been coded with nature and spirituality throughout this and other episodes, these forces apparently provide the impetus for Michaela's self-awakening. In light of the importance of this exchange, it is worth quoting at length:

DR. MIKE:	There's still so much we don't know about the heart.
SULLY:	Maybe that ain't the problem.
DR. MIKE:	No, her circulation is good. I don't detect any blockages. I'm certain the irregular heartbeat has something to do with it. I just, I just don't understand why the digitalis isn't helping.
SULLY:	Ask for some help. I've seen you do it before.
DR. MIKE:	The answer is here, Sully. I just haven't seen it.
SULLY:	Maybe Hank was right [about your stubbornness].
DR. MIKE:	How could you suggest such a thing?
SULLY:	Well, what would happen if they didn't pick you?
DR. MIKE:	Honestly Sully.
SULLY:	What would happen if the Denver Suffrage League said that you weren't their "Woman of the Year"? [*brief pause*] What?
DR. MIKE:	Well, I'd disappoint everyone – Dorothy, the Reverend, the whole town, Colleen. They expect so much from me. They always want me to be so strong and decisive – know everything about everything. They don't see the other side of me.
SULLY:	They see what you want them to see.
DR. MIKE:	It took me so long to win their confidence that sometimes I think if I let it down for one second . . . I know it's silly.
SULLY:	No it ain't.
DR. MIKE:	Some mornings I just want to stay in bed and hide under the covers, or take a buggy ride out to the lake, not let anyone know where I am – just let life go on without Dr. Mike.
SULLY:	It would you know.
DR. MIKE:	It's so easy for you, Sully. Always being yourself. But you pay a price too. I mean when Hazen comes to the reservation, you'll . . .
SULLY:	I gotta live with myself first. I figure that we all got to.

To live meaningfully, Sully suggests that persons must accept their contradictions rather than hide them behind images and false appearances. We must be true to ourselves, to the multiplicity of ourselves. Michaela will only be able to achieve a sense of harmony when she accepts that she is strong and fragile, decisive and uncertain. Similarly,

Hank will only be happy when he accepts that he can be both respectable and a saloon owner.

The following morning when Hank shows up at the telegraph office, Horace refuses to allow him to enter. Horace announces he is "taking back *his life*" (emphasis added) and he urges Hank to do the same by telling his nanna the truth. Hank leaves to find his grandmother, as Michaela arrives at the telegraph office to wire a colleague in Boston. Although viewers do not hear the content of the wire, the interaction between Dr. Mike and Sully the previous evening invites the perception that Michaela is seeking assistance in diagnosing Hank's nanna. On the other side of town, Hank finds his grandmother and confesses his lie. Explaining his motives, he says, "I told you all of them things so you wouldn't have to be ashamed of your grandson." His honesty is validated by his grandmother, who responds, "It is good to know the truth. I should have told the truth about fainting." With no more lies between them, the two are finally able to relax and enjoy one another's company. Whereas keeping up appearances distressed their relationship, the "truth" about themselves draws them closer to one another despite self-perceived shortcomings.

After Michaela contacts her colleague in Boston, she seeks out Hank and his nanna. Along the way, Dr. Mike spies Beatrice and invites her to come along and listen to what she has learned concerning nanna's condition. Addressing Hank's grandmother, Michaela admits her error in judgment and apologizes for her shortsightedness:

DR. MIKE: I wired a colleague who treats people with problems specific to the heart. He does suggest that fainting is related to your irregular heartbeat, but he also says that the digitalis can't manage the problem alone. He recommends another medicine – quinadine sulfate, which I have.

HANK: Will it stop Nanna from fainting?

DR. MIKE: Both medicines will stabilize her heart until she can see the right doctor. There's this one in St. Louis who's had great success. If you leave on the afternoon train, you should be there by tomorrow night.

HANK: [*to his nanna*] You gotta see this doctor. I'll take you.

DR. MIKE: It was poor medical judgment for me not to seek consultation earlier. I hope you'll accept my apologies.

When Hank and his grandmother leave, Dr. Mike turns to Beatrice and concedes that her effort to "appear" perfect was misguided. While Beatrice confirms this sentiment, initially suggesting to the audience that she will not recommend Michaela for "Woman of the Year," she goes on to say that she does intend to recommend Dr. Mike:

DR. MIKE: I allowed myself to put a patient at risk because of professional pride. That was wrong of me.
BEATRICE: Yes, it was. My work here is completed. I'll be leaving on the next train.
DR. MIKE: Well, I have a medicine to prepare. Excuse me.
[*Michaela turns to leave, but then comes back*]
DR. MIKE: I'm sure there is a woman somewhere who could do everything, Ms. Cartwright. Raise children, be a wife, friend, have a career, and probably do it all quite well. But that woman isn't me.
BEATRICE: You're wrong again, Dr. Quinn – which is precisely why I'm recommending you receive our award.

Apparently, Michaela achieved the "perfection" she so deeply desired when she admitted her own "imperfection." It is that depth of character, that substance rather than surface that makes her whole, and in this episode, that makes her the complete woman. Looked at from another angle, Michaela achieves the perfect harmony of her many selves when she stops trying to be what others want her to be and she merely is herself.

In both form and content, the episode's final scene functions to impose psychological unity and closure. The scene takes place where the narrative began, at the train depot; the two unfamiliar women whose arrival on the train had set the narrative in motion, are now preparing to leave. Both of their visits have validated the search for an essential self over the fabrication of an image-based identity. As nanna prepares to board the train, Hank volunteers to accompany her, but she declines, reminding him of his responsibilities in Colorado Springs:

NANNA: You have a business to run.
HANK: [*ashamed*] You mean the saloon?
NANNA: Oh, Hank. I know you Hank [*pointing to his heart*] in here. This is all that matters to me.

Nanna's closing words to her grandson explicitly identify an innate essence, and elevate it over image and appearance in assessing a person's worth and identity. It seems that Hank has learned, and by extension the audience has learned, that being true to one's "self" is the preferred way to resolves the pressure of fragmentation or the pressure persons often feel to be different things to different people. Free from the semiotic excess of media cultures, the Western landscape allows characters to be judged by who they are at heart.

In Michaela's case, the intervention of a spiritual force (Sully) helped her to achieve a meaningful sense of self. In the context of a simplified, frontier landscape, that "true" if multiple self made Dr. Mike a clear choice for Colorado Territory's "Woman of the Year." Indeed, whether or not Beatrice would recommend Michaela was only ever in serious doubt when image (despite being a remarkably positive image) was allowed to supplant authenticity as the defining characteristic of Michaela's identity. As Colleen escorts Beatrice to the train, Beatrice reaffirms what regular viewers knew all along – that Dr. Quinn is the ideal combination of professional and private woman:

BEATRICE: I suppose you expect me to say something wonderful like, "Colorado needs more women like your mother."
COLLEEN: Only if you mean it.
BEATRICE: I won't be saying that. I happen to believe we need more women like your mother everywhere.

Upon Beatrice's departure, Sully turns to Michaela and invites her to take a buggy ride out to the lake. She agrees. Coincidentally, it is the same request Michaela had to decline when she was "maintaining outward appearances" and helping Colleen with her science project. Here again, nature (in the form of the lake) is linked to a process of self-actualization and legitimated by the character's expressions of happiness and narrative closure. The final scene offers the perfect resolution of each character's personal trials, and leaves the characters at peace with nature and themselves. In the remainder of this chapter, I probe more closely the symbolic equipments that viewers might derive from this message to make sense of their own lives in the Information Age.

Symbolic Equipments in Nostalgia TV

In response to the fears and anxieties brought on by the dramatic social, political, and economic changes underlying the shift from the Industrial Age to the Information Age, nostalgia television emerged as an important mode of public discourse in the 1990s. Its overall orientation toward the changing landscape was one of rejection, offering escape from the perceived threats and challenges of the Information Age by (re)inventing a simpler, holistic, and safer vision of the world through the rhetorical devices of purity, unity, and security. Operating principally in a melodramatic mode involving heterodiegetic narration, it storied a world of clear values, certain truths, and coherent being. To better appreciate the specific symbolic equipments this discourse provides individuals for living meaningful, fulfilling lives in the Information Age, it is vital to examine the ontological and epistemological resources afforded by nostalgia television. Thus, I turn first to an examination of its privileged model of identity and, then, to its fundamental mode of logic and information-processing.

As the previous chapter illustrates, the rise of the new information technologies and the subsequent information explosion undermined the rationalist and existentialist accounts of identity that had dominated the (modernist) Industrial Age. Whether discovered or developed, both the rationalist and existentialist subjects assume a singular, unitary self. But in *The Protean Self: Human Resilience in an Age of Fragmentation* (1993), psychology professor Robert Jay Lifton argues that such a self is no longer possible. In a world "beset by contradiction," "social uncertainties," and instantaneous global communication, Lifton contends that the self is always multiple and variable (1). Drawing on the mythology of Proteus, the Greek Sea God of many forms, he terms this multiplicitous self the "protean self." Elaborates Lifton (1993), "The essence of the protean self lies in its odd combinations. There is a linking – often loose but functional – of identity elements and subselves not ordinarily associated with one another to the point of even seeming (in Max Ernst's words) 'mutually irreconcilable'. . . . But it continually combines its fragments in order to avoid fragmentation" (50). The protean self differs considerably, however, from the image-based personae privileged by hyperconscious television. Whereas Gergen's "multiphrenic self" *embraces* fragmentation, appropriating existing images and styles in an outward performance of identity, Lifton's "protean self" *resolves* fragmentation, combining disparate elements into a coherent sense of self.

Coherence should not be confused with singularity though. The protean self is coherent because it is intelligible to its author/creator. It is multiple because it integrates diverse, often seemingly contradictory elements. To the extent that multiphrenia and proteanism recognize the multiplicity and contingency of the self, both models reflect postmodern or constructivist accounts of identity (Lifton 1993: 8). But they are very different accounts. The multiphrenic self of hyperconscious television is a "surface staging" of appearances. The protean self of nostalgia television is a "deep storying" of essential, if multiple and variable, elements. "Though variation is the essence of the protean self," clarifies Lifton (1993), "that self has certain relatively consistent features" (5). In other words, the protean self is *grounded* in essential "elements" or fundamental building blocks. These building blocks are combined, sometimes in "odd combinations," to form a coherent identity. The process by which these elements are successfully combined is rooted in storytelling. Storytelling, as we have already seen, entails both events (actions) and existents (characters and setting). Through the sequential unfolding of events in the simplified, homogenous setting of the frontier or local community, nostalgia television programs such as *Dr. Quinn, Medicine Woman* are able to story coherent identities.

Dr. Michaela Quinn effectively combines, for instance, the "odd" subselves or elements of nurturing mother and devoted wife with strong-willed professional and pioneering feminist. Similarly, in the episode "Woman of the Year," Hank effectively combines morally respectable and concerned grandson with tavern and brothel owner. In both instances, these protean selves are made possible by narrative and setting. As Karin Esders (2000) writes, "the conceptual components of narrative – character, causality, intelligibility, credibility – bestow identity on individuals" (77). If nostalgia television privileged image over narrative as hyperconscious television does, then it would be difficult to *reconcile* the so-called "odd combinations" that comprise protean selves. An image-based personae is about surface rather than depth; since it has no "essential" elements, it has no "need" to reconcile disparity. The protean self, by contrast, has a need for coherence, which it attains by narratively reconfiguring its essential elements as context demands. A series of events may narratively construct an identity that is *both* dependent *and* independent, but in which one element is featured more prominently in a given context. The frontier setting of *Dr. Quinn, Medicine Woman* enhances this capacity for combining disparate elements by purifying and simplifying the setting. Against the backdrop of a downsized, elemental folk culture or an uncontaminated, natural landscape, one is free to be oneself in all of one's complexity, for the erasure of external difference renders internal complexity intelligible.

Exposure to cultural difference and otherness functions rhetorically to highlight the arbitrariness of cultural categories, norms, and beliefs. If the underlying form of a television show consistently foregrounds difference, as hyperconscious television does through eclecticism and intertextuality, then it becomes more difficult to articulate "core" principles, because such principles are seen as selective, constructed, and arbitrary. If a form erases difference through unity – either the depiction of an uncorrupted landscape or a homogenous community, however, then certain principles may *appear* to be universal. The appearance of universals, of that which is beyond doubt or question, can be profoundly comforting in a time of rapid, fundamental change. Universals serve as anchors, as fixed reference points for negotiating semiotic excess. Nostalgia television offers not only a model for reconciling identity fragmentation, but also an escape from a world of cultural fragmentation into a (story)world of purity and innocence. By storying certain absolutes, whether "traditional" family values or spirituality, nostalgia television affords viewers symbolic anchors or tethers to ground themselves and to resist identity drift. *Highway to Heaven, Touched by an Angel,* and *Promised Land,* for instance, all assure viewers that no matter how chaotic and threatening the world may seem, God is always present to guide them. Meanwhile, *Cheers, The Golden Girls, Friends,* and *Beverly Hills 90210* provide the ever-present comfort of family and friends who share similar values.

The audience for nostalgia television during the 1990s was heavily skewed toward older and often female viewers. *Dr. Quinn, Medicine Woman, Walker, Texas Ranger, Touched by an Angel, Promised Land,* and *Murder, She Wrote* all aired on CBS, whose key demographic during the decade was described by UPN's senior executive VP Lenn Grossi as "50-plus." Series such as *Matlock* and *Murder, She Wrote* were especially attractive to older viewers. As media scholar Karen Riggs (1996) explains:

> It is no accident that mystery and detective programs tend to skew toward older audiences, who may find the genre comfortable compared with more experimental programs. For example, the Fox network has purposely attracted younger viewers through programs with brassy, quick-paced styles and, occasionally, radical or fused forms, such as *The Simpsons*. Programs with their roots in the mystery, lawyer, or detective genre, such as *Moonlighting*, *L.A. Law*, and *Twin Peaks*, were able to attract younger viewers to various degrees because they broke from hackneyed formulas. (312)

In explaining why older viewers are drawn to certain programs, Riggs identifies genre purification and recognizable formulas as central elements – elements that foster a sense of comfort or safety. Meanwhile, she suggests that (hyperconscious) programs such as *The Simpsons*, *Moonlighting*, and *Twin Peaks* tend to appeal to younger viewers because of their quick-paced, eclectic style.

Many nostalgia television series, such as *The Golden Girls* and *Designing Women*, appealed disproportionately to both older (over 50) *and* female viewers. The casting of many of these series offers, at least, a partial explanation for this demographic trend. "*The Golden Girls* was," for instance, "the first successful modern sitcom in which all of the stars were female. Even more surprisingly was that all were well over age fifty" (McNeil 1996: 333). "Like *The Golden Girls*," notes McNeil (1996), "*Designing Women* was a sitcom in which all of the stars were female" (213). But not all nostalgia television shows were targeted to or attracted older viewers. Shows such as *Beverly Hills 90210* and *Friends* had largely young, female fan bases. This raises an interesting question. Why did nostalgia television *tend* to appeal to older and/or female viewers, but less so to young, male viewers in the 1990s? One possible answer has to do with the unique symbolic equipments afforded by nostalgia television. As I argued earlier, nostalgia television is typically critical of (post)modern technologies. Discursively, then, it constructs a world – a social hierarchy – in which the new information technologies are either nonexistent or far less important than what one can do with her/his hands and mind. Such a discourse will be especially attractive to those individuals "guilty" of not keeping with technological innovation because it resolves that guilt through transcendence. By creating a social hierarchy in which technological literacy has low social value, technological illiteracy is no longer a source of guilt.[2]

The digital divide describers the disparity between technological haves and technological have-nots. Throughout the 1990s, age was a key predictor of access to technology, as seniors (55+) "trail[ed] all other age groups with respect to computer ownership (25.8 percent) and Internet access (14.6 percent)" (Falling Through the Net 1999). Indeed, according the United States Department of Commerce, "Individuals age 50 and older [were] among the least likely to be Internet users with [an] Internet use rate of 29.6 percent in 2000" (Falling Through the Net 2000). At a time when access to and proficiency with information technologies was being heralded in the business world as absolutely essential, it is not hard to see why a lack of access to or proficiency with such technologies would be a significant source of guilt. A popular advertisement for WebTV from Phillips Magnavox in the late 1990s lends additional support to the premise that older Americans are technologically illiterate. The advertisement boldly features the heading, "Now, getting on the internet is so easy, even an adult can do it." The ad suggests that prior to WebTV, logging onto the Internet was beyond the capability of many adults – a message it insultingly reinforces with the following illustrated steps: "Fig. 1 – Place on TV. Fig. 2 – Plug in. Fig. 3 – Click remote. Fig. 4 – You're on the Web." The ad also suggests that internet access is vital to a better world in its closing tag line, "Let's make things better. Phillips Magnavox." Apparently, "things" are not so good when one does not know how to access the internet.

Like age, gender was a key feature of the digital divide during the 1990s. Unlike seniors, however, women closed this gap by the decade's end. Historically, information technology and computer-mediated communication have been *represented* as male domains. Throughout much of the decade, print and TV advertisements for computing hardware and software depicted women as technologically incompetent, featuring them as modelers of technology rather than users. As Robert Burnett and P. David Marshall (2003) explain, "Early adoption of the Internet upheld this [gendered] conception of Web identity; however, more recently and specifically in countries with high Internet usage the [gender] bias of use has virtually disappeared" (79). But prior to the turn of the millenium, access to and proficiency with the new information technologies was a source of guilt for women as well as seniors. The scope and character of nostalgia television's online fandom provides further evidence that part of this genre's appeal lies in its resolution of guilt about techno-illiteracy. In December of 1997, *The Simpsons* had over 100 fan websites, while *Dr. Quinn, Medicine Woman* had only one. The sole fan website was maintained by Barney Jernigan and located at http://matrix.cis.ecu/dqmw.html. Two official *Dr.* Quinn websites also existed at the time: http://www.cbs.com/primetime/dr_quinn.html (maintained by CBS) and http://www.drquinn.com/ (maintained by the show's producers). This disparity in online activity is even more noteworthy when one considers that *Dr. Quinn* was consistently drawing a larger audience share than was *The Simpsons*. Although more viewers were seeing *Dr. Quinn*, far fewer of them were expressing their pleasure or interest in the show on the Web.

The underlying "form" of the World Wide Web is rooted in hypertext, which philosopher Michael Heim (1993) defines as "nonsequential writing with free user movement" (33). In terms of form, hypertext, which "fosters a literacy that is prompted by jumps of intuition and association" (Heim 1993: 30), is homologous with hyperconscious television, which through intertextual references also fosters a nonlinear, associative logic. Since the underlying logic of the Web is much more similar to the logic of hyperconscious television than to the logic of nostalgia television, online fan cultures for hyperconscious television tend to be greater in size, scope, and complexity than those connected with nostalgia television. Nostalgia television arranges and patterns information in a manner that is dramatically different than that of hyperconscious television. Whereas hyperconscious TV privileges the logic of PO, nostalgia television cultivates a mode of information processing that I term "SO." The logic of SO is predicated on three key principles: consequence, closure, and consumption. By examining each of these principles, I aim to isolate the epistemological resources that nostalgia TV affords viewers for addressing the challenges of life in the Information Age.

SO *as Consequently*

In common usage, the word "so" implies temporality and, in particular, linear, causal temporality. "So" is often used as a substitute for or in conjunction with the words "then," "next," or "subsequently." It can be synonymous with the words "thus" and "therefore," which suggest a particular relationship between the events or facts they introduce and the events or facts that preceded them. That relationship is one of cause and effect, of rational, deductive reasoning. If one were writing a story, s/he might say, "Elliot witnessed a crime. *So*, he called the police." By privileging linear narrative, in which one event leads to the next, nostalgia television fosters a causal, linear mode of information-processing.[3] For every action in a story, there are *consequences*, actions and events that *follow* logically *from* earlier actions and events. Nostalgia TV is, like hyperconscious TV, a visual medium. But the images in nostalgia television are always in the *service* of the story. They are arranged sequentially to advance the plot, to move it toward conclusion and resolution. In hyperconscious TV, the plot is frequently an afterthought, as the images *dominate* the story.

When Beatrice Cartwright announces that she is in town to observe Dr. Quinn in the episode "Woman of the Year," and then Dr. Mike is shown carefully attending to the medical needs of a young girl, it (consequently) creates an appetite to see her nominated for Colorado's Woman of the Year. When Homer Simpson phones NASA from Moe's Tavern to complain about the space program in the episode "Deep Space Homer," it does not "causally" follow that he would become an astronaut. That Homer does become an astronaut in the episode is purely a vehicle for intertextual allusions to various space fictions such as *The Right Stuff*, *Planet of the Apes*, *2001: A Space Odyssey*, and *Star Trek*; it is not the fulfillment of a formal appetite created by logically and temporally prior events in the story. What matters when watching *The Simpsons* is being able to recognize the allusions, to mentally "jump" from the images on the screen to the vast array of media images external to the narrative. What matters when watching *Dr. Quinn, Medicine Woman*, by contrast, is being able to mentally "follow" the internal, unfolding images. Since hyperconscious and nostalgia television involve different mental activities, their viewers necessarily view them quite differently. One sits down for the expressed purpose of watching nostalgia programs from beginning to end. Indeed, given their sequential character, it is difficult to understand the story if one tunes in "late." Nostalgia TV, then, offers an escape from the hyper-saturated world of conflicting messages and transports viewers to an imaginary realm where information is processed step-by-step.

so as Closure

The word "so" can also mean true or factual, as in the phrase, "It is so." Nostalgia television assures viewers of fundamental truths, ultimate grounds, and unified meanings by privileging semiotic closure. Unlike hyperconscious programs, which continuously invite viewers to make their own interpretive choices, associations, and thus meanings, nostalgia television shuts down signification and privileges the meaning of the Author-God. Umberto Eco (1979) describes this class of messages as "closed texts," which he defines as:

> Those texts that obsessively aim at arousing a precise response on the part of... precise empirical readers... They apparently aim at pulling the reader along a predetermined path, carefully displaying their effects so as to arouse pity or fear, excitement or depression at the due place and at the right moment. Every step of the "story" elicits just the expectation that its further course will satisfy. They seem to be structured according to an inflexible project. (8)

Eco is fully aware that some readers may resist the specific structured invitations of a text, and he terms such readings "aberrant" decodings. Nostalgia television is closed, nevertheless, precisely because it is *equally* open to all aberrant decodings – meaning that it does not prefer one aberrant decoding (e.g., misreading) to another; they are all equally incorrect.

The psychological appeal of semiotic closure is directly related to the challenges and anxieties of living in the Information Age. At a time of cultural fragmentation and relativism, when long-standing traditions and social institutions appear to be giving way beneath our feet, the guarantee of certain constants is profoundly comforting. Each week, series such as *Touched by an Angel* and *Promised Land* testified to the existence of a higher, spiritual force. These shows quite literally narrated that there are some certainties in the world that can always be counted on. Similarly, *Matlock, Murder, She Wrote*, and *Walker, Texas Ranger* offered viewers the weekly assurance that good will triumph over evil and that justice will be served. Unlike hyperconscious television, which equips viewers to *adapt* to an endlessly changing social landscape, nostalgia television offers viewers the *assurance* that certain principles, values, and beliefs are beyond doubt even in a period of great change. Hyperconscious television teaches viewers to be *flexible*; nostalgia television teaches viewers to be *faithful*.

SO *as Consumption*

In nostalgia television, the Author-God occupies a privileged position. The story is hers/his to tell, which places the viewer on the receiving end of a finished message or product. Consumption describes a specific mode of interpretive practice in which the viewer accepts (typically without any critical reflection) the boundaries of the show or "text" as established by producers and writers. To consume something is to ingest it in the "form" in which it is "packaged." Though viewers of nostalgia television certainly bring their own experiences and knowledge to the interpretive process, it is a different type of knowledge than that utilized in viewing hyperconscious television. Whereas hyperconscious television encourages viewers to draw upon specific or selective knowledge of popular culture, biographical information about actors in the series, and production history of the show, nostalgia television invites viewers to exercise general or common knowledge of broad cultural codes. Though not *passive*, this mode of interpretation generally is unreflective. Because it requires only general cultural knowledge to appreciate (such as the meaning of nonverbal expressions), viewers are scarcely aware that they are involved in interpretation at all.

Since consumption is a specific interpretive mode, it can be understood by looking at how consumer-viewers employ technology such as remote control devices (RCDs). As we have already seen, the audience for nostalgia television tends to be older than the audience for hyperconscious television. Not only are these audiences drawn to different types of programming, but they also employ RCDs in different ways. A 1989 study of RCD use found the following:

> The youngest viewers were about 20% more likely than the oldest viewers to change channels during a program (the definition of *grazing* used in this study) and to zap when ads come on. A third of the youngest viewers reported that they flipped through channels when they began to view (orienting search) compared to only about 5% of viewers over 50. Younger viewers flipped more because they enjoyed flipping more. Nearly half of viewers aged 18–24 enjoyed television as

much when they were flipping, while only 17% of viewers 50 or older did.... The conclusions from the study are clear: the young click more than the old. (Bellamy & Walker 1996: 97)

This and other studies of RCD use indicate that older viewers use the remote control primarily to turn on and off the television set and to switch between channels when a program concludes, meaning that they accept the boundaries of "programs" as defined by producers. In short, older viewers tend to use technology to reinforce a temporal or sequential logic, rather than a spatial logic in which multiple programs are viewed at once. Their resistance to and displeasure with using the remote control to "produce" an intertextual viewing experience re-inforces the notion that they are drawn to nostalgia television because they find its form epistemologically more comfortable. Adopting the interpretive role of *consumer* places the onus for organizing the vast array of semiotic material circulating in society into meaningful patterns onto message creators. This alleviates the sense of information overload by allowing viewers to dismiss "unpackaged" signs as semiotic noise.

Nostalgia television's fearful "no" attitude toward the emerging Information Age works rhetorically to offer escape from and resolution to the social anxieties of the 1990s. Through the devices of purity, unity, and safety, it stories a sentimentalized world of comfort and certainty. Nostalgia television models a way of being that is multiple and adaptive, but rooted in "core" principles. It offers a terrain that resolves the guilt of techno-illiteracy. It privileges a logic of so that provides organization in the face of chaos, certainty in the face of change, and closure in the face of fragmentation. Although the form and attendant attitude of nostalgia television differ greatly from that of hyperconscious television, the symbolic resources it provides for "living" in the Information Age are no less valuable to the viewers who adopt them. The ways in which both hyperconscious and nostalgia television have changed or intensi-fied since their emergence in the 1990s is the focus of the final chapter.

Notes

1 The teens on *Beverly Hills 90210* represent a "nostalgic community" in three senses. First, they are homogenous. In the words of Kaleda Stokes, "There's no blacks. There's no Asians. No Hispanics. There's nothing

I can relate to" (quoted in Blumenfeld 1992: D5). Second, the "gang's" principal hangout is a fifties-style diner called the "Peach Pit." Third, the adult Walshes "play" parents to the whole gang, instilling their "wholesome family values" (see Kile 1993).

2   The other means by which to resolve the "guilt" of not keeping up with technological innovation is to become proficient. That many seniors chose this mode of resolution is evidenced by the proliferation of organizations such as the Silver Fox Computer Club – a group designed to teach seniors to use computers – in the 1990s (see Dickerson 1995: 41).

3   Traditionally, books have fostered a similar linear logic. So, I find it interesting that one reviewer would shower the nostalgia television series, *Northern Exposure*, "with praise by saying, 'Watching *Northern Exposure* is a lot like reading a good book' " (Thompson 1996: 164).

Chapter 5
Television and the Future

When we have overcome the naive vision of television, we begin to understand the history of television as a tool with which to approach other questions. . . . We should carefully chronicle the changes in television in order to move toward those larger questions, and . . . a history of formulas or larger patterns of action . . . provides the major services of establishing the appropriate field of reference. . . . An appropriate history of television, then, would be a history of those major stylistic shifts that are also shifts in meaning, and would lead toward a very different conception of the medium and its role in American culture. (Newcomb 1978: 12–13)

Thus, it becomes the task of the Burkean critic to identify the modes of discourse enjoying currency in society and to link discourse to the real situations for which it is symbolic equipment. (Brummett 1984a: 161)

(Re)Viewing the Small Screen

For nearly 50 years now, the Western world has been in the throws of dramatic social change, in *transition* from one social paradigm to another. The age of production, homogeneity, standardization, mass marketing, nationalism, and industrialism has steadily and rapidly given way to the age of reproduction, heterogeneity, diversification, niche marketing, globalism, and informationalism. In the United States, the decade of the 1990s was crucial to this transition, for it located culture's inhabitants more in the new paradigm than in the old. Within this context of fundamental social, political, and economic reorganization, society's prevailing cultural forms were, as cultural forms are apt to do, undergoing equally dramatic changes. They increasingly, for instance, began to name, order, and express our social fears and anxieties, and to furnish formal strategies for confronting and addressing the psychological displacements associated with the shift to the Information Age. Chief among the cultural forms and technologies to offer such symbolic resources was television. But television was, like most other modes of public discourse, split in its response – torn between embracing and rejecting the new paradigm, between the basic human attitudes of yes and no.

As W. J. T. Mitchell (1994) explains in *The Pictorial Turn*, the great paradox of the Information Age is that it is simultaneously the era of images, of visuals with unprecedented power, and the era of iconophobia, of fear and anxiety about the power of images (15). This paradox is readily apparent in the two great symbolic forms of prime-time television in the 1990s: hyperconscious and nostalgia TV. The former *revels* in the image, endlessly (re)circulating and (re)combining cultural styles in a playful dance. The latter *recoils* at the image, (re)turning to and (re)investing in a melodramatic mode of storytelling. To understand these two forms is to understand the diverse ways that citizen-viewers negotiated a meaningful sense of themselves and their world in the face of paradigmatic social change. Thus, I begin the concluding chapter by comparing and contrasting the unique symbolic equipments that hyperconscious and nostalgia TV afford viewers for living in the Information Age. I, then, investigate recent changes in television and speculate about the possibility that the next great social change may already be underway.

In the late 1980s when the concept of postmodernism was coming into academic vogue, the (modernist) impulse of many cultural critics and scholars was to draw up a list of what is in and what is out. Some studies of television even published charts, locating shows such as *Moonlighting*, *Twin Peaks*, and *The Simpsons* in the postmodern column and programs such as *Hart to Hart*, *Dynasty*, and *The Cosby Show* in the modern column (Campbell & Freed 1993: 82–3). But according to Glenn Hendler (2000), "to find postmodernism on television, we need to go beyond the either/or dichotomy, the idea that some individual shows are postmodern and some are not" (181). As Hendler (2000) elaborates, the "television apparatus" (175) has never been modern; thus, rather than going in search of postmodern programs, critics ought "to look at the surface of television, at the screen, at the medium and not just the message" (182; see also Storey 1998: 193).

If the medium of television is postmodern and postmodernism is, as Fredric Jameson (1991) argues, the "cultural logic of late capitalism," then the important question is how does the cultural logic of late capitalism as screened and articulated through television equip us to live in the Information Age?

Answering that question has been the central aim of this book. In chapter 1, I argued that television is the postmodern medium *par excellence* and that it therefore "screens" the social world through a postmodern lens – a lens that is, at once, unique and multiple. It is unique in its skepticism of classical notions of universal progress, in its flattening of history, and in its privileging of simulations, but it is multiple in its attitude toward the social world. Television "speaks" (e.g., it addresses itself to viewers) in two voices. One voice – that of hyperconscious television – displays self-awareness about the rise of informationalism, which it welcomes. The other voice – that of nostalgia television – favors self-denial about ongoing social changes and seeks to recuperate a social world of pre-informationalism that never existed. Although the first voice may appear more practical than the second, both voices have been vital in assisting citizen-viewers to live their everyday lives in meaningful and fulfilling ways. I turn now to an overview of those voices and to the specific sets of resources they provide individuals for negotiating the trials and tribulations brought on by the transition to the Information Age.

Hyperconscious and nostalgia TV describe the two principal symbolic forms of primetime US American television in the 1990s. Although divergent in their codes and conventions, these two forms both represent public responses to the same set of sociohistorical conditions, namely those fueled by the information explosion. The individual and social functions of those responses derive from the particularities of their form. Hyperconscious television is characterized by the traits of eclecticism, intertextuality, and self-reflexivity, while nostalgia television is characterized by the traits of purity, unity, and security. Structurally, these two forms might be imagined as opposing poles on a continuum of textual possibilities. *Textuality* is a product of the manner in which a structured set of signs encourages or activates "cooperation from" its readers or viewers (Eco 1979: 4). As chapters 3 and 4 illustrate, the forms of hyperconscious and nostalgia TV encourage dramatically different modes of viewer cooperation.

Through the blending of popular genres, allusions to and appropriations of other cultural texts, and reflection on its own codes and conventions, hyperconscious television invites viewers to actively participate in "text" construction. In other words, hyperconscious televisual texts are *open* and unfinished. I am using the term "open" in the sense supplied by Italian semiotician Umberto Eco (1979). He contends that the open text "not only calls for the cooperation of its own reader, but also wants this reader to make a series of interpretive choices which even though not infinite are, however, more than one" (4; see also Eco 1989: 1–23). This textual beckoning for viewer participation appeals to some viewers more than others, because it requires viewers to supply particular kinds of knowledge and semiotic resources. According to John Fiske (1989), self-reflexivity is one of the key ways that television delegates semiotic power to viewers (70). A meaningful viewing of *The Simpsons*, for instance, requires a vast knowledge of current events, celebrity and popular culture, and other media texts, as well perhaps as the show's production history. Furthermore, it entails competency with pastiche, montage, and irony. It asks viewers to "read" laterally, to actively draw upon extratextual material in the production of pleasure and meaning. Viewers who lack the cultural resources to "produce" texts will likely turn to those that more readily lend themselves to consumption.

Nostalgia television is well suited to consumption, because through appeals to simplicity and spirituality, narrative and community, and authenticity and sincerity, it presents *closed* texts. The text is closed when it aims, notes Eco (1979), "at eliciting a sort of 'obedient' cooperation" from the viewer (7). Central to nostalgia television's creation of closed texts are its appeals to sincerity and authenticity, to its careful construction of the illusion of realism, "[f]or realism is essentially a unifying, closing strategy of representation, it is necessarily authoritarian" (Fiske 1989: 70). A meaningful viewing of *Dr. Quinn, Medicine Woman* requires knowledge of only *general* cultural codes related to gesture and expression, not to *specific* extratextual information. It asks the viewer to obediently "follow" the story along a predetermined path, and to passively "submit" to internal structures of the text. Such passiveness is obviously a matter of degree. All texts are partially open and call upon readers or viewers to engage in interpretation, to supply "a set of tastes, personal inclinations, and prejudices" (Eco 1989: 3). Nevertheless, some texts are *strategically* open, left unfinished, so as to function more like "the components of a construction kit" than "a balanced organic whole" (Eco 1989: 4).

These variations in form – from highly open to highly closed texts[1] – position viewers differently in relation to the medium of television, and therefore provide viewers quite different symbolic strategies and resources for managing their sense of themselves and their world. With regard to the matter of identity, hyperconscious and nostalgia television model distinctive modes of identity and subsequently provide unique equipments for fashioning a sense of self. Such equipments are addressed, however, to the same set of psychological anxieties. As the new information technologies fueled the information explosion and altered our sense of time and space, individuals increasingly began to experience identity drift or placelessness along with a feeling of fragmentation. To more fully understand these social anxieties, it is helpful to situate them within a broader historical narrative.

Prior to the rise of the modern mass media, community or a shared sense of collective identity was closely tied to geography (Vitanza 1999: 60–2). Persons who shared a similar set of spatial-temporal experiences tended also to share a common set of values and interests. Since individuals were quite literally surrounded by others who were like themselves, their beliefs, values, and practices often passed as natural rather than cultural. Within this context, individuals had a deep faith in the norms and conventions of their communities; social and cultural roles seemed to be universal and absolute rather than constructed and contingent. One's individual identity, then, was simply a *reflection* of a core set of social roles. Thus, "the forms of identity in modernity [and the Industrial Age] are," argues Douglas Kellner (1995), "relatively substantial and fixed; identity...comes from a circumscribed set of roles or norms: one is a mother, a son, a Texan, a Scot, a professor, a socialist, a Catholic, a lesbian – or rather a combination of these social roles and possibilities" (231). The conception of a stable, innate self-identity, therefore, depends upon being in real places (Vitanza 1999: 61). But it is precisely this strong sense of *place* that new information technologies such as networked computers and broadcast television radically undermine.

In chatrooms and on nightly news broadcasts, the internet and television highlight the arbitrary and constructed character of social norms and roles by repeatedly exposing viewers to cultural difference. Thanks to the new information technologies, both the workplace and the home have become electronic portals through which one can instantaneously be transported around the globe. Satellites, broadcast signals, phone lines, and optical fibers obliterate the traditional constraints of physical distance. The mutability and heterogeneity of *space* – of televisual space, cyberspace, and virtual space – supplants the stability and homogeneity of *place*. I have something on the order of Michel de Certeau's distinction between space and place in mind here. He writes:

> The law of the "proper" rules in the place: the elements taken into consideration are *beside* one another, each situated in its own "proper" and distinct location, a location it defines. A place is thus an instantaneous configuration of positions. It implies an indication of stability. A *space* exists when one takes into consideration vectors of direction, velocities, and time variables. Thus space is composed of intersections of mobile elements. . . . In contradistinction to the place, [space] has none of the univocality or stability of a "proper." (de Certeau 1984: 117)

Within the space of global information flows and cultural difference, it becomes more and more difficult to believe blindly in universal and absolute Truth, for as Walter Truett Anderson (1990) explains, "The postmodern individual is continually reminded that different peoples have entirely different concepts of what the world is like" (8). Suddenly, individuals recognize, if only subconsciously, that their values and beliefs are *their* values and beliefs. Confronted by the denaturalization of social roles and norms, place and geography decline in importance as predictors of identity, and neighbors and neighborhoods no longer define the contours of community. In psychological terms, the Information Age fosters a sense of placelessness and a growing feeling of fragmentation.

Paradoxically, the same technologies fueling these "threats" to identity offer symbolic resources for confronting and managing them. In the case of 1990s television, those resources can be plotted on a continuum ranging from hyperconscious television's multiphrenic personae crafted from the endless array of available cultural styles and images to nostalgia television's protean self grounded in story and essential elements. The characters found in hyperconscious TV model a multiphrenic persona in which identity is fluid, multiple, and performed. Homer Simpson, for instance, is defined not by the socially prescribed roles of father, husband, or safety inspector at the local power plant (roles he is utterly inept at), but instead by his participation in the culture industries. His identity is performed from week to week in relation to *consumption*, and not just consumption of food, beer, and television, but also consumption of styles and images. Indeed, it is the availability and recognizability of mediated images that allow Homer to be an astronaut one week and a traveling circus performer another. Homer models a mode of identity that is highly adaptive and contextual. Through intertextual references to other cultural texts, he can become anything at a moment's notice. From this perspective, fragmentation is transformed from a threat into a type of play and performance. As viewers watch, they learn to perform their own identities in relation to media images, styles, and looks.

Homer, as well as the other characters on *The Simpsons*, do more than merely model a particular mode of identity, however. They provide "actual" resources in the form of mediated images for viewers to utilize in their own performances of identity. As a popular "image" of rebellion, for instance, Bart has been widely appropriated by various individuals and subcultural groups to articulate their identities. Bart Simpson T-shirts featuring sayings such as "Don't have a cow, man!" and "Underachiever and proud of it" became so popular among young boys as an anti-authoritarian statement in the early 1990s that they were banned in many grade schools (Rebeck 1990: 622). Meanwhile, "Black Bart" became a popular icon in the African-American community and a poncho-clad "Mexican Bart" was utilized as part of a resistive, performance-art piece titled "The Temple of Confessions" (see Gomez-Pena & Sifuentes 1996: 19; Parisi 1993: 125–42). Toys and T-shirts featuring other Simpsons' characters continue to be widely available 17 years after the show's initial launch. That the television series *Dr. Quinn, Medicine Woman* has not produced its own clothing and merchandise line and that Dr. Michaela Quinn has not been adopted as an icon by any subcultural group suggests that a very different mode of identity is being modeled in nostalgia television. Before turning to that model, however, it is worth mentioning that one reason *why* viewers may be drawn to the television programs that they are is because those programs showcase a mode of identity with which they are comfortable and able to identify.

For the characters on nostalgia television, identity is not an image-based, surface-level performance, but a narratively constructed reconciliation of deep-seated, constitutive elements. Although these elements are sometimes in tension and flux, the stylistic traits of purity and unity provide a context in which fundamental values and beliefs can meaningfully be storied. Since nostalgia TV's protean self requires regular work and commitment, the plots found in this genre far more often revolve explicitly around identity issues than do the plots of hyperconscious television. The characters on *Beverly Hills, 90210* and *Touched by an Angel* are far more likely to "struggle" over their sense of selfhood than the characters on *Seinfeld* and *Beavis and Butt-head*. Jerry Seinfeld has no need for struggle, for he is little more than a copy of an image – a reflection of the celebrity persona of comedian Jerry Seinfeld. Likewise, Homer Simpson never seems to experience a "crisis" of identity despite his wild shifts in social experience. Dr. Quinn, by contrast, must continually work at maintaining a coherent sense of self. She must endlessly juggle the rudimentary and multiplicitous elements of her identity. In the context of a downsized folk culture and simplified western landscape, she ultimately emerges as the perfect composite of professional, wife, mother, feminist, and friend.

Like hyperconscious television, nostalgia television not only models a particular mode of identity (e.g., the protean self), but also provides viewers resources for its enactment. Since the protean self is not pregiven, but discursively constructed, it requires continual work. This work comes in the form of a protective self-narrative – an ongoing, reflexive biography. According to sociologist Anthony Giddens (1991) in his book *Modernity and Self-Identity: Self and Society in the Late Modern Age*, "A person's identity is not to be found in behavior, nor – important though this is – in the reactions of others, but in the capacity *to keep a particular narrative going*. The individual's biography . . . must continually integrate events which occur in the external world, and sort them into an ongoing 'story' about the self" (54). One of the widely available resources for storying a coherent sense of self in the Information Age is the world of television. "Talk about fictional characters and situations," explains media scholar E. Graham McKinley (1997), "both produces and makes possible certain ways of being in the world" (52). Through discussion of characters and their actions with friends, viewers can articulate their own sets of values and commitments. This mode of identity stresses language over look and story over style. Unlike the multiphrenic self which embraces fragmentation, the protean self overcomes fragmentation by storying an "ideal self" – one in which its multiple elements exist in harmony (McAdams 1997: 46–78).

Despite their differences, the multiphrenic self modeled by hyper-conscious television and protean self modeled by nostalgia television share a number of commonalties. As constructivist rather than essen-tialist perspectives on identity, both furnish symbolic equipments for negotiating a meaningful sense of self in the semiotic saturated land-scape of the Information Age. Second, both perspectives locate media culture, and in particular television, as a central symbolic resource for managing identity. Their key difference, then, lies not in *what* they do, but in *how* they do it. For hyperconscious television, image and surface are central, while for nostalgia television, narrative and depth domin-ate. Since "depth" has historically been the more positive signifier in the depth/surface binarism, it is worth noting that I do not view one model as superior to the other. Indeed, as the two models reflect extremes on a continuum of possibilities and are not mutually exclu-sive, many if not most individuals probably utilize aspects of both models in negotiating their identities today. To the extent that there is political "danger" in postmodern identity, it lies not with a particu-lar model, but with fanaticism for either model. The multiphrenic self, when carried to the extreme, can potentially yield a radical relativism in which collective action is rendered improbable and a workable notion of justice impossible. But taking the protean self to an extreme (in which only a select group of values are legitimated) can be equally disconcerting, leading to an intolerance for competing values and ultimately to fundamentalism. Tragically, in our current world, neither of these extremes appears to be simply hypothetical. Hyperrelativism and extreme fundamentalism are both present within national and global politics (see Anderson 1990).

In addition to providing resources for managing identity in the Information Age, the symbolic forms of hyperconscious and nostalgia television equip persons to resolve the various types of guilt common to our current sociohistorical matrix. Guilt, as Kenneth Burke explains, is a consequence of violating social hierarchy. Since individuals are unable to conform to all social hierarchies all the time, guilt is an inevitable part of the human condition – a part for which we are always seeking resolution. Living in a rapidly changing high-tech media cul-ture fosters a situation ripe for particular types of guilt. In a society that endlessly bombards citizens with imagery, but that generally values print literacy over visual literacy, watching television is often a signifi-cant source of guilt. In privileging and therefore valuing eclecticism, intertextuality, and reflexivity, hyperconscious TV erects an alternative social hierarchy in which heavy media and television consumption is not a source of guilt, but a source of pride. Heavy viewing and the media savvy it creates is rewarded with a sense of in-group superiority, rather than stigmatized as a mindless waste of time. On the opposite end of the spectrum are those individuals who avoid both our media culture and the information technologies that animate it. In the workforce, where proficiency with information technologies is highly valued, a lack of proficiency can also be a key source of guilt. Nostalgia television functions to assuage such guilt by celebrating a social world marked by simplicity and the drama of human relations. Hence, viewers may be drawn to the programs that they are not simply because of the modes of identity that they model, but also because of the symbolic resources they provide for resolving guilt.

As television viewers accumulate resources for managing identity and resolving guilt, they also begin to internalize the underlying logic of the programs they watch. In the early 1960s, Canadian media scholar Marshal McLuhan (1964) observed that speech, writing, radio, film, television, and other media are unique forms that emphasize certain aspects of communication over others. Based on this observation, he argued that "seeing" the world and processing information differs from one medium to another. For McLuhan, the medium or technology of communication is central, then, to the way people experience and therefore know their world. Extending this line of inquiry, Walter Ong, as well as Harold Innis, studied how the character of thought is shaped by the prevailing communication technologies of a given society. Near the conclusion of his landmark study on orality and print literacy, Ong (1988) suggested that new electronic media are transforming expression once again, and bringing with them a whole new consciousness (135). Although this emergent mode of thought, which Ong terms "secondary orality," has received considerable attention from media scholars, it has been plagued thus far by two biases.

The first bias has been the tendency to treat this emergent mode of thought as relatively singular and homogenous *across* the new information technologies. Based on a set of traits common to a wide array of electronic communication technologies, James Chesebro and Dale Bertelsen (1996) maintain that knowing in an electronic culture differs from knowing in a literate (writing and print) culture (14–20). But they have painted the contours of that way of knowing with rather broad, indiscriminate brush strokes. A second bias has been to see the new logic of the Information Age as multiple, but only *among* different mediums of communication. Operating from a McLuhanite perspective, for example, David Altheide and Robert Snow (1991) contend that select media, or what they term "media formats," such as radio and television each have their own logic (12, 19–50). Although both approaches have generated valuable insight into the logic(s) of the Information Age, they have tended to ignore how various forms and genres *within* a particular medium may also produce distinct logics. But as chapters three and four demonstrate, a single communication medium such as television can foster diverse logics, which if experienced habitually can begin training the mind to process information is specific ways.

The symbolic forms of hyperconscious and nostalgia television are both incarnations of electronic media generally and the apparatus of television specifically. As such, they do share certain structural similarities that influence how people process information. Both forms depend upon electricity for their transmission – a structural feature of digital media that has been linked to the speed with which people process and manage information (Chesebro & Bertelsen 1996: 140). Furthermore, as televisual formats, hyperconscious and nostalgia TV combine sound and images, and thus require mental faculties to decode both aural and visual stimuli. Despite these similarities though, hyperconscious and nostalgia television are remarkably dissimilar forms that organize thought and expression differently. Therefore, the more frequently and selectively a viewer watches hyperconscious or nostalgia television, the more likely he or she is to process information in ways related to the underlying symbolic form of that genre. Like textuality and identity, hyperconscious television's logic of PO and nostalgia television's logic of SO do not reflect "either/or" options, but are poles on a spectrum of thinking, knowing, and information-processing. The extent to which one learns and exercises a PO logic, for instance, is related to how much hyperconscious television one watches.

To frequent viewers, hyperconscious television offers provocation, provisionality, and prosumption as patterning devices for processing information. These devices stress spatial and nonlinear, contingent and local, and active and creative ways of knowing. The logic of PO is closely related to hyperconscious television's form. Its privileging of the image and its use of eclecticism, intertextuality, and reflexivity encourage viewers to make lateral, associative, and simultaneous connections, rather than linear, causal, and sequential connections. The meaning and pleasure of shows like *South Park* and *The Simpsons* is generated when viewers "catch" the extratextual references or recognize the conventions of television that are being toyed with. Since narrative is secondary to image, viewers can "enter" the story at virtually any point and still have a meaningful and pleasurable experience. Like the World Wide Web, hyperconscious television is highly participatory and invites viewers to choose their own pathways, to create their own experiences. The structural homology between the Web and hyperconscious television may be central to why the programs within this genre had such large, active internet followings in the 1990s. Given hyperconscious television's general orientation of acceptance, its yes attitude toward the Information Age – an age fueled by the new information technologies – its generally technofriendly stance is hardly surprising.

Nostalgia television, by contrast, is at best skeptical of the transition to the Information Age and the information technologies animating it. As such, its formal properties are themselves reflective of a pretelevision era, of a world rooted in a print-oriented paradigm. Through rhetorical appeals to purity, unity, and security, nostalgia television reflects a unique mode of televisual expression that fosters a logic distinct from that of hyperconscious television. Downplaying the importance of its images, nostalgia television privileges language and story. Since words and narrative are structured sequentially, repeated viewing of nostalgia television favors temporal and linear, causal and closed, and passive and receptive ways of knowing. As Edward Soja (1989) explains, "The discipline imprinted in a sequentially unfolding narrative predisposes the reader to think historically...[just as] language dictates a sequential succession, a linear flow of sentential statements" (1–2). In chapter 4, I labeled nostalgia television's logic as that of so and identified its central patterning mechanisms as consequently, closure, and consumption. Like the printed word, nostalgia television programs such as *Touched by an Angel* and *Dr. Quinn, Medicine Woman* are relatively autonomous and self-contained texts. They supply the codes necessary for interpretation, and ask the reader to follow the text rather than to stray from it. In viewing such texts, the Author-God occupies a privileged position, exercising heightened control over meaning and pleasure. Since that act of viewing is closer to consumption than production, the desire and need to "extend" the text in other media such as the Web is diminished. In short, nostalgia TV offers refuge from the rapidly changing, increasingly fragmented, hypertechnological, semiotic saturated landscape of the Information Age. Its uncorrupted landscapes, supportive communities, formulaic patterns, and holistic structures offer reassurance that the old paradigm is not yet lost by seemingly (re)creating it (e.g., by simulating it).

Throughout the 1990s, but especially at the start of the decade, gender and age were relatively reliable predictors of television likes and dislikes. As noted in chapters 3 and 4, male and/or younger viewers were disproportionately drawn to hyperconscious television, while female and/or older viewers tended to gravitate toward nostalgia television. One interesting correlation with this trend is the digital divide. The phrase "digital divide" describes the gap in access to and/or proficiency with the new information technologies, particularly computing, around social categories such as gender, age, income, geographic region, and race or ethnicity (JANUS Project 2003: 1). As society transitioned from the Industrial Age to the Information Age, male workers under 40 dominated the "core" information technology (IT) professions – computer scientists, computer engineers, systems analysts, and computer programmers (Meares & Sargent 1999: 4). According to computer software expert Kathleen Vail (1997), "From the beginning, computers have been a sort of technology magnet, attracting boys and repelling girls. . . . In 1984, according to a US Department of Education Study, 17 percent of boys used a computer at home compared to only 9 percent of girls" (A19). Over the course of the decade, however, the gender gap in computer use steadily began to close.

The generally welcoming attitude of hyperconscious television toward the new social paradigm and information technologies may partially account for the dramatic demographic overlap, then, between its viewers and moderate to heavy IT users. Although the core IT professions continue to be heavily skewed toward men, many other professions now demand IT competency. As information technology has become increasingly central to a diverse array of work environments, the digital divide has narrowed along lines of gender and to some extent age, though IT use still drops off substantially at age 55

(Falling Through the Net 1999: 35; Falling Through the Net 2000: 33). The once prevalent gender and age divisions among hyperconscious and nostalgia television viewers have today all but disappeared.

Life and Television in the Twenty-First Century

The closing of the 1990s coincided both with the start of the twenty-first century and a new millennium – a symbolic if not actual break with the past. Society no longer seemed to be *in transition* from the Industrial Age to the Information Age so much as *transitioned*. That the new social paradigm had fully arrived could be seen in three key events. The first event was the dot-com boom and subsequent NASDAQ crash in 2000. In contrast to traditional brick and mortar stores, dot-coms are internet or e-based businesses such as America Online, Amazon.com, or eBay. In the latter half of the 1990s, dot-com companies were popping up almost as quickly as they could be thought up. Individuals and businesses, hoping to get in on the ground floor of the next Microsoft, invested widely and heavily in computing and networking technologies as well as internet-based businesses. As a result, the NASDAQ exchange – an index of technology stocks – was rising at an unprecedented rate, turning many twentysomething CEOs into millionaires virtually overnight. Between 1996 and 2000, the NASDAQ grew in value from 600 to more than 5,000, peaking on March 10, 2000, at 5048.62, before beginning its historic fall. The frenzied investment in internet-based businesses resulted in an overvaluation of many stocks. When the dot-com bubble burst, many companies went bankrupt, others sustained severe financial and job losses, and investors lost billions. The NASDAQ crash of 2000 serves as a cautionary tale about the dangers of unbridled optimism in new technologies.

The second key event was the public reaction to the apocalyptic predictions surrounding the Y2K bug. The Y2K bug referred to a design flaw in computer programming that might cause some date-related processing to operate incorrectly for dates and times on or following January 1, 2000. By 1999, information technologies had so come to dominate virtually every aspect of our lives that media predictions about the effects of this programming flaw included financial institutions sending out bogus billing information, hospitals and electric companies losing power, airplanes falling from the sky, and nuclear reactors melting down. Although the actual problems caused by the Y2K bug were relatively minor, due in part to careful planning, the public *fear* fueled by media predictions led some people to withdraw their life savings, stockpile essentials like toilet paper and canned food, and purchase Y2K survival kits. These behaviors, though certainly not representative of everyone, do suggest just how deeply some individuals perceived their lives to be bound up with the new information technologies. In retrospect, the Y2K bug was significant not because of its effect on computing systems, but because of its effect on the collective unconsciousness of our society. The Y2K bug served as its own cautionary tale about the hysteria of unrestrained pessimism over information technologies.

The third and most dramatic event to signal the arrival of the new social paradigm was the September 11, 2001, terrorist attacks on the Pentagon and World Trade Center. Both the planning and execution of the attacks as well as the media response that followed confirmed that we now live in a radically different era. The 9/11 terrorists highjacked four commercial airliners, which they used as missiles to attack the World Trade Center and Pentagon – symbolic symbols of US economic and political power. Prior to the attack, none of the terrorists had ever actually flown a commercial jetliner; their training had come exclusively in the form of flight simulators. It was an attack not by another government or nation-state, but by a terrorist network whose strategic planning and operational funding were carried out largely over global information networks. US citizens were, as the news media constantly reminded us by endlessly replaying the gruesome images of that day, no longer safe even at home. The new information technologies had shrunk our world to such an extent that no *place* any longer offered security. To combat this new decentered, flexible, high-tech enemy, the US government itself quickly turned to IT. The passage of the Patriot Act and, as we would learn years later, the government's secret wiretapping program, changed the nature of warfare. Information, we were now told, was our best tool in "the war on terror." It is a state of affairs the eerily resonates with Lyotard's prediction in 1984 that "It is conceivable that the nation-states will one day fight for control of information, just as they battled in the past for control over territory" (5).

The dot.com bust, Y2K bug, and terrorist attacks of 9/11 each, in their own way, urge a moderate view of technology, one of cautious, calculated, and conditional acceptance. The dot-com bust resulted from an overly optimistic view of the new information technologies, while the Y2K bug signaled the pitfalls of unrestrained pessimism. The events of 9/11 also favor a centrist view of technology in the Information Age by demonstrating that IT can be both friend and foe, defense and threat. It is increasingly becoming clear that the new information technologies are neither a panacea, nor a plague. They are, however, critical elements of our social, political, and economic system. As such, it no longer makes sense to blindly accept or utterly reject the new paradigm. Living *in* the Information Age means learning to say both "yes" and "no" depending upon the context. In the past few years, audiences have become far more likely to watch a combination of both hyperconscious and nostalgia television, depending on their specific moods and needs. When viewers desire to have their media savvy legitimated and valued, they still regularly turn to hyperconscious television. When viewers feel overwhelmed by the endless semiotic array, they still seek escape in nostalgia television. What is different today is that audiences are seeking out both types of mental equipments as they try to find a "balance" that helps them negotiate the contours of contemporary life.

The televisual landscape continues to be marked largely by the general "yes" and "no" orientations, though hyperconscious and nostalgia television have begun to mutate into two new symbolic forms. The hyperconscious television of the 1990s is slowly being reconfigured into the hyperreality television of the twenty-first century. Whereas Fox and MTV were central to the rise of hyperconscious television, Comedy Central has been vital to the development and spread of hyperreality TV. Hyperreality television retains elements of eclecticism, intertextuality, and self-reflexivity, but it foregrounds these stylistic devices even more explicitly and deepens the "ironic" attitude of hyperconscious TV. Hyperreality television is principally TV *about* TV. *The Daily Show with Jon Stewart* (1998–), for instance, is a self-described "fake" news program *about* the news. Although critics often describe the show as a "spoof," many viewers consider it a trustworthy source for news (Fenton 2005: 13). A study of 18- to 29-year-olds conducted by the nonpartisan group "Declare Yourself," found that young people who got their news primarily from nontraditional outlets like the internet rated John Stewart ahead of Peter Jennings, Tom Brokaw, and Dan Rather as TV's most trustworthy news anchor (Brown 2005). "Stewart's success," argues media scholar David T. Z. Mindich (2005), "is that the show is very, very funny and drips with the kind of irony that many young people tell me they appreciate" (125).

The Daily Show with Jon Stewart is not alone in its "ultrahip" ironic attitude, however. *Son of a Beach* (2000–1) is a TV show that mocks fluff TV shows, specifically by parodying *Bay Watch* (1989–2001). *Reno 911* (2003–) and *Drawn Together* (2004–) are both "fake" reality TV shows that comment on reality TV. *Reno 911* is modeled on reality television shows like *Cops* and *Rescue 911*. But whereas those reality shows are silent about their own conventions, *Reno 911* continually highlights them. Similarly, *Draw Together* is modeled on MTV's various iterations of the *Real World* and other "picked to live in the same house" reality shows such as *Big Brother* (2000–). The pleasure and meaningfulness of shows like *Son of a Beach*, *Reno 911*, and *Drawn Together* depends upon intertextual knowledge of the history of specific television genres, just as appreciation of *The Daily Show* requires knowledge of the codes and conventions of traditional broadcast news. Another television program about television is the animated series *South Park* (1997–). Where *South Park* differs from the aforementioned programs is that it refers to and comments upon a range of television genres as opposed to just one. As a crudely animated series, the show also lends itself to quick production, a fact that has allowed the series to allude to current events far more quickly than more traditional programs. *South Park* is about what is happening with and on television now. In other words, hyperreality television combines the "already said" with the "what is being said."

Like hyperconscious television, nostalgia television has undergone its own mutations since the turn of the millennium. Much of what is popularly described today as "Reality TV" is a reconfiguration of nostalgia television. Reality shows such as CBS's *Survivor* (2000–), MTV's *Sorority Life* (2002), Fox's *Temptation Island* (2001–3), the WB's *High School Reunion* (2003–5), and PBS's *Frontier House* (2002) are all about creating a sense of nostalgia, in which a downsized community is stripped of any modern conveniences in favor of the (melo)drama of human relations. *Survivor* is premised, for instance, on dividing the participants into tribes – a gesture to "primitivism" – and denying them technologies they are accustomed to. Moreover, it constructs situations such as voting off one's own tribe members that will lead to conflict. In manufacturing interpersonal conflict, reality TV privileges story and particularly the storying of identity. What are each cast members' values? How easily can those values be swayed by others or context? How do we form social bonds and relationships? How do they change?

Not all nostalgia television programs today erase or downplay technology, however. The CBS series *CSI: Crime Scene Investigation* (2000–) and its numerous spin-offs reflect a unique post-1990s, pro-technology nostalgia. Each week, senior Las Vegas forensics officer Gil Grissom (William Petersen) employs "all the advanced techniques available to analyze evidence found at crime scenes and determine how the crimes, mostly gruesome murders, had been committed" (Brooks & Marsh 2003: 179). In 2006, *CSI, CSI: Miami* (2002–) and *CSI: New York* (2004–) frequently garnered three of the top 10 spots in the weekly Nielsen ratings. As a television critic, I strongly suspect that this show is tapping into some profound psychological need. In a post-9/11 culture with the ever-present threat of terrorism (experienced as fear, confusion, insecurity, and chaos) looming in our unconscious, *CSI* assures viewers week after week that governmental agencies have the skills and advanced technology to locate, stop, and convict those who would wreak havoc on US society. Programs such as *CSI* suggest that the government can adapt to and outsmart even the most high-tech criminals (terrorists). This formula, then, combines technology with downsized community to foster a sense of safety and security.

Other technology-friendly nostalgia programs included ABC's legal drama *The Practice* (1997–2004), NBC's political drama *The West Wing* (1999–2006), Fox's teen drama *The O.C.* (2003–), and CBS's procedural drama *Without a Trace* (2002–). These shows recognize the centrality of technology (from computers to cell phones) in everyday life, but they are rooted in melodramatic storytelling, authenticity, and sincerity. Like the previous generation of nostalgia television programs, they are strong on community and closure. Where programs such as *CSI* and *The O.C.* differ from their 1990s predecessors such as *Walker, Texas Ranger* and *Beverly Hills, 90210* is that the new information technologies are a means to achieve community and closure, rather than an impediment to it. The highly rated series *Without a Trace* marries technology with advanced psychological profiling techniques to locate missing persons. I find it more than coincidental that at the historical moment when citizen-viewers are suffering from identity drift and a feeling of placelessness, that a drama about the New York Missing Persons Squad of the FBI, whose job it is to bring together the many components of a person's personality so as to locate him or her, would experience such tremendous popularity. Each episode of the show *locates* – which is to say, furnishes identity coordinates for – a lost or missing person, and in the process, provides a weekly model for managing the threats to identity.

The symbolic forms of hyperreality and reality television are, in many ways, simply adaptations of hyperconscious and nostalgia television. The more fundamental change currently transforming television is occurring at the level of technology. "In fact," explains Ronald Grover (2004), "TV is confronting the biggest turning point in its more than 60-year history. The most profound change underway is one of technological upheaval" (158). In particular, three trends are (re)shaping the medium of television: convergence, interactivity, and mobility. Convergence describes the integration and synthesis of previously distinct technologies such as computers, radio, television, and video games into one medium. "As digital movies and television programs become increasingly common," technology analyst Mark Fischetti (2001) explains, "they are morphing with video games, Internet video and music into one stream of digital content. At the same time, the distribution channels for that content – cable TV, satellite and the Internet – are widening into one big broadband pipe into your home" (35; see also Elmer-Dewitt 1992: 39). The need for multiple devices that perform different functions from playing music to providing email access is rapidly dwindling. Technological convergence is fueled by two main forces, the transition of analog technologies such as television to digital (creating a common format) and the ever-expanding bandwidth, or channel capacity, for moving information.

The convergence of various digital technologies is fueling a second trend, interactivity. During the 1990s, the interactivity of television was mainly a product of the remote control and VCR, which allowed for channel surfing and time-shifting. But thanks to a host of innovative new technologies, viewers have even more power to manipulate the "content" of television. This trend is evident in digital video recorders such as TiVo and ReplayTV (both introduced in 1999), which allow viewers to produce their own programming schedules, pause live-action, and fast-forward through commercials. Microsoft's UltimateTV, launched in March 2001, goes further, allowing viewers to display Web pages and email on their TVs using WebTV software (see Day 1998: 116; Fischetti 2001: 37.) Soon, viewers will be able to call up statistics about their favorite players *as* they watch a sporting event or learn more about their favorite actors *as* they watch them on TV. According to Richard Zoglin (1992a), "People will be able to call up on their screen virtually everything the culture produces, from the latest Hollywood movie to lessons in chess, from an old episode of *The Twilight Zone* to this morning's newspaper, custom-edited for individual readers" (70). Existing examples of television's increasing interactivity include Fox's phone-in and text-in voting on *American Idol* (2002–) and NBC's live phone-a-friend on *Who Wants to Be A Millionaire* (1999–).

The third key trend transforming television is mobility. Until recently, television has been a large "box" containing a heavy cathode ray tube. Because television sets are cumbersome and therefore inconvenient to move, they usually remain in one place, where they receive a broadcast signal or are wired to receive cable. The invention of flat screens (both digital and plasma) along with the development of high-speed wireless technology are making TV more mobile, however. In the twenty-first century, "The box with wires coming out of it will be just one way folks will see TV programs. Cell phones, PDAs, and computers will also receive shows" (Grover 2004: 160). This will forever change the nature of television viewing, which has historically occurred almost exclusively in the home or in the occasional town pub. "In the last six years," according to iLoop Mobile CTO Michael Becker (2005), "the United States has seen a 56% increase in the adoption of mobile phone subscribers, [bringing the total number of subscribers to] nearly 194 million" (1–2). With individual television episodes already available for download at websites like iTunes, TV is now on the go. Convergence, interactivity, and mobility will give viewers unprecedented power to watch what they want, when they want, how they want, and where they want. The ability of viewers to control scheduling and content will transform mass TV into custom TV, and force major changes in the way content providers operate. Heightened viewer control potentially signals an end to the importance and very notion of "primetime" TV as well as to the traditional 30-second advertising spot (Grover 2004: 158).

The Next Great Paradigm Shift?

The development, emergence, and adoption of new technology drives social, political, and economic change. As we pass the mid-point of the first decade of the twenty-first century, some social analysts believe that the next great paradigm shift may already be underway, and that the days of the Information Age are waning quickly. As incredible as this claim may seem, there are good reasons to take it seriously. As a consequence of the massive computational and processing power of computers, technological innovation and scientific discovery are occurring at an unprecedented pace. Groundbreaking advances in mathematics, biology, and physics have become almost as regular as turning on the television set. If we are entering a new era, then what are its contours and its consequences? Although it may be too soon to answer that question with precision and certainty, observers agree that the concept of "networks" is central. According to Harry Dent, Jr. (1998), "The most critical changes coming in the next decade and beyond will affect where and how we work and live. We are about to establish a new network-driven society that will elevate relativistic and nonlinear, right-brain skills that are necessary to build new organizational structures based on the network model" (202–3). Recent research in the area of science known as "complexity theory" has demonstrated that what were formerly thought to be random patterns in nature and social behavior may actually emerge in identifiable and (even more importantly) predictable ways (Barabási 2003; Buchanan 2004). From the motion of atoms and the movement of storms to the paths of pedestrians and the trading of stocks, the laws of networks may govern all things big or small. If supercomputers allow us to map these natural and social networks, then the culture of connection, and of webs, may soon come to replace the culture of fragmentation, and of splintering.

Scholars in fields ranging from sociology to physics have variously dubbed the coming revolution and emergent era "Network Culture," the "Network Society," the "Connected Age," and the "Conceptual Age" (see Pink 2005; Shaviro 2003; Taylor 2001; Watts 2003). Recounting the paradigm shifts from the Agricultural Age to the Industrial Age to the Information Age to the Conceptual Age, social analyst Daniel H. Pink writes, "In short, we've progressed from a society of farmers to a society of factory workers to a society of knowledge workers. And now we're progressing yet again – to a society of creators and empathizers, of pattern recognizers and meaning makers" (2005: 50). Paradigm shifts, such as those from the Industrial Age to the Information Age and from the Information Age to the Conceptual Age, signal a fundamental change in social organization. Table 5.1 summarizes how the central structuring principle of society has transitioned from "place" to "pace" to "pattern."

Leading cultural and technology authority Howard Rheingold also identifies "networks" as key to the next great shift. In his book *Smart Mobs: The Next Social Revolution* (2002), Rheingold contends that wireless technologies such as cell phones, pagers, PDAs, and hand held computers are creating "smart mobs" – new forms of social connectivity – that "enhance the power of social networks" by enabling "*people to act together in new ways and in situations where collective action was not possible before*" (xviii). At the start of the twenty-first century, it appears that links, nodal relations, connectivity, and networks mark the way ahead. But the coming age, as with others, will not be ushered in without its own fears and anxieties.

Students have already expressed to me concerns about being detached, cut-off, or understimulated. They feel a pressing need to be constantly connected and endlessly engaged. Merely forgetting one's cell phone, pager, or PDA often prompts intense feelings of disconnection, isolation, and boredom. As individuals increasingly "plug-in" to digital and social networks, it will likely heighten existing anxieties about the loss of humanity to technology – a fear recently

Table 5.1: Structuring principles of historical epochs

	Industrial Age	Information Age	Conceptual Age
Central structuring principle	*Place*: The social is shaped by geography, by the distribution of natural resources and the nation-state.	*Pace*: The social is shaped by the speed of information exchange and technological development.	*Pattern*: The social is shaped by networks, links, connectivity, ties, and nodal relations.

dramatized in *The Matrix* trilogy – and the loss of individual agency to network structure. But in response to these social anxieties, television will develop new and relevant symbolic forms. The job for critics and scholars will be to chart the various ways that television, as a prominent mode of public discourse, equips individuals to confront and resolve the anxieties that are just now beginning to take shape. Television, it turns out, is neither simply a mirror nor a creator of social reality, and viewers not merely its patrons. TV is also a therapist, and viewers its patients. Just as viewers once adjusted their TV antennas for better reception, TV adjusts us to better receive our ever-changing social world.

Note

1   Umberto Eco's distinction between open and closed texts is mirrored closely by the French semiotician Roland Barthes's distinction between readerly (*lisible*) and writerly (*scriptible*) texts in his book *S/Z*. According to Barthes (1974), a readerly text, much like Eco's closed text, shuts down signification; it restricts the "proper" meaning of a text by plunging the reader into idleness (4). Barthes terms these texts readerly because they are designed, which is to say "structured," to be read (passively consumed), but not to be written (actively produced). The goal of the writerly text, by contrast, "is to make the reader no longer a consumer, but a producer of the text" (Barthes 1974: 4). See also Barry Brummett's (1994) discussion of discrete and diffuse texts (80–1).

References

Adorno, T. W. (1954). How to Look at Television. *The Quarterly of Film, Radio and Television* 8(3), 213–35.

Alcaly, R. (2004). *The New Economy.* New York: Farrar, Straus and Giroux.

Allen, R. C. (1992). Introduction to the Second Edition, More Talk about TV. In: Allen, R. C. (ed.), *Channels of Discourse, Reassembled: Television and Contemporary Criticism.* 2nd ed. Chapel Hill, NC: The University of North Carolina Press, pp. 1–30.

Anderson, W. T. (1990). *Reality Isn't What It Used to Be: Theatrical Politics, Ready-to-Wear Religion, Global Myths, Primitive Chic, and Other Wonders of the Postmodern World.* San Francisco, CA: Harper & Row, Publishers.

Anderson, W. T. (1995). *The Truth about the Truth: De-confusing and Re-constructing the Postmodern World.* New York: Penguin Putnam Inc.

Anderson, W. T. (1997). *The Future of the Self: Inventing the Postmodern Person.* New York: Penguin Putnam Inc.

Appelo, T. (1999). *Ally McBeal: The Official Guide.* New York: HarperPerennial.

Altheide, D. L. & Snow, R. P. (1991). *Media Worlds in the Postjournalism Era.* New York: Aldine de Gruyter.

Auster, A. (1996). It's Friendship . . . *Television Quarterly* 28, 2–7.

Baker, K. (1988, Jan. 30). Wonder Years Looks at '60s Through Eyes of a Pre-Teen. *The Associated Press,* 7C.

Barabási, A. (2003). *Linked: How Everything Is Connected to Everything Else and What It Means for Business, Science, and Everyday Life.* New York: Plume.

Barber, B. R. (2001). *Jihad vs. McWorld: Terrorism's Challenge to Democracy.* New York: Ballantine Books.

Barker, J. A. (1988). *Discovering the Future: The Business of Paradigms.* 2nd ed. St. Paul, MN: ILI Press.

Barthes, R. (1974). *S/Z.* Trans. R. Miller. New York: Hill and Wang.

Barthes, R. (1988). *Image-Music-Text.* Trans. S. Heath. New York: Hill and Wang.

Batra, N. D. (1987). *The Hour of Television: Critical Approaches*. Metuchen, NJ: Scarecrow Press, Inc.

Baudrillard, J. (1983). *Simulations*. Trans. P. Foss, P. Patton, & P. Beitchman. New York: Semiotext(e).

Becker, M. (2005, Sept. 12). Research Update: The Effects of Adding Mobile Initiatives for Increased Brand Satisfaction. iLoop Mobile. Available online at: http://www.iloopmobile. com/news/effects_research_update_0905.pdf

Bell, D. (1973). *The Coming of Post-Industrial Society: A Venture in Social Forecasting*. New York: Basic Books.

Bellamy, R. V. & Walker, J. R. (1996). *Television and the Remote Control: Grazing on a Vast* Wasteland. New York: Guilford.

Bennett, W. L. (2005). *News: The Politics of Illusion*. 6th ed. New York: Pearson.

Best, S. & Kellner, D. (1991). *Postmodern Theory: Critical Interrogations*. New York: The Guilford Press.

Best, S. & Kellner, D. (1997). *The Postmodern Turn*. New York: The Guilford Press.

Best, S. & Kellner, D. (2001). *The Postmodern Adventure: Science, Technology and Cultural Studies at the Third Millennium*. New York: The Guilford Press.

Bianculli, D. (1992). *Teleliteracy: Taking Television Seriously*. New York: A Touchstone Book.

Bianculli, D. (1996). *Dictionary of Teleliteracy: Television's 500 Biggest Hits, Misses, and Events*. New York: The Continuum Publishing.

Bianculli, D. (2000, Jan. 13). Hurray for 'Simpsons' Family Values! Under-Achieving Bart and His Kooky TV Clan Celebrate 10 Happily Dysfunctional Years. *Daily News*, 46.

Bignell, J. (2004). *An Introduction to Television Studies*. New York: Routledge.

Biocca, F. (2000). New Media Technology and Youth: Trends in the Evolution of New Media. *Journal of Adolescent Health* 27, 22–9.

Bitzer, L. F. (1986). The Rhetorical Situation. *Philosophy and Rhetoric* 1, 1–14.

Bloom, A. (1987). *The Closing of the American Mind*. New York: Simon & Schuster Inc.

Blumenfeld, L. (1992, Feb. 17). When a Television Drama . . . 'Beverly Hills, 90210' Strikes a Popular Chord. *The Washington Post*, D5.

Borgman, A. (1995, June 18). Suburbia's Signs of Stressful Times. *The Washington Post*, B01.

Brooks, T. & Marsh, E. (2003). *The Complete Directory to Prime Time Network and Cable TV Shows 1946–Present*. 8th ed. New York: Ballantine Books.

Brown, M. (2005, Spring). Abandoning the News. *Carnegie Reporter* 3. Available online at: http://www.carnegie.org/reporter/10/news/index.html

Brummett, B. (1980). Symbolic Form, Burkean Scapegoating, and Rhetorical Exigency in Alioto's Response to the 'Zebra' Murders. *Western Journal of Communication* 44, 64–73.

Brummett, B. (1984a). Burke's Representative Anecdote as a Method in Media Criticism. *Critical Studies in Mass Communication* 1, 161–76.

Brummett, B. (1984b). Burkean Comedy and Tragedy, Illustrated in Reactions to the Arrest of John Delorean. *Central States Speech Journal* 35, 217–27.

Brummett, B. (1985). Electric Literature as Equipment for Living: Haunted House Films. *Critical Studies in Mass Communication* 9, 247–61.

Brummett, B. (1991). *Rhetorical Dimensions of Popular Culture*. Tuscaloosa, AL: The University of Alabama Press.

Brummett, B. (1994). *Rhetoric in Popular Culture*. New York: St. Martin's Press.

Brunsdon, C. (2006). Television Studies. *The Museum of Broadcast Communications*. Chicago, IL. Available online at: http://www.museum.tv/archives/etv/T/htmlT/televisionst/televisionst.htm

Buchanan, M. (2004). *Nexus: Small Worlds and the Groundbreaking Theory of Networks*. New York: W. W. Norton & Company.

Burgin, V. (1996). *In/Different Spaces: Place and Memory in Visual Culture*. Berkeley, CA: University of California Press.

Burke, K. (1941). *The Philosophy of Literary Form: Studies in Symbolic Action*. Baton Rouge: Louisiana State University Press.

Burke, K. (1953). *Counter-Statement*. 2nd ed. Los Altos, CA: Hermes Publications.

Burke, K. (1968). *Language as Symbolic Action: Essays of Life, Literature, and Method*. Berkeley, CA: University of California Press.

Burke, K. (1984). *Attitudes Toward History*. 3rd ed. Berkeley, CA: University of California Press.

Burnett, R. & Marshall, P. D. (2003). *Web Theory: An Introduction*. New York: Routledge.

Cali, D. D. (2000). The Logic of the Link: The Associative Paradigm in Communication Criticism. *Critical Studies in Media Communication*, 17, 397–408.

Campbell, R. & Freed, R. (1993). 'We Know It When We See It': Postmodernism and Television. *Television Quarterly* 26, 75–87.

Cantor, P. A. (1997). The Greatest TV Show Ever. *American Enterprise* 8, 34–7.

Cantor, P. A. (2003). *Gilligan Unbound: Pop Culture in the Age of Globalization*. Lanham, MD: Rowman & Littlefield.

Cashmore, E. (1994). . . . *And There Was Television*. New York: Routledge.

Castells, M. (2000). *The Rise of the Network Society.* 2nd ed. Malden, MA: Blackwell Publishing.

Castells, M. (2001a). Epilogue: Informationalism and the Network Society. In: Himanen, P. *The Hacker Ethic and the Spirit of the Information Age.* New York: Random House, pp. 155–78.

Castells, M. (2001b). *The Internet Galaxy: Reflections on the Internet, Business, and Society.* Oxford: Oxford University Press.

Cathcart, R. S. (1993). Instruments of His Own Making: Burke and Media. In: Chesebro, J. W. (ed.), *Extensions of the Burkeian System.* Tuscaloosa, AL: University of Alabama Press, pp. 287–308.

Chatman, S. (1978). *Story and Discourse: Narrative Structure in Fiction and Film.* Ithaca, NY: Cornell University Press.

Chesebro, J. W. & Bertelsen, D. A. (1996). *Analyzing Media: Communication Technologies as Symbolic and Cognitive Systems.* New York: The Guilford Press.

Collins, A. (1994). Intellectuals, Power and Quality Television. In: Giroux, H. A. & McLaren, P. (eds.), *Between Borders: Pedagogy and the Politics of Cultural Studies.* New York: Routledge, pp. 56–73.

Collins, J. (1992). Television and Postmodernism. In: Allen, R. C. (ed.), *Channels of Discourse, Reassembled: Television and Contemporary Criticism.* 2nd ed. Chapel Hill, NC: The University of North Carolina Press, pp. 327–53.

Collins, J. (1995). *Architectures of Excess: Cultural Life in the Information Age.* New York: Routledge.

Columbia Tri-Star Television: Walker, Texas Ranger. (2006). Sony Pictures Digital, Inc. Available online at: http://www.sonypictures.com/tv/shows/walker/

Connor, S. (1997). *Postmodern Culture: An Introduction to Theories of the Contemporary.* 2nd ed. Cambridge, MA: Blackwell Publishers.

Conrad, M. T. (2001). Thus Spake Bart: On Nietzsche and the Virtues of Being Bad. In: Irwin, W., Conrad, M. T. & Skoble, A. J. (eds.), *The Simpsons and Philosophy: The D'oh! of Homer.* Chicago, IL: Open Court, pp. 59–78.

Consalvo, M. (2000). Reality Television. In: Pendergrast, T. & Pendergrast, S. (eds.), *St. James Encyclopedia of Popular Culture.* vol. 4: P–T. Detroit, MI: St. James Press, pp. 181–3.

Corliss, R. (1994, May 2). Simpsons Forever! *Time,* 77.

Corliss, R. (1998, June 8). The Cartoon Character Bart Simpson. *Time,* 204.

Corner, J. (1999). *Critical Ideas in Television Studies.* New York: Oxford University Press.

Croteau, D. & Hoynes, W. (2003). *Media/Society: Industries, Images, and Audiences.* 3rd ed. Thousand Oaks, CA: Pine Forge Press.

Curry, J. (1986, May). Can 'Moonlighting' Save ABC? *American Film*, 49.

Davidson, J. D. & Rees-Mogg, L. W. (1999). *The Sovereign Individual: Mastering the Transition to the Information Age*. New York: A Touchstone Book.

Davis, D. (1993). *The Five Myths of Television Power or Why the Medium is Not the Message*. New York: Simon & Schuster.

Davis, S. & Meyer, C. (1998). *Blur: The Speed of Change in the Connected Economy*. Reading, MA: Perseus Books.

Day, N. (1996). *Sensational TV: Trash or Journalism*. Springfield, NJ: Enslow Publishers.

Day, R. (1998, April). Screen Saviors. *World Traveler*, 78, 81, 83, 116.

de Bono, E. (1970). *Lateral Thinking: Creativity Step by Step*. New York: Harper & Row, Publishers.

de Bono, E. (2005). *De Bono's Thinking Course*. Rev. ed. New York: Barnes & Noble Books.

de Certeau, M. (1984). *The Practice of Everyday Life*. Trans. S. Rendell. Berkeley, CA: University of California Press.

Debord, G. (1995). *The Society of the Spectacle*. Trans. D. Nicholson-Smith. New York: Zone Books.

Dent, H. S., Jr. (1998). *The Roaring 2000s: Building the Wealth and Lifestyle You Desire in the Greatest Boom in History*. New York: Simon and Schuster.

Dickerson, J. F. (1995, March 1). Never Too Old: Millions of Seniors are Getting Connected Through the Internet. *Time*, 41.

Dizard, W. P. (1982). *The Coming Information Age: An Overview of Technology, Economics, and Politics*. New York: Longman.

Dockery, D. S. (1995). The Challenge of Postmodernism. In: Dockery, D. S. (ed.), *The Challenge of Postmodernism*. Grand Rapids, MI: Baker Book House, pp. 13–18.

Doherty, T. (1987). MTV and the Music Video: Promo and Product. *Southern Speech Communication Journal* 52, 352–3.

Douglas, D. (1993). *The Five Myths of Television Power: Or, Why the Medium is Not the Message*. New York: Simon and Schuster.

Douglas, M. (2002). *Purity and Danger: An Analysis of Concept of Pollution and Taboo*. New York: Routledge.

Dow, B. (1996). *Prime-Time Feminism: Television, Media Culture, and the Women's Movement Since 1970*. Philadelphia, PA: University of Pennsylvania Press.

Dr. Quinn Medicine Woman Official Website. (2006). CBS Entertainment Productions and The Sullivan Company. Available online at: http://www.drquinnmd.com/index.html

Dunne, M. (1992). *Metapop: Self-referentiality in Contemporary American Popular Culture*. Jackson, MS: University Press of Mississippi.

Dylan, B. (1964). The Times They Are A-Changin'. *The Times They Are a Changin'*. Columbia Records/CBS Records Inc. compact disc CK 8905.

Eagleton, T. (1996a). *Literary Theory: An Introduction*. 2nd ed. Minneapolis, MN: The University of Minnesota Press.

Eagleton, T. (1996b). *The Illusions of Postmodernism*. Malden, MA: Blackwell Publishers.

Eco, U. (1979). *The Role of the Reader: Explorations in the Semiotics of Texts*. Bloomington, IN: Indiana University Press.

Eco, U. (1984). Postscript to *The Name of the Rose*. New York: Harcourt Brace Jovanovich.

Eco, U. (1989). *The Open Work*. Trans. A. Cancogni. Cambridge, MA: Harvard University Press.

Eco, U. (2004). Intertextual Irony and Levels of Reading. In: Eco, U. (ed.), *On Literature*. Trans. M. McLaughlin. New York: Harcourt, pp. 212–35.

Edmunds, A. & Morris, A. (2000). The Problem of Information Overload in Business Organisations: A Review of Literature. *International Journal of Information Management* 20, 17–28.

Elkins, J. (2003). *Visual Studies: A Skeptical Introduction*. New York: Routledge.

Ellin, N. (1999). *Postmodern Urbanism*. Rev. ed. New York: Princeton Architectural Press.

Ellin, N. (ed.) (1997). *Architecture of Fear*. New York: Princeton Architectural Press.

Elm, J. (1990, March 17). Are the Simpsons America's TV Family of the '90s? *TV Guide*, 8.

Elmer-Dewitt, P. (1992, Oct. 15). Dream Machines: Technology Watchers Foresee a World Filled with Multisensual Media, Smart Roads and Robots That are Almost Alive. *Time*, 39.

Erickson, H. (1995). *Television Cartoon Shows: An Illustrated Encyclopedia, 1949 Through 1993*. Jefferson, NC: McFarland and Company, Inc.

Esders, K. (2000). (The) Playing Author: Narrativity and Identity in Literature and Interactive Media. In: Kraus, E. & Auer, C. (eds.), *Simulacrum America: The USA and the Popular Media*. Rochester, NY: Camden House, pp. 75–83.

Falling Through the Net II: New Data on the Digital Divide. (1998, July). US Department of Commerce, NTIA. Available online at: http://www.ntia.doc.gov/ntiahome/net2/falling.html

Falling Through the Net: A Survey of the 'Have Nots' in Rural and Urban America. (1995, July). US Department of Commerce, NTIA. Available online at: http://www.ntia.doc.gov/ntiahome/fallingthru.html

Falling Through the Net: Defining the Digital Divide. (1999, July). US Department of Commerce, NTIA. Available online at: http://www.ntia.doc.gov/ntiahome/fttn99/FTTN.pdf

Falling Through the Net: Toward Digital Inclusion. (2000, Oct.). US Department of Commerce, NTIA. Available online at: http://search.ntia. doc.gov/pdf/fttn00.pdf

Featherstone, M. (1991). *Consumer Culture and Postmodernism*. Newbury Park, CA: Sage Publications.

Fenton, T. (2005). *Bad News: The Decline of Reporting, the Business of News, and the Danger to Us All*. New York: HarperCollins.

Feuer, J. (1984). The MTM Style. In: Feuer, J., Kerr, P., & Vahimagri, T. (eds.), *MTM: 'Quality Television'*. London: British Film Institute, pp. 32–60.

Feuer, J. (1992). Genre Study and Television. In: Allen, R. C. (ed.), *Channels of Discourse, Reassembled: Television and Contemporary Criticism*. 2nd ed. Chapel Hill, NC: The University of North Carolina Press, pp. 138–60.

Fischetti, M. (2001, Nov.). The Future of TV. *Technology Review*, 35–40.

Fiske, J. (1987). *Television Culture*. New York: Routledge.

Fiske, J. (1989). Moments of Television: Neither the Text Nor the Audience. In: Seiter, E., Borchers, H., Kreutzner, G., & Warth, E. (eds.), *Remote Control: Television, Audiences and Cultural Power*. New York: Routledge, pp. 56–78.

Fiske, J. (1991). Postmodernism and Television. In: Curran, J. & Gurevitch, M. (eds.), *Mass Media and Society*. New York: Edward Arnold, pp. 55–67.

Fiske, J. (1992). British Cultural Studies and Television. In: Allen, R. C. (ed.), *Channels of Discourse, Reassembled: Television and Contemporary Criticism*. 2nd ed. Chapel Hill, NC: The University of North Carolina Press, pp. 284–326.

Fiske, J. (1994). *Media Matters: Everyday Culture and Political Change*. Minneapolis, MN: University of Minnesota Press.

Flitterman-Lewis, S. (1992). Psychoanalysis, Film, and Television. In: Allen, R. C. (ed.), *Channels of Discourse, Reassembled: Television and Contemporary Criticism*. 2nd ed. Chapel Hill, NC: The University of North Carolina Press, pp. 203–46.

Foucault, M. (1980). *Power/Knowledge: Selected Interviews and Other Writings 1972–1977*. Trans. C. Gordon. New York: Pantheon Books.

Fox, J. (2001). *Chomsky and Globalization*. Duxford, Cambridge: Totem Books.

Fukuyama, F. (1999). *The Great Disruption: Human Nature and the Reconstitution of the Social Order*. London: Profile Books Ltd.

Gardner, H. (1983). *Frames of Mind: The Theory of Multiple Intelligences*. New York: Basic Books, Inc., Publishers.

Gerbner, G., Gross, L., Morgan, M., & Signorielli, N. (1982). Charting the Mainstream: Television's Contribution to Political Orientations. *Journal of Communication* 30, 100–26.

Gergen, K. J. (2000). *The Saturated Self: Dilemmas of Identity in Contemporary Life*. New York: Basic Books.

Gianoulis, T. (2000). *The Simpsons*. In: Prendergast, T. & Prendergast, S. (eds.), *St. James Encyclopedia of Popular Culture*. vol. 4: P–T. Detroit, MI: St. James Press, pp. 408–9.

Gibbs, N. (1989, April 24). How America Has Run Out of Time. *Time*, 58.

Giddens, A. (1991). *Modernity and Self-Identity: Self and Society in the Late Modern Age*. Stanford, CA: Stanford University Press.

Gitlin, T. (1983). *Inside Prime Time*. New York: Pantheon Books.

Gitlin, T. (2001). *Media Unlimited: How the Torrent of Images and Sounds Overwhelms Our Lives*. New York: Metropolitan Books.

Gleick, J. (1987). *Chaos: Making a New Science*. New York: Penguin Books.

Gleick, J. (1999). *Faster: The Acceleration of Just About Everything*. New York: Pantheon Books.

Glick, I. O. & Levy, S. J. (1962). *Living with Television*. Chicago, IL: Aldine Publishing.

Gomez-Pena, G. & Sifuentes, R. (1996). *Temple of Confessions: Mexican Beasts and Living Santos*. New York: powerHouse Books.

Grenz, S. J. (1996). *A Primer on Postmodernism*. Grand Rapids, MI: Wm. B. Eerdmans Publishing.

Grossman, L. K. (1995). *The Electronic Republic: Reshaping Democracy in the Information Age*. New York: Viking.

Grover, R. (2004, Oct. 11). How Will TV Survive Its Own Reality Show? *Business Week*, 158, 160.

Haithman, D. (1988, April 24). Wonder Years Captures 1968 in a Child's Eyes. *The Los Angeles Times*, 8G.

Hall, S. (2006). Encoding/Decoding. In: Durham, M. & Kellner, D. (eds.), *Media and Cultural Studies: Key Works*. Rev. ed. Malden, MA: Blackwell Publishers, pp. 163–73.

Hardt, M. & Negri, A. (2001). *Empire*. Harvard, MA: Harvard University Press.

Harms, J. B. & Dickens, D. R. (1996). Postmodern Media Studies: Analysis or Symptom? *Critical Studies in Mass Communication* 13, 210–27.

Hart, R. P. (1994). *Seducing America: How Television Charms the American Voter*. Oxford, MA: Oxford University Press.

Hartley, J. (2002). *Communication, Cultural and Media Studies: The Key Concepts*. 3rd ed. New York: Routledge.

Harvey, D. (1990). *The Condition of Postmodernity: An Enquiry into the Origins of Cultural Change*. Cambridge, MA: Blackwell Publishers.

Harvey, D. (1991). Flexibility: Threat or Opportunity? *Socialist Review* 21, 66–77.

Heide, M. J. (1995). *Television Culture and Women's Lives: "Thirtysomething" and the Contradictions of Gender*. Philadelphia, PA: University of Pennsylvania Press.

Heim, M. (1993). *The Metaphysics of Virtual Reality*. Oxford: Oxford University Press.

Hendler, G. (2000). Channel Surfing: Postmodernism on Television. In: Carmichael, T. & Lee, A. (eds.), *Postmodern Times: A Critical Guide to the Contemporary*. DeKalb, IL: Northern Illinois University Press, pp. 173–98.

Hiltbrand, D. (1994, March 21). Picks and Pans: Duckman. *People Weekly*, 15.

Hilton-Morrow, W. & McMahan, D. T. (2003). *The Flintstones* to *Futurama*: Networks and Prime Time Animation. In: Stabile, C. A. & Harrison, M. (eds.), *Prime Time Animation: Television Animation and American Culture*. New York: Routledge, pp. 74–88.

Hirsch, E. D., Jr. (1987). *Cultural Literacy: What Every American Needs to Know*. New York: Houghton Mifflin.

Hoesterey, I. (2001). *Pastiche: Cultural Memory in Art, Film, Literature*. Bloomington, IN: Indiana University Press.

Hoffer, E. (1963). *The Ordeal of Change*. New York: Harper & Row.

Horkheimer, M. & Adorno, T. W. (2001). *Dialectic of Enlightenment*. Trans. J. Cumming. New York: Continuum.

Hornblower, M. (1997, June 9). Great Xpectations. *Time*, 66.

Horowitz, J. (1986, March 30). The Madcap Behind "Moonlighting." *The New York Times Magazine*, 26.

Hudson, H. E. & Leung, L. (1988). The Growth of the Information Sector. In: Williams, F. (ed.), *Measuring the Information Society*. Newbury Park, CA: Sage Publications, pp. 35–54.

Huff, R. (1999, Oct. 1). TV Males "Violent": Kids, Boys Don't See Selves in Small-Screen Guys. *Daily News*, 130.

Hutcheon, L. (2002). *The Politics of Postmodernism*. 2nd ed. New York: Routledge.

Iyer, P. (1990, May 14). History? Education? Zap! Pow! Cut! *Time*, 85.

Jacobs, A. J. (1996, March 8). Heaven Can Rate. *Entertainment Weekly*, 38.

Jameson, F. (1983). Postmodernism and Consumer Society. In: Foster, H. (ed.), *The Anti-Aesthetic: Essays on Postmodern Culture*. Port Townsend, WA: Bay Press, pp. 111–25.

Jameson, F. (1991). *Postmodernism, or, The Cultural Logic of Late Capitalism*. Durham, NC: Duke University Press.

JANUS Project. (2003, Oct.). Information Society Technologies Programme of the European Commission. *The Digital Divide*, 1–12.

Jenkins, H. (1988). Star Trek Rerun, Reread, Rewritten: Fan Writing as Textual Poaching. *Critical Studies in Mass Communication* 5, 85–107.

Jhally, S. & Lewis, J. (1992). *Enlightened Racism: The Cosby Show, Audiences, and the Myth of the American Dream*. Boulder, CO: Westview Press.

Joyrich, L. (1992). All that Television Allows: TV Melodrama, Postmodernism, and Consumer Culture. In: Spigel, L. & Mann, D. (eds.), *Private Screenings: Television and the Female Consumer*. Minneapolis: University of Minnesota Press, pp. 227–51.

Kaminisky, S. M. & Mahan, J. H. (1985). *American Television Genres*. Chicago, IL: Nelson-Hall.

Kanaley, R. (1997, Nov.). Many Forced to Cope with Computers in Mid-Career. *Centre Daily Times*, Connected 2.

Kaplan, E. A. (1985). A Post-Modern Play of the Signifier? Advertising, Pastiche and Schizophrenia in Music Television. In: Drummond, P. & Paterson, R. (eds.), *Television in Transition: Papers from the First International Television Studies Conference*. London: BFI Publishing, pp. 146–63.

Kaufman, J. (1997, March 29). Tuning into God. *TV Guide*, 33.

Kellner, D. (1989). *Critical Theory, Marxism and Modernity*. Baltimore, MD: The Johns Hopkins University Press.

Kellner, D. (1990). *Television and the Crisis of Democracy*. Boulder, CO: Westview Press, Inc.

Kellner, D. (1995). *Media Culture: Cultural Studies, Identity and Politics Between the Modern and the Postmodern*. New York: Routledge.

Keveney, B. (2000, Nov. 3). Oakily Dokily! "Simpsons" Hits 250. Who Says Dysfunctional Families Can't Get Ahead? *USA Today*, 11E.

Kilday, G. (1993, Oct.). Lady Lane. *Lears*, 108.

Kile, C. (1993). Recombinant Realism/Caliutopian Re-Dreaming: *Beverly Hills 90210* as Nostalgia Television. Paper presented at the annual meeting of the National Popular Culture Association, New Orleans, LA.

Kimmel, D. M. (2004). *The Fourth Network: How Fox Broke the Rules and Reinvented Television*. Chicago: Ivan R.

Kohrs Campbell, K. & Jamieson, K. H. (1978). *Form and Genre: Shaping Rhetorical Action*. Falls Church, VA: Speech Communication Association.

Kozloff, S. (1992). Narrative Theory and Television. In: Allen, R. C. (ed.), *Channels of Discourse, Reassembled: Television and Contemporary Criticism*. 2nd ed. Chapel Hill, NC: The University of North Carolina Press, pp. 67–100.

Lash, S. (2002). *Critique of Information*. Thousand Oaks, CA: Sage Publications.

Lasswell, M. & Weiner, E. (1997, March 29). Getting Religion. *TV Guide*, 28.

Lifton, R. J. (1993). *The Protean Self: Human Resilience in an Age of Fragmentation*. New York: Basic Books.

Lyotard, J.-F. (1984). *The Postmodern Condition: A Report on Knowledge*. Trans. G. Bennington & B. Massumi. Minneapolis, MN: University of Minnesota Press.

Mander, J. (2002). *Four Arguments for the Elimination of Television*. New York: Perennial.

Mandese, J. (1993, Feb. 15). "Dr. Quinn" Could Cure CBS' Blues on Saturday. *Advertising Age*, 61.

Mann, V. (1991, Oct. 6). How History Repeats Itself on Television. *The Record* (Bergen County, NJ), E01.

Marc, D. (1995). *Bonfire of the Humanities: Television, Subliteracy, and Long-Term Memory Loss*. Syracuse, NY: Syracuse University Press.

Mason, M. S. (1998, April 17). "Simpsons" Creator on Poking Fun. *The Christian Science Monitor*, B7.

Matheson, C. (2001). *The Simpsons*, Hyper-Irony, and the Meaning of Life. In: Irwin, W., Conrad, M. T., & Skoble, A. J. (eds.), *"The Simpsons" and Philosophy: The D'oh! of Homer*. Edited by. Chicago, IL: Open Court, pp. 108–25.

Maurstad, T. (1997, Feb. 6). "Star Wars" is Nation's Latest Trip Down Memory Lane. *Centre Daily Times*, C1.

Mazarr, M. J. (2001). *Global Trends 2005: An Owner's Manual for the Next Decade*. New York: Palgrave.

McAdams, D. P. (1997). The Case for Unity in the (Post)Modern Self: A Modest Proposal. In: Ashmore, R. D. & Jussim, L. (eds.), *Self and Identity: Fundamental Issues*. New York: Oxford University Press, pp. 46–78.

McAllister, M. P. (1994). The Simpsons: US Cartoon Situation Comedy. In: Newcomb, H. (ed.), *Museum of Broadcast Communications Encyclopedia of Television*. vol. 3: Q–Z. Chicago, IL: Fitzroy Dearborn Publishers, pp. 1493–5.

McCain, T. A. (1998). Information and Knowledge On-line: Teaching and Learning in the Communication Age. 1998 B. Aubrey Fisher Memorial Lecture. University of Utah, Department of Communication.

McCarroll, T. (1991, Aug. 12). Technology: What New Age? *Time*, 45.

McGee, M. C. (1990). Text, Context, and the Fragmentation of Contemporary Culture. *Western Journal of Speech Communication* 54, 274–289.

McIntyre, N. (1995, June 9). All the News That's Fit to Make You Fret. *The Arizona Republic*, E14.

McKinley, E. G. (1997). *Beverly Hills, 90210: Television, Gender, and Identity*. Philadelphia, PA: University of Pennsylvania Press.

McLuhan, M. (1964). *Understanding Media: The Extensions of Man*. New York: McGraw-Hill.

McNeil, A. (1996). *Total Television: A Comprehensive Guide to Programming from 1948 to the Present*. 4th ed. New York: Penguin Books.

McQuail, D. (2000). *McQuail's Mass Communication Theory*. 4th ed. Thousand Oaks, CA: Sage Publications.

Meares, C. A. & Sargent, J. F., Jr. (1999, June). The Digital Workforce: Building Infotech Skills at the Speed of Information. US Department of Commerce. Technology Administration. Office of Technology Policy.

Meier, R. L. (1962). *A Communication Theory of Urban Growth*. Cambridge, MA: MIT Press.

Meier, R. L. (1963). Communication Overload: Proposals from the Study of a University Library. *Administrative Science Quarterly* 4, 521–44.

Meiksins Wood, E. (1996, July–Aug.). Modernity, Postmodernity, or Capitalism. *Monthly Review*. Available online at: http://www.findarticles.com/p/articles/mi_m1132/is_n3_v48/ai_18484828

Meyrowitz, J. (1985). *No Sense of Place: The Impact of Electronic Media on Social Behavior*. Oxford: Oxford University Press.

Mindich, D. (2005). *Tuned Out: Why American's Under 40 Don't Follow the News*. New York: Oxford University Press.

Minow, N. N. (1995). Address to the National Association of Broadcasters, May 9, 1961. In: Minow, N. N. & Lamay, C. L. (eds.), *Abandoned in the Wasteland: Children, Television, and the First Amendment*. New York: Hill and Wang, pp. 185–96.

Mitchell, W. J. T. (1994). *Picture Theory: Essays on Verbal and Visual Phenomena*. Chicago, IL: The University of Chicago Press.

Moody, R. (2000). *The Real World*. In: Pendergrast, T. & Pendergrast, S. (ed.), *St. James Encyclopedia of Popular Culture*. vol. 4: P–T. Detroit, MI: St. James Press, p. 181.

Morley, D. (1980). *The "Nationwide" Audience: Structure and Decoding*. London: British Film Institute.

Morrison, I. & Schmid, G. (1994). *Future Tense: The Business Realities of the Next Ten Years*. New York: Morrow.

Morrow, L. (1991, Jan. 14). Old Paradigm, New Paradigm. *Time*, 65.

Morrow, L. (1992, Sept. 21). Folklore in a Box. *Time*, 50.

Naisbitt, J. (1982). *Megatrends: Ten New Directions Transforming Our Lives*. New York: Warner Books.

Newcomb, H. (1978). Toward Television History: The Growth of Styles. *Journal of the University Film Association* 30, 9–14.

Nietzsche, F. (2000). *The Birth of Tragedy*. Trans. D. Smith. Oxford: Oxford University Press.

O'Day, M. (1999). Postmodernism and Television. In: Sim, S. (ed.), *The Routledge Critical Dictionary of Postmodern Thought*. New York: Routledge, pp. 112–20.

O'Keeffe, M. E. & Waller, K. (2003). Hollywood's Absent, Impotent, and Avenging God in the Classroom. *Horizons* 30, 92–110.

O'Sullivan, T., Hartley, J., Sanders, D., Montgomery, M., & Fiske, J. (1994). *Key Concepts in Communication and Cultural Studies*. 2nd ed. New York: Routledge.

Okrent, D. (1999, May 10). Raising Kids Online: What Can Parents Do? *Time*, 38.

Ong, W. J. (1988). *Orality and Literacy: The Technologizing of the Word*. New York: Routledge.

Ott, B. (2003a). "I'm Bart Simpson, Who the Hell Are You?" A Study in Postmodern Identity (Re)Construction. *The Journal of Popular Culture* 37, 56–82.

Ott, B. (2003b). "Oh My God, They Digitized Kenny!" Travels in the *South Park* Cybercommunity V4.0. In: Stabile, C. A. & Harrison, M. (eds.), *Prime Time Animation: Television Animation and American Culture*. New York: Routledge, pp. 220–42.

Ott, B. & Walter, C. (2000). Intertextuality: Interpretive Practice and Textual Strategy. *Critical Studies in Media Communication* 17, 429–46.

Owen, R. (1997). *Gen X TV: The Brady Bunch to Melrose Place*. Syracuse, NY: Syracuse University Press.

Parisi, P. (1993). "Black Bart" Simpson: Appropriation and Revitalization in Commodity Culture. *Journal of Popular Culture* 27, 125–142.

Pelton, J. N. (1992). *Future View: Communications Technology and Society in the 21st Century*. Boulder, CO: Baylin Publications.

Pink, D. H. (2005). *A Whole New Mind: Moving from the Information Age to the Conceptual* Age. New York: Riverhead Books.

Pinsky, M. I. (2001, Feb. 5). How Big is *The Simpsons? Christianity Today*, 34.

Pinsky, R. (2000, Nov. 5). Creating the "Real," in Bright Yellow and Blue. *The New York Times*, 12.

Postman, N. (1985). *Amusing Ourselves to Death: Public Discourse in the Age of Show Business*. New York: Viking Penguin.

Postman, N. (1999). *Building a Bridge to the Eighteenth Century: How the Past Can Improve Our Future*. New York: Alfred A. Knopf.

Pourroy, J. (1995). *Behind the Scenes at ER*. New York: Ballantine Books.

Press, A. L. (1991). *Women Watching Television: Gender, Class, and Generation in the American Television Experience*. Philadelphia, PA: University of Pennsylvania Press.

Pritchett, P. (1994). *The Employee Handbook of New Work Habits for a Radically Changing World: 13 Ground Rules for Job Success In the Information Age*. Dallas, TX: Pritchett & Associates.

Putnam, R. D. (2000). *Bowling Alone: The Collapse and Revival of American Community*. New York: Simon & Schuster.

Quittner, J. (1999, May 10). Are Video Games Really So Bad? *Time*, 50.

Rebeck, V. A. (1990, June 27). Recognizing Ourselves in the Simpsons. *The Christian Century*, 622.

Rheingold, H. (2002). *Smart Mobs: The Next Social Revolution*. Cambridge, MA: Perseus Publishing.

Rifkin, J. (2000). *The Age of Access: The New Culture of Hypercapitalism Where All of Life is a Paid-For Experience*. New York: Jeremy P. Tarcher/Putnam.

Riggs, K. E. (1996). The Case of the Mysterious Ritual: Murder Dramas and Older Women Viewers. *Critical Studies in Mass Communication* 13, 309–23.

Riggs, K. E. (2006). Murder, She Wrote. *The Museum of Broadcast Communications*. Chicago, IL. Available online at: http://www.museum.tv/archives/etv/M/htmlM/murdershew/murdershew.htm

Robert V. B., Jr. & Walker, J. R. (1996). *Television and the Remote Control: Grazing on a Vast Wasteland*. New York: The Guilford Press.

Robertson, Ed. (2006). *Walker, Texas Ranger* on Home Video. Available online at: http://www.edrobertson.com/walker.htm

Robinson, J. P. & Godbey, G. (1997). *Time for Life: The Surprising Ways Americans Use Their Time*. University Park, PA: The Pennsylvania State University.

Romanyshyn, R. D. (1993). The Despotic Eye and Its Shadow: Media Images in the Age of Literacy. In: Levin, M. D. (ed.), *Modernity and the Hegemony of Vision*. Berkeley, CA: University of California Press, pp. 339–60.

Rosen, J. (1993, Oct. 9). Beavis and Butt-head are Cool, huh-huh, huh. *Centre Daily Times*, 1E.

Rosenau, P. M. (1992). *Post-Modernism and the Social Sciences: Insights, Inroads, and Intrusions*. Princeton, NJ: Princeton University Press.

Rowe, J. C. (1994). Spin-off: The Rhetoric of Television and Postmodern Memory. In: Carlisle, J. & Schwarz, D. R. (eds.), *Narrative and Culture*. Athens: The University of Georgia Press, 97–120.

Sarup, M. (1993). *An Introductory Guide to Post-Structuralism and Postmodernism*. 2nd ed. Athens: The University of Georgia Press.

Sarup, M. (1996). *Identity, Culture, and the Postmodern World*. Athens, GA: The University of Georgia Press.

Schatz, T. (1992). The New Hollywood. In: Collins, J., Radner, J., & Preacher Collins, A. (eds.), *Film Theory Goes to the Movies*. New York: Routledge, pp. 8–36.

Schement, J. R & Curtis, T. (1995). *Tendencies and Tensions of the Information Age: The Production and Distribution of Information in the United States*. New Brunswick, NJ: Transaction Publishers.

Schindehette, S. (1993, Feb. 25). What's Up, Doc? *People*, 74.

Schramm, W., Lyle, J., & Parker, E. B. (1961). *Television in the Lives of Our Children*. Stanford, CA: Stanford University Press.

Scott, A. O. (2001, Nov. 4). Homer's Odyssey. *The New York Times Magazine*, 44.

Seabrook, J. (1997, Oct. 20). The Big Sellout. *The New Yorker*, 182.

Shaviro, S. (2003). *Connected, or What it Means to Live in the Network Society.* Minneapolis: University of Minnesota Press.

Shenk, D. (1997). *Data Smog: Surviving the Information Glut.* New York: HarperCollins Publishers.

Signorielli, N. (1991). *A Sourcebook on Children and Television.* New York: Greenwood Press.

Silverstone, R. (1994). *Television and Everyday Life.* New York: Routledge.

Snierson, D. (2000, Nov. 3). The Ups And Downey of "Ally McBeal." *Entertainment Weekly*, 31.

Soja, E. W. (1989). *Postmodern Geographies: The Reassertion of Space in Critical Social Theory.* New York: Verso.

Spigel, L. (1992). *Make Room for TV: Television and the Family Ideal in Postwar America.* Chicago, IL: University of Chicago Press.

Sreberny-Mohammadi, A. (1995). Forms of Media as Ways of Knowing. In: Downing, J., Ali Mohammadi, A., & Sreberny-Mohammadi, A. (eds.), *Questioning the Media: A Critical Introduction.* 2nd ed. Thousand Oaks, CA: Sage Publications, pp. 23–38.

Stabile, C. A. & Harrison, M. (2003). Introduction: Prime Time Animation – An Overview. In: Stabile, C. & Harrison, M., *Prime Time Animation: Television Animation and American Culture.* New York: Routledge, pp. 1–11.

Stallybrass, P. & White, A. (1986). *The Politics and Poetics of Transgression.* Ithaca, New York: Cornell University Press.

Stein, H. (1993, March 6). *Dr. Quinn* Should Shrink from New Age Nonsense. *TV Guide*, 43.

Stephens, M. (1998). *The Rise of the Image The Fall of the Word.* New York: Oxford University Press.

Storey, J. (1998). *An Introduction to Cultural Theory and Popular Culture.* 2nd ed. Athens, GA: The University of Georgia Press.

Strinati, D. (1995). *An Introduction to Theories of Popular Culture.* New York: Routledge.

Swerdlow, J. L. (1995, Oct.). Information Revolution. *National Geographic* 188, 5–18.

Taylor, E. (1989). *Prime Time Families.* Berkeley: University of California Press.

Taylor, M. C. (2001). *The Moment of Complexity: Emerging Network Culture.* Chicago, IL: The University of Chicago Press.

Tetzeli, R. (1994, July 11). Surviving Information Overload. *Fortune*, 60.

The Digital Decade: The 90s. (2000). Richmond, VA: Time-Life Books.

The Technological Reshaping of Metropolitan America. (1995, Sept.). US Congress, Office of Technology Assessment. OTA-ETI-643. Washington, DC: US Government Printing Office.

Thompson, R. J. (1996). *Television's Second Golden Age: From Hill Street Blues to ER*. New York: Continuum.

Thompson, T. N. & Palmeri, A. J. (1993). Attitudes toward Counternature (with Notes on Nurturing a Poetic Psychosis). In: Chesebro, J. W. (ed.), *Extensions of the Burkeian System*. AL: The University of Alabama Press, pp. 269–83.

Thurow, L. C. (1996). *The Future of Capitalism: How Today's Economic Forces Shape Tomorrow's Word*. New York: Penguin Books.

Toffler, A. (1970). *Future Shock*. New York: Random House.

Toffler, A. (1980). *The Third Wave*. New York: William Morrow and Company.

Toulmin, S. (1990). *Cosmopolis: The Hidden Agenda of Modernity*. New York: The Free Press.

Turner, C. (2004). *Planet Simpson: How a Cartoon Masterpiece Defined a Generation*. Cambridge, MA: De Capo Press.

Vail, K. (1997, June). Girlware. *Electronic School*, A18–21.

van Poecke, L. (1996). Media Culture and Identity Formation in the Light of Postmodern Invisible Socialization: From Modernity to Postmodernity. *Communications* 21, 183–98.

Vancil, D. L. & Pendell, S. D. (1987). The Myth of Viewer–Listener Disagreement in the First Kennedy–Nixon Debate. *Central States Speech Journal* 38, 16–27.

Vande Berg, Leah R. (1989). Dramedy: Moonlighting as an Emergent Generic Hybrid. *Communication Studies* 40, 13–28.

Vattimo, G. (2004). *Nihilism and Emancipation: Ethics, Politics, and Law*. New York: Columbia University Press.

Verespej, M. A. (1995, June 19). Communication Technology: Slave or Master. *Industry Week*, 18–24.

Vitanza, V. J. (1999). *Cyberreader*. 2nd ed. Boston: Allyn and Bacon.

von Bayer, H. C. (2004). *Information: The New Language of Science*. Cambridge, MA: Harvard University Press.

von Busack, R. (1996, March 28). Walker on the Mild Side. *Metro*. Available online at: http://www.metroactive.com/papers/metro/03.28.96/walker-9613.html

Waters, M. (2001). *Globalization*. 2nd ed. New York: Routledge.

Watson, J. & Hill, A. (1997). *A Dictionary of Communication and Media Studies*. 4th ed. New York: Arnold.

Watts, D. J. (2003). *Six Degrees: The Science of the Connected Age*. New York: W. W. Norton & Company.

Williams, F. (1988). The Information Society as an Object of Study. In: Williams, F. (ed.), *Measuring the Information Society.* Newbury Park, CA: Sage, pp. 13–31.

Williams, J. P. (1988). When You Care Enough to Watch the Very Best: The Mystique of *Moonlighting. Journal of Popular Film and Television* 16, 90–9.

Williams, K. (2003). *Understanding Media Theory.* New York: Oxford University Press.

Williams, R. (1974). *Television: Technology and Cultural Form.* Hanover: Wesleyan University Press.

Wilson, J. L. (2005). *Nostalgia: Sanctuary of Meaning.* Lewisburg: Bucknell University Press.

Wood, D. (1992). *The Power of Maps.* New York: The Guilford Press.

Wurman, R. S. (1989). *Information Anxiety.* New York: Doubleday.

Zehme, B. (1990, June 28). The Only Real People on TV: At Home with the Simpsons. *Rolling Stone*, 41.

Zoglin, R. (1992a, Oct. 15). Beyond Your Wildest Dreams: TV Will Dazzle Us With Choices, But Will We Be Happy in Our Cocoons? *Time*, 70.

Zoglin, R. (1992b, Sept. 21). Sitcom Politics. *Time*, 44.

Zoglin, R. (1996, Oct. 21). The News Wars. *Time*, 61.

Index